AUDIENCE AND AUTHORITY IN THE MODERNIST THEATER OF FEDERICO GARCÍA LORCA

AUDIENCE AND AUTHORITY IN THE MODERNIST THEATER OF FEDERICO GARCÍA LORCA

C. Christopher Soufas

The University of Alabama Press

Tuscaloosa and London

C. Christopher Soufas's English-language translations of
excerpts from Federico García Lorca's Spanish-language works
© Herederos de Federico García Lorca and C. Christopher Soufas
1996. Federico García Lorca's drawing, "Clown with a double
face," catalog number 198, from Line of Light and Shadow, The
Drawings of Federico García Lorca © 1991 Duke University
Press. Translations and drawing used with permission of
Herederos de Federico García Lorca. For information regarding
rights and permissions for works by Federico García Lorca,
please contact William Peter Kosmas, Esq., 77 Rodney Court,
6/8 Maida Vale, London W9 1TJ, England.

∞

The paper on which this book is printed meets the minimum
requirements of American National Standard for Information
Science-Permanence of Paper for Printed Library Materials,
ANSI Z39.48-1984.

Library of Congress Cataloging-in-Publication Data

Soufas, C. Christopher.
    Audience and authority in the modernist theater of Federico
García Lorca / C. Christopher Soufas.
        p.   cm.
    Includes bibliographical references and index.
    ISBN 0-8173-0817-2 (alk. paper)
    1. García Lorca, Federico, 1898–1936—Dramatic works. I. Title.
PQ6613.A763Z8855 1996
862'.62—dc20   95-32239

British Library Cataloguing-in-Publication Data available

For Teresa

CONTENTS

PREFACE

THE PAST TWENTY years have witnessed notable developments in the study of the theater of Federico García Lorca. The most significant is the publication of *The Public* (*El público*) and *Play Without A Title* (*Comedia sin título*), which strongly challenges earlier assumptions about his theater, as well as other previously unavailable material, the outlines, notes, or partial drafts for a variety of theater projects (collected in *Teatro inconcluso* [*Uncompleted Theater*]), much of which has been included in a three-volume revised edition of the *Obras completas* (*Complete Works*) from which most of the quotations in this study are taken. This has been accompanied by the appearance of previously unpublished poetry (especially the *Sonnets to Dark Love* [*Sonetos del amor oscuro*]), personal correspondence, juvenilia, and drawings.[1] The appearance of more reliable accounts of the playwright's life, especially regarding his assassination and his homosexual orientation, has served to provide a more objective basis for critical observations about his theater.[2] Equally significant have been some of the more recent performances of the plays themselves—numerous stagings of a variety of his plays during the 1980s in Spain and elsewhere, notable among which are the 1987 premiere of *The Public* and a musical-dramatic adaptation of the *Sonnets to Dark Love*—which have also served to expand discussion and interpretation of Lorca's theater.

There are also, however, the more dubious contributions of postformalist criticism that have added new adjectives to the bewildering array that currently invokes "essential" qualities of Lorca's theater. Earlier descriptions—conservative, tradition-minded, realistic, "Spanish"; social, liberal, avant-garde; mythic, archetypal, existential—have been surpassed by characterizations like psychoanalytic, personalistic, homoerotic, and transgressive. During the middle decades of this century, critics tended to organize Lorca's theater around two distinct and contradictory paradigms: one which viewed him as a socially concerned liberal whose mature art returns to the realistic conventions of theater after a brief flirtation with experimental theater;[3] and another which considered Lorca's art to epitomize tradition and conservatism, an agenda dedicated to the representation of the "Spanish essence."[4] These views in turn were copiously supplemented by a variety of psychological/archetypal readings that have themselves become more refined and sophisticated since the vogue of their popularity during the seventies.[5]

In a July 16, 1992, commentary in the *New York Review of Books* on the persistence of an apparently unreconcilable critical double focus, Michael Wood considers that Lorca

> remains a curiously elusive figure, restless and changing in his work as in his life. . . . Does he belong to tradition or to the avant-garde? Are his strengths his simplicity and closeness to the popular imagination, or his elegance, sophistication, and learning? Did the author of so many delicate children's songs also create those poems and drawings riddled with ugly sexual fear? Can the poet of the darkly tormented homoerotic sonnets really have produced the shrill railing against "fairies" that stains the "Ode to Walt Whitman"? Is there a way to get from the haggard drama of *The House of Bernarda Alba* to the Pirandellian high jinks of *The Public?* (36)

Recasting the persistent questions of nearly sixty years in relation to the recent candor about the playwright's homosexuality, Wood offers compelling testimony to the enduring power of attitudes and critical assessments of the artist that, rather than the consequence of consistent critical positions, continue to reflect attitudes brought to Lorca's texts about his person, political beliefs, and, most recently, his sexual orientation.

In the aftermath of publication of the long-suppressed *The Public*, the view of Lorca as a theatrical innovator has provided a certain impetus to rethink long-standing assumptions, especially about his later theater. For example, a play such as *The House of Bernarda Alba* (*La casa de Bernarda Alba*) that has been used matter-of-factly to exemplify Lorca's embrace of a mature realism, greater social consciousness, and his desire to critique repressive Spanish social institutions and sexual roles, etc., has in recent years been viewed as loaded with ironies and contradictions, so much so that "queerness" (Ronald Cueto) rather than faithfulness to conventional standards of imitation has been used to characterize what appears to be a much more problematical content. As newer critical assumptions have entered the mainstream of Hispanic criticism, the formalist prohibitions against affectivity have ceded to observations about the role of the audience, in a narrow sense, as a structural extension of the script (see Edwards, especially 60–124), and in a more expansive sense as a historical barometer of standard expectations and originality (Fernández Cifuentes 11–26). While acknowledging the contribution of recent developments, this study also approaches the evolution of Lorca's theater as deriving significant authority from its association with the artistic paradigms of Modernism that achieves its fullest moment in Europe during the 1920s and 1930s.

Lorca's conscious mission as a mature dramatist is to restore the prestige of a Spanish theater that has conditioned its audiences to predictable expectations as it has also acquiesced in their demands for a safe and restricted range of theatrical experience. Even more than the conservative tastes of theater audiences, Lorca criticizes those in the institution of theater who have acted as its de facto extensions—actors, writers, producers, and even theater critics—in tolerating a situation in which the imaginative insufficiencies of theater audiences have been accompanied by a lack of direction and stage leadership:

> In this theater full of actors and authors and critics, I am declaring that there exists a grave crisis of authority. The theater has lost its authority, and if it continues this way and if we let it continue, we will allow new generations to lose faith and, therefore, the precious source of the vocation itself. . . .
> The theater has lost its authority because there presently exists a great imbalance between art and business. Theater needs money, and it is fundamental and just for its continued existence that it be a motive for profit; but only halfway and no more. The other half is purification, beauty, care, sacrifice for the superior goal of emotion and culture. . . . It is necessary to demand a minimum of decorum and to remember always theater's artistic and educative function. . . .
> The public is not to blame; the public is attracted, fooled, educated, entertained without realizing it, not to trick them but for their money. But the fact must not be lost sight of that the theater is superior to the public and not inferior, as happens today with lamentable frequency. (III 452–53)[6]

The continuing lack of critical consensus suggests the need for a fuller and more integrated account of the direction in which Lorca's Modernist sensibilities take his theater. For Lorca, the reestablishment of stage authority requires a thorough rethinking of then-current premises of theater and the imposition of a greater discipline upon all participants in the theater experience, including complacent, conservative audiences with a limited appreciation of its possibilities, as Lorca asserts in "Theater Chat":

> Theater should be imposed on the public and not the public on the theater. For this reason, authors and actors must attire themselves, even at the cost of blood, with great authority, because the theater public is like children in school: they adore the serious and austere teacher that demands from them and does them justice, and they fill with cruel needles the chairs where the timid and cringing teachers sit, the ones that neither teach nor allow others to be taught. (III 460)

Although Lorca's position as one of the preeminent literary figures of the Spanish twentieth century seems unassailable, the effective hegemony of a text-centered tradition of criticism, which has largely confined discussion of his work to a specifically Spanish context, has also rendered invisible the fuller dimension of an extended dialectical struggle for stage authority within the wider context of Modernist Europe.

This study examines the development of Lorca's comprehensive relationship with the theater, which includes other relevant aspects of the act of theater, the full "circuit of reception"—the dramatic script transformed by stage director and others into a performance text before a theater audience—but also the personal dimension of authority upon which Lorca's theater project draws its force. In opposition to the domesticating power of theater audiences from a vantage point in the darkness beyond the space of the stage, Lorca situates the center of his quest for dramatic authority in an unconventional offstage space and force, an alternative agenda that the forces of convention—not simply theater audiences but also those within the theater who cater to the status quo—have relegated to invisibility and unstageability.

This study examines the rather steady evolution of Lorca's theater toward the full validation of such a renovative agenda. I have chosen to examine his plays largely in chronological order because, although his reputation as a spontaneous talent is not without merit, Lorca himself was quite insistent upon the evolutionary character of his theater: "In the theater I have followed a well-defined trajectory" (III 674).[7] The early theater is framed by his only major dramatic failure, *The Butter-*

fly's Spell (El maleficio de la mariposa), and his first significant success, *Mariana Pineda*. Between these plays are puppet and other minor farces which to my view mark a moment of self-examination in the aftermath of his early failure. The two subsequent major farces, *The Shoemaker's Prodigious Wife (La zapatera prodigiosa)* and *The Love of Don Perlimplín with Belisa in His Garden (El amor de don Perlimplín con Belisa en su jardín)*, form a logical unit, and it is clear that Lorca's misgivings about his relation to the commercial stage in these plays motivate, at least in part, his explicitly experimental moment in *As Soon As Five Years Pass (Así que pasen cinco años)* and *The Public*.

Although nearly all of Lorca's critics attest to the strong evolutionary quality of his most mature theater during the 1930s—the "rural dramas" are often thought of, if perhaps not correctly, as a trilogy—it seems equally clear that such an evolution also proceeds as a consequence of insights gained from the experimental theater and considerable practical experience as principal director of the La Barraca theater group. Finally, as Lorca began to attain the type of personal authority that he believed essential to the renovation of the Spanish stage, he had also begun to understand and acknowledge his theater more fully in relation to developments elsewhere in Europe. Not only had he actually begun to collaborate with prominent European playwrights such as Pirandello (and others in his circle) who had taken a sincere interest in his work, but his last work, *Play Without A Title*, clearly embraces a wider and more universal vision of theater. The surviving fragments of his theater in preparation, collected in *Teatro inconcluso*, while surely attesting to a continuation of certain earlier themes (e.g., *The Dreams of My Cousin Aurelia [Los sueños de mi prima Aurelia]*) also suggest the possibility of a theater substantially different in content from the productions upon which Lorca's reputation had once squarely rested before the publication of *The Public*. Notable among these works in preparation is *The Black Ball (La bola negra)*, in which Lorca seems to be affirming a more realistic portrayal of the homosexual themes that had, at the time of his death, relegated such scripts, finished or unfinished, to the category of the unstageable.

While this study acknowledges that a not inconsiderable part of Lorca's present reputation and popularity is a direct consequence of the many often innovative stage performances over the more than half-century since his death and, indeed, that through performance a playwright's work is given a renewed existence as the interpretations of dramatic scripts by stage directors and theater groups add to the body of opinion and criticism of a given work, the present study is nevertheless concerned primarily with Lorca's specific attitudes toward theater during his lifetime and in relation to his historical audience. Present-day performance models, which have incorporated into their paradigms the considerable historical evolution of the institution of theater over the course of this century, provide valuable assistance in the task of situating Lorca's plays in both the formal and the ideological theater agenda of Modernist Europe. It is from this double focus that my study begins.

ACKNOWLEDGMENTS

I SHOULD LIKE to thank the Fundación Federico García Lorca (Madrid) for allowing me to use their extensive library and manuscript holdings and the Program for Cultural Cooperation Between Spain's Ministry of Culture and United States' Universities for their generous support.

Parts of articles on *Bodas de sangre (Blood Wedding)* and *La casa de Bernarda Alba (The House of Bernarda Alba)* are reprinted from "*Bodas de sangre* and the Problematics of Representation" © 1987 by *Revista de Esudios Hispánicos* and "Dialectics of Vision: Pictorial vs. Photographic Representation in *La casa de Bernarda Alba* © 1990 by *Ojáncano,*" by C. Christopher Soufas. Used by permission.

Portions of the introduction previously appeared in Soufas, "Lorca's Theatre in a Modernist/Performance Context," *Gestos* 19 (April 1995).

I should also like to acknowledge my parents, Charles C. Soufas and Clara Davis Soufas, whose love and support over the years, at so many levels, have provided more than words can adequately express.

Finally, I wish to acknowledge my son Paul who has learned so much—and taught me even more—during the time that this book was attaining form.

I

INTRODUCTION

T HE CONTINUING LACK of consensus about the theater of Federico
García Lorca is in significant measure a consequence of a critical un-
willingness to understand his literary production in relation to Mod-
ernism, as a full participant in a multifaceted international movement
that dominated artistic expression in Europe (and elsewhere) between
the two world wars. To varying degrees of intensity and with different
emphases within specific national literatures of Europe, Modernist
writers and artists formulate a new artistic paradigm significantly dif-
ferent from the empirically oriented representational models of real-
ism-naturalism, often accompanied with great irreverence, frequent
polemics in the form of manifestos and position papers, and at times
even physical violence. The open hostility of Modernist artists to bour-
geois values and standards of artistry closely parallels developments
in continental politics in which a corollary antagonism toward bour-
geois forms of parliamentary government, in the form of revolutionary
activity and/or position-taking from both the left and the right, even-
tually culminates in the violence that engulfs Spain, Europe, and in
due course the world and which claims Lorca himself as one of its
prominent casualties. Although there emerges a variety of Modern-
ist subschools throughout Europe, the many "isms" that succeed each
other with often dizzying frequency and with varying degrees of suc-
cess, underlying the movement as a whole is a desire to subvert, dis-
rupt, or even to sever the connection with a more publicly available
mimetic representational mode no longer considered an adequate me-
dium for art.

Fredric Jameson, in fact, has characterized the most significant for-
mal impulses of canonical Modernism as wills to style: "strategies of
inwardness, which set out to reappropriate an alienated universe by
transforming it into personal styles and private languages" (2). Peter
Bürger has also noted that, historically, avant-garde artistic movements

have typically dedicated themselves to overturning positions that assign art to an objective or autonomous status (53). Indeed, Modernist artists strive invariably to create alternative realities, private understandings that are not faithful imitations of an observed or public reality and that, to a greater or lesser degree, supersede the working assumptions of realistic representation with a sensibility that affirms a preference for

> compartmentalized spaces of lived time over against clock time, bodily or perceptual experience over against rational and instrumental consciousness, a realm of "originary" or creative language over against the daily practice of a degraded practical speech, the space of the sexual and the archaic over against the reality- and performance-principles of "le sérieux" and of adult life, and of the growing independence of the various senses from one another—in particular the separation of the eye from the ear. (Jameson 14)

During Modernism, the conventional supposition that verbal (symbolic) and visual (iconic) signs function as mutually interdependent mirrors is progressively abandoned in favor of a new configuration that privileges one of these sign systems over the other. At least in the rhetoric of position papers, manifestos, and polemical essays, some of the more radical Modernists advocate the full or partial severance of their mode of production altogether from one of these primary groups of signs in favor of the creation of an eye- or ear-dominated art.

Thus, for example, under the leadership of Ezra Pound, many of the representational assumptions of Imagism are premised on a theory of language that does not consider verbal signs to be conventional, arbitrary constructs or meaning to be simply the consequence of a tacit agreement among the speakers of a language that a given sign will signify one thing and not another. Rather, language is, or should be, iconic in nature. For Imagism, the verbal sign becomes a visual word, a real presence that establishes an isomorphic relationship with its referent in the manner that Pound and Ernest Fenollosa, erroneously, considered Chinese ideograms to function (in *The Chinese Written Character as a Medium for Poetry*), as a pictorial language that "resists reductive analysis . . . [that] is holistic, intuitive, creative rather than referential or duplicative" (Sherry 63). The meanings of words, therefore, are not conventional, arbitrary, or open to more than one meaning. They should be understood to mean fundamentally only one thing because of their inherent iconicity. Also implicit in this view of language, of course, are the seeds of Pound's political extremism. If there is little sympathy for situations in which words can have more than one meaning, if the epiphanic visual experience, one's own privileged point of view, is primary or exclusive, then this also suggests the need for an elitist, authoritarian political structure to accommodate such visual values: "The optical discrimination Pound extols is . . . at the top of a hierarchy of sensory merit, the lower reaches of which are marked by the ear's openness to fluid, continuous sound (la synérèse)—emblem and medium of the undistinguished, undistinguishing masses" (Sherry 73).

At the other extreme of the Modernist critique of mimeticism are Surrealism and André Breton, again, at least at a theoretical level, in the advocacy of automatic writing and related techniques as means to transcend ordinary reality. Automatic writing is considered the antithesis of mimetic representation and the idea of the easy translatability of visual and verbal signs. Indeed, the desire is to transcend altogether the need for dependence upon semiotic systems: "Automatism may be writing, but it is not, like the rest of the written signs of Western culture, representation. It is . . . 'spoken thought.' Thought is not a representation but is that which is utterly transparent to the mind, immediate to experience, untainted by the distance and exteriority of signs" (Krauss 12).

In contradistinction to the high value that Imagism ascribes to the eye, vision, and seeing in order to free art from its association with musicality and sentimental impressionism that are invariably communicated by means of the ear, Breton privileges a special type of hearing, independent of empirically articulated speech and unencumbered by the need to contextualize that message further in a scene or vision. Indeed, for the Surrealists "human eyesight was, simply, defective, weak, impotent" (Krauss 32), which also explains their fascination with photography, valued for its indexical and not its iconic qualities— the camera's ability to render a given slice of reality automatically by means of point-to-point correspondences that bypass mimesis altogether (Krauss 26). The abandonment of voluntary control in the process of art brought with it a sympathy not only for the enhanced values of a special mode of hearing over those of vision but also, at least for a time, for antibourgeois political movements—namely, revolutionary

Socialism—with which they seemed to share a common ground. Thus as the eye-dominated, aristocratic aesthetic of Pound and Wyndham Lewis extolled, at one end of the political spectrum, the authoritarian virtues of Fascism and Nazism, Breton and many Surrealists placed their ear-dominated art at the service of extreme left-wing political movements whose postulations about the inexorable movement of the uncontrollable forces of history seemed to parallel and confirm their artistic agenda.

As I have developed at greater length (*Conflict*), most of the significant poetry of the 1920s and 1930s in Spain, whether or not it acknowledges a sympathy or affiliation with a specific Modernist subschool, fully participates in the new artistic paradigm. Jorge Guillén's declaration that "the American name *Imagists* could well be applied to certain writers that wrote with imagination here or there during the twenties," that this poetry affirms a "reality not . . . reduplicated in copies but recreated in the very freest manner" ("Generación" 20), is an after-the-fact acknowledgment that his early poetry shares much in common with the vision-centered positions of Pound and Imagism. The typical poem of the initial editions of *Canticle* (*Cántico*) does not at all seek to imitate faithfully an object/landscape but rather, by an act of the intellectual will, to transform or hybridize it into a more direct or fully present picture of heightened consciousness that relegates the nominal subject of the poem to a secondary status. Guillén privileges vision in the sense that an active imagination-consciousness seeks out objects from the empirical world that confirm its existential-aesthetic agenda in act of representation. Poetry becomes an occasion for the collapse of empirical space into a heightened plane of imagination-consciousness that confirms the poet's private agenda, to transcend mimesis and to affirm the presence of being (Soufas 32–62). For example, Pound's and Guillén's mutual fascination with the "perfect" form of the circle—compare Guillén's sentiments in one of his best known poems, "Perfection of the Circle," to Pound's statement that "[i]t is the universal, existing in perfection, in freedom from space and time" (*Visual* 207)—is not coincidental. The circle epitomizes a mutual aesthetic ideal, a form whose very representation transcends mimesis to become a type of presence.

At the other side of the scale of the Modernist visual-verbal revaluation are significant moments in the poetry of Luis Cernuda and Rafael Alberti. Of the major Spanish poets identified to any significant degree with Surrealism, Cernuda is alone in acknowledging a sympathy with and debt to his French counterparts (see "Historial" 905–13). When in a poem from *A River, A Love* (*Un río, un amor*) significantly entitled "Complete Darkness" Cernuda expresses his confusion as an overpouring of words not only from the conventional source of their production, his lips, but also from his eyes and dreams (*Realidad* 47), he is expressing his experience of an involuntary center of production, represented as a gushing or overpouring of words that overwhelms the conventional sites, lips and eyes, where words and images had previously been closely associated. Likewise, Alberti in "Somnambular Angels" from *Concerning the Angels* (*Sobre los ángeles*) describes a new and unconventional association between invisible, interior "ears" that slowly descend to the throat (356), that is, to a new ear-centered locus of production that has surpassed empirical discourse. During these intense moments in their poetry, Cernuda and Alberti are affirming an explanation for artistic production more in sympathy with the official position of the Surrealists than with the vision-centered aesthetic of Imagism. The most typical effect of these visual-verbal disruptions is the fusion into a common plane of the functions of image and language, that is, the creation of a new form of hieroglyph, succinctly summarized by Wyndham Lewis's statement that "the word-picture of the writer is a hybrid of the ear and eye" (218). Neither abstract nor imitative, yet also not self-referentially autonomous, the typical Modernist artifact offers itself to its beholder to trace, or decipher, a trajectory away from empirico-referential experience to an alternative understanding that is simultaneously a critique of ordinary reality.

Although perhaps not so evidently positioned on one or the other side of the visual-verbal rupture that epitomizes the Modernist artistic paradigm, Lorca is aware from an early stage of the insufficiencies of empirico-mimeticism that is often expressed in his poetry in terms of an existential cost (contrasting sharply with Guillén's experience of existential plenitude). In "Song of the Departing Day," the poet addresses the day, an emblem of ordinary reality that quantifies and phantomizes, the poet's being, which exists in a different dimension:

You depart full of me,
you return without knowing me.
How much it costs me
to leave upon your breast
possible realities
of impossible minutes!

(I 390)

This intuition is intensified in "Symbol," the initial segment of "Suite of the Mirrors," as the figure of Christ further personifies the untenability of existence within an empirico-mimetic context:

Christ
had a mirror
in each hand.
He multiplied
his own specter.
He projected his heart
in the black stares.

(I 667)

Christ's experience is also Lorca's, fully conscious of the price paid for representing his absent specter in the destructive, fragmenting medium of "the black stares" of others. The need is for a less "costly" mode of representation that affords a more hospitable climate for the private realm of the heart and the public context in which the heart's message is so inhospitably received.

Lorca moves toward a more explicitly Modernist position in the "Ode to Salvador Dalí" and *Gypsy Ballads* as he consciously rejects the phantom images of mimeticism, "the mountain of impressionist mist" (I 953), in favor of a medium of greater visual denseness that, especially in *Gypsy Ballads*, functions in the manner of a buffer between public and private realities. This is certainly the most important role of the gypsies of *Gypsy Ballads*, dense visual pretexts that allow Lorca both to dramatize the heart's private message and to disguise it in a manner that allows him to avoid the costly existential and public consequences he lamented in his earlier poetry. The newer mode is perhaps most evident in the celebrated "Somnambular Ballad," in which the initial verse "Green that I love you green" ("Verde que te quiero verde" [I 400]) epitomizes the Modernist disruption of word and image. Although it is possible to consider the verse a mysterious yet fully articulated thought, it more succinctly exemplifies the word-picture, or hieroglyph, typical of high Modernism: the dependent clause "that I love you," which characterizes the fragmented desire of the poem's three principals, is physically framed on either side by the word-color green. As a frame-juxtaposition rather than a component of a syntagmatic unit, "green" more intensely emphasizes the separation of the empirical landscape of the father and lover and the private world of the gypsy girl whose frustrated desire for the lover persists even after her departure from the public domain.

Lorca employs essentially the same technique with far less voluntary precision in *Poet in New York* (*Poeta en Nueva York*), in which the empirical landscape becomes a much more transparent pretext for meditations on the state of the poet's private world. The visual denseness of *Gypsy Ballads* effectively disappears in a poem like "Girl Drowned in a Well," in which the anecdote contained in the title is little more than an anchoring device that affords the poem a nominal "rural" setting. This "well," however, is but another aspect of the private world to which the gypsy girl of "Somnambular Ballad" also belongs (as suggested explicitly by the subtitle "Granada and Newburg"). The difference lies in the shift in formal emphasis from the visual to the verbal, from the "great stars of frost" (I 400) of "Somnambular Ballad" to a much different evocation of the nocturnal landscape in "Girl Drowned in a Well," in which "the tender stars croak" (I 498), the involuntary production of cacophonous sounds being likened to the croaking of frogs.

Like that of his European contemporaries, Lorca's art is also dedicated to the exploration of a private, hybrid, more significant reality impossible to affirm through conventional modes of understanding. Perhaps more so than for others in his circle of artistic associates, however, Lorca's Modernist sympathies have not been emphasized because of his tendency to limit his landscapes to rather familiar, often identifiably Andalusian settings. Lorca's apparent traditionalism was, indeed, a source of friction between him and his much more flamboyant associates, Luis Buñuel and Salvador Dalí. Both criticize *Gypsy Ballads* and, more severely, in a prelude to the breakup of their friendship, *Love of Don Perlimplín with Belisa in His Garden*.

Lorca evinces his concern about a divergence in artistic focus with his friends at least as early as 1925 in the "Dialog with Luis Buñuel,"

which features a discussion by three characters—who bear the names
Federico García Lorca, Luis Buñuel, and Augusto Centeno—on pre-
cisely the issue of artistic space and its expressive geography, commu-
nicated in the dialog in terms of the necessity for taking trips. The
character Buñuel has a "thirst for travel . . . [that] . . . constitutes an
obsession. . . . The earth itself is too small" (II 303). The character
Lorca prefers to "travel around my garden" (II 303). Thanks to the
mediation of the character Centeno—who bears the name of one of
Lorca's many friends at the Residencia de Estudiantes (Gibson *Lorca* I
368)—these differences are declared reconciled by the observation that
what the two artists are disputing is not the avant-garde direction or
content of their art but rather the physical scenario in which the imagi-
nation manifests itself visually. Centeno recognizes the validity and
fundamental compatibility of both artists: "I believe that the two of
you can travel in your worlds without having to know which will be
carrying his suitcases fuller" (II 304). The Lorca character strongly sec-
onds this idea by observing that "from North to South on the weather-
vane on the roof there is the same distance as from one Pole to the
other Pole," with which the character Buñuel concurs: "Absolutely
the same" (II 304). The dialog vividly illustrates a major dilemma of
the new artistic paradigm beginning to manifest itself in the personal
styles of these artists. While affirming the new mode of expression,
Lorca is also aware that it is bringing to light differences among his
circle of friends that this dialog is intended to ameliorate. Buñuel's
scenarios are much more expansive and thus require a greater visual
vocabulary while Lorca prefers to work within a more reduced and
private visual geography. Although his aim in this piece is to reiter-
ate—to the flesh-and-blood Buñuel—that the goals of both artists are
indeed compatible, it nevertheless reflects Lorca's equally earnest alle-
giance to the particular terms of his commitment to the new mode of
production.

Lorca's preference for a more reduced and "traditional" physical
geography does not in any way detract from a Modernist sensibility
firmly anchored in a "tradition" which has less to do with folklore or
"Spanishness" than with the facilitation of an imaginative evasion of
the inadequacies of mimetically determined representation.[1] The no-
tion of tradition in the expansive and universalist sense that Modern-
ists like T. S. Eliot, James Joyce, Pound and many others understand it

becomes a significant aspect of the new aesthetic. In Eliot's seminal "Tradition and the Individual Talent," tradition becomes the foundation stone of modernity, a new expressiveness conscious of its uniqueness and originality by virtue of the awareness of its continuity, and discontinuity, with the past. Others, like the Surrealists much less in awe of tradition (although they are also concerned with tracing their artistic genealogy, to Goya, Baudelaire, Lautréamont, and others), nevertheless make extraordinary efforts, via pronouncements and manifestos, to establish a foundational position. Thus, "traditionalists" like Eliot and iconoclasts like the Surrealists are engaging in a fundamentally similar enterprise when they invoke or denigrate tradition, that of authorizing their very modernity.

Critics of Lorca's theater have also been reluctant to advance the view that his production is specifically Modernist.[2] Although the preponderance of theater criticism, both formalist and poststructuralist, continues to be dominated by textual strategies, the phenomenon of verbal-visual realignment during Modernism affords a significant methodological point of departure for a study of Lorca's theater. One of the principal aspects of criticism of Lorca's theater is the difficulty that critics have in making his plays conform to a strict realist paradigm, even in his so-called socially motivated "rural dramas." A frequent strategy is to ascribe those elements that are not easily assimilable into a realist format (e.g., symbolic figures and even the motivations of specific characters) to the intrusion of the dramatist's personality in the work, that is, a "realism"—often qualified by adjectives such as "magical," "poetic," etc.—accompanied by the "real" presence of the playwright. Such a position has been most succinctly stated by Ricardo Gullón, who understands form and posits closure in Lorca's theater by means of identifying the implicit configuration of the playwright's personality in his productions. For Gullón, what is normally a component of narrative, the phenomenon of point of view, becomes prominent in Lorca's theater because the audience is able to recognize the work as taking its form from a specific personality, the product of an unmistakable source. Lorca's maturing vision aims to expose explicit truths, including truths about himself. Thus the New Critical idea of the literary work as a "verbal icon" acquires personalistic connotations as the plays become vehicles for the emergence of the playwright's person and personality. The language of the text refers the audience or reader to yet another more intimate self-referential dimension that strongly associates the meaning of Lorca's theater with the artist's signature. This tendency to see Lorca in his dramatic texts has proven irresistible to many critics, especially in relation to the issue of his homosexuality, which also implicitly underlies Gullón's argument.[3]

From a poststructuralist perspective, Paul Julian Smith argues against these very proprietary attachments to Lorca's name, replacing the person of Lorca with a Foucauldian model of depersonalized authorship. For the form and meaning that Gullón understands to cluster around the name Lorca are substituted an impersonal equivalent that, while it addresses the issue—as opposed to the "problem"—of sexuality and desire in Lorca, does so in such a manner as to erase any distinction among forms of writing. Lorca's theater is thus assimilated into an iconoclastic paradigm that takes a view of Lorca's theater that effectively stops at the script. Well-intentioned as these exercises are, I consider that the significant issues, formal and ideological, in Lorca's theater may be more fully addressed by recent advances in performance criticism that approach theater as both a visual and verbal phenomenon—that is, not only as the product of historical, ideological, psychological, and sociocultural factors that move the pen of the playwright in a given direction and not another but also as a public, physical activity inextricably wed to an equally intense intellectual activity, the dialectical engagement of the minds and imaginations of a body of spectators by the playwright's words in specific visual scenes.

Performance models generally recognize that the act of theater includes two distinctive components, the theater script, the verbal province of a playwright, and the scenario, the visual-physical domain of the stage director who takes the script, including its specific staging directions, and transforms it—via the use of actors, acting styles, costume, props, and transformations of the script itself—into a viable performance text (or *mise-en-scène*) intended for an audience (see Alter 31–90; Elam 208–10; Hornby 40–67; Issacharoff 138–43; Pavis 133–61; Ubersfeld 11–19). Although the models are numerous and varied, each emphasizing specific dimensions within a wide repertoire of possibilities (see Hornby 92–109 for an overview and discussion), in general, the performance text emphasizes the connectedness between script and performance as it attempts to account for and to integrate directorial input into the elaboration of the performance text. Performance criticism thus tends to understand the act of interpretation as having to do with both the use made of the stage and the response of the theater audience to an actual performance. Especially significant in the evolution of Lorca's theater is the idea-function, and reality, of the audience, an especially prominent aspect of his more mature theater.

Although nearly all performance models consider the theater audience to be an integral component of the performance, there is presently a spectrum of opinion regarding the prominence of the audience function, ranging from the historical response model of Jauss premised on the audience's "horizon of expectations" to more stage-centered notions of response that understand the audience's function more in terms of interpreting a stage director's intentions (Alter 213–18; Pavis 71–78).[4] An advantage of performance-text models, which are themselves responses both to the need to account for the iconic dimension of theater already implicit in the script and to the historical emergence and prominence of the strong stage director during the twentieth century, is the potentially greater sensitivity to the visual-verbal (symbolic-iconic) contentiousness that characterizes Modernist art in general and that is also significant in the evolution of Lorca's theater.

Francisco Ruíz Ramón (*Historia* 177) has postulated that the underlying theme of all of Lorca's theater is the conflict between authority and freedom, that is, an unyielding moral-social code that clashes with the desperate desire for a release from its oppressive obligations. Such a view, however, contrasts sharply with Lorca's abovementioned pleas for greater authority for the stage. This is because authority in its fullest sense connotes the ability to command obedience without recourse to coercion or even to persuasion. Acceptance of authority means conformity to the will of another without having to be ordered, convinced, or forced.[5] According to this more exact application of the term, therefore, Lorca's stage more accurately depicts the disintegration of traditional authority into struggles for power. This is a significant distinction that more exactly characterizes as well the tension between the activity on the performance stage and its real antagonist, the theater audience and its extensions inside and beyond the institution of theater. Lorca makes his entrance upon the Madrid theater scene at a moment when stage discipline is in short supply. Even the most serious theater companies were largely undisciplined and typically directed not by professional stage directors but by lead actors, who often pandered to audiences for the sake of greater profits and applause.[6] The reestablishment of stage authority requires, therefore, that everyone involved in theater—actors, entrepreneurs, and theater critics as well as the immediate theater audience—accept the professionalizing authority of qualified stage directors and scriptwriters no longer willing to acquiesce in conventional theater fare. The power struggles represented on Lorca's stage are thus paralleled by an equally intense conflict between two offstage spaces, the audience's and that of a more authoritative theater agenda demanding a hearing.

The most succinct expression of this new alignment of forces, which impacts directly upon the relationship between the visual and the verbal aspects of theater, is offered by the Director near the end of *The Public* where he confesses that his efforts to build a tunnel to the subterranean location where the most intimate truths about himself and his theater reside, the "theater beneath the sand," have ultimately been directed to revealing "the profile of a hidden force when the audience has no further recourse except to pay full attention, filled with spirit and overpowered by the action" (II 665). Lorca's mission as a dramatist is shaped by his acknowledgment of the demands upon him by forces that cannot be represented under realist theater models and conventions that presuppose a convenient interdependence between the visual and verbal dimensions of theater. The standard components of story, plot, character development, and the "four-wall" interior setting[7] become decidedly secondary to the exposition of the more intense private reality, here characterized in relation to a theater whose audience consists of but a single character and his phantoms. Expanding upon the Director's insights, Lorca's stage becomes the physical site for a revitalized theater that acknowledges the more significant existential-artistic authority embodied in this hidden force. Well before he writes *The Public*, however, Lorca gives strong indications that he understands that the significant issues in his life, especially his homosexuality, are not choices but rather responses to the direction provided by a more sublime form of authority. Lorca's theater thus emerges in response to the authority of two offstage domains, the audience (in an ideologically charged sense, a diverse group of spectators

with specific points of view) and the existential-artistic imperatives of
the hidden force, which make the stage the site of an ongoing dialectic.

I wish to use the idea of a hidden force primarily as a focusing devise
in order to suggest that in the rather hierarchical theater model that
Lorca envisions for the reform of an anarchic Spanish stage, there is a
need to differentiate between the source of authority, typically sepa-
rate from the governing apparatus, and the visible exercise of power
undertaken in the name of that authority (Arendt 111). The artistic
consequences of Lorca's relationship to a hidden source of authority
may be compared to the intimate scene in Velázquez's *The Maids of
Honor (Las meninas)* in which the court painter appeals for artistic
authority by virtue of his intimate association with the royal house-
hold, of which the key members—the Spanish king and queen—are
not directly represented in the painting. They are part of the extended
space of the picture but not of the representation. A similar relation-
ship obtains between Lorca and the authority of the hidden force
whose invisible presence exercises a considerable effect upon the space
of the stage, extending it in unconventional directions, while the
source of those effects remains separate from what is visually repre-
sented. Authority, therefore, provides a foundation and framework, a
certain direction from which there ensues a progressive willingness
to acknowledge that authority and thus to follow its imperatives. The
hidden force is an integral aspect of an alternative theatrical structure,
which produces a struggle for dominance over the stage between the
dramatist and the theater audience in all its extensions. This structure
and the resulting struggle bring into greater visual profile an agenda for
theater relegated to the status of the unstageable.

A significant consequence of Lorca's empathy with the view of such
a multivalent idea of an extended theatrical reality is the creation of a
supporting cast of metafictional characters. Rather than interjecting
his own personality or using the stage to refer specifically to him-
self, as Gullón and others have suggested he does, Lorca progressively
dramatizes the theater functions, as forces and/or personalities, which
under strictly realist conventions would not be part of the act of thea-
ter. Although numerous critics of Lorca's theater (for example, Farris
Anderson in "Metatheatre," Silver, and most recently Vitale) have
made reference to "metatheater" to characterize specific moments, en-
tire plays, or aspects of Lorca's productions, this concept made popular

by Lionel Abel has been expanded upon in more recent discussions by performance critics (notably De Marinis 121–36, Hornby 110–26, Schlueter 1–17, Schmelling 47–98).

In fact, a form of metatheatricality is an almost inherent aspect of any actual performance since the very presence of human actors and real objects on stage, according to Anna Whiteside (expanding upon Ubersfeld 19–29 and the concept of "ostension" offered by Elam 30 and Eco 225), means that theatrical signs function as both signs and referents, indeed, as "a hyphenated sign-referent: at once a sign of something and the thing or things referred to by the actors. Thus, the concrete theatrical referent seen onstage refers, in turn, to itself as a mimetic theatrical sign . . . [and] to theatre as theatre. . . . Self-reference . . . concerns all artistic creation and re-creation and is the inevitable correlate of our awareness of the poetic function" (27). Lorca himself was also well aware of the close proximity of the metadramatic in every performance, even the most seemingly realistic, as the Autor ironically indicates in *Play Without A Title:* "Reality begins because the author does not want you to feel that you are in the theater, but rather in the middle of the street" (II 1070). Rather than to emphasize specific references to overt theatricality or play-life metaphors of the type that have characterized previous discussions of metatheatrics in Lorca's plays, I shall instead accentuate situations in which the dramatic characters display characteristics that associate them with the self-critical examination and evolution of the principal theater functions. Although there are numerous, and extended, metadramatic moments in Lorca's theater, this dimension is perhaps most significant as a more generalized intertextual system of reference and/or reflection upon the evolution of the theory and practice of his own theater.

Lorca was confronted by a Madrid theater scene already "metatheatricalized" in a negative sense by the decline in professional standards, a significant consequence of which was the effective breakdown in the demarcation line between the space of the stage and the audience (see Dougherty and Vilches). Lorca responds by dramatizing, through characters (or more explicitly in spokespersons in prologs), the essential functions of theater and their relationship to the audience. Responsibility for the theater script, consistently referred to as the function of the "poet," is complemented by the "stage director" responsible for transforming the text into a readily available visual spectacle for an audience. Lorca, of course, uses the script to indicate some of his ideas for an actual performance, as do virtually all playwrights, by means of his staging instructions, or didascalia, which in addition to the physical setting can also include the naming of characters, their actions, location, gestures, and objects of address (Ubersfeld 17; Issacharoff 63). Emerging fully only at the end of Lorca's career is the more authoritative synthesis of these two functions, in both a theoretical and practical sense, the *autor*, the embodiment of fuller stage authority. The evolution of these personalities/functions offers an ongoing view of Lorca's thinking about the theoretical and practical dynamics of his theater as well as the possibilities and limitations inherent in a view of life bound to the interventions of the hidden force.

At the outset of Lorca's career, in *The Butterfly's Spell* and other early plays, there is a disequilibrium, if not yet a fully defined dialectical tension, between the primary theater functions. Perhaps still somewhat under the influence of his juvenile dialogs, Lorca demonstrates at this early point that he has little consciousness of audience, that theater centers squarely in the poetic function, the script, and that he is indulging a private agenda rather than creating a viable circuit of reception. The dramatic potential of this private agenda, however, does not become fully apparent until after Lorca is forced to acknowledge, in *The Public*, the imposing authority of the audience and its negative implications for the type of theater that he wishes to develop. The early theater also witnesses, however, the growing prominence of the director function, with its authority inextricably wed to the audience. The imagined consequences of a test of audience tolerance are explored in *The Public*, in which the shortcomings of the dramatic theory of the Director are exposed. As Lorca's private agenda begins to confront the public reality, stageability becomes a progressively more central concern. As a consequence of both his experimental theater and his practical experience as principal director with La Barraca, Lorca further refines his understanding of theater in the face of social and artistic circumstances during the 1930s. The dialectic between the theater functions—conflicting goals of dramatic authority (the "poet") and the necessity for commercial viability before approving audiences (the director)—reaches a sublime moment in the "rural tragedies" and culminates in the *Play Without A Title* (written at the same period as *The House of Bernarda Alba*) as Lorca achieves a synthesis in the Autor, who assumes authority over the stage in the multiple role of script-writer, stage director, and theoretician-critic.[8] The final phase in Lorca's theater thus signals his own recognition of his growing authority as a dramatist and his greater confidence in his creative powers.

In the box-office failure of *The Butterfly's Spell* Lorca learns the essential lesson that the audience is an absolutely necessary component of the theater equation. By the end of his career, the audience had become both multidimensional in its range—for Lorca the different types, levels, and prices of seating in the theater reflected the multiple divisions within Spanish society—and synonymous with vision itself. By the "rural dramas" Lorca had embarked upon a strategy to confront the power of vision of his audience, ironically, by enhancing audience vision to the point of omniscience, by allowing the spectator to assume what amounts to "directorial" authority as regards the unfolding scenario. The visual domain of the theater stage is thus effectively conflated with the imagination-consciousness of the spectator while the verbal authority of the script becomes more intimately associated with an offstage discourse that represents itself to characters on stage unconstrained by the visual anecdotes that acquire prominence in the spectator's mind. Lorca achieves his fullest metadramatic synthesis in the "rural" plays as the act of theater becomes the occasion to confront mutual antagonists, the audience and the "hidden force," which in turn dramatize the disruption of visual-verbal complementarity that typifies Modernist expression.

As Lorca's dramatic authority grows during the thirties, he also begins to acknowledge his activities in an expanded and more European context. In *Don Cristobal's Little Puppet Stage* (*El retablillo de don Cristóbal*), he envisions his puppet theater in solidarity with the farcical traditions of the rest of Europe. Indeed, the Director of this piece equates Cristobal (along with his Spanish compatriots Bululú and Aunt Norica) as a "brother of Monsieur Guiñol, of Paris, and uncle of Mr. Harlequin, of Bergamo, as one of the characters in which the original essence of theater remains pure" (II 697). As Lorca explores the roots of his own theatrical intuitions and inspiration, he also understands his sympathies and compatibilities with developments in other parts of Europe. Indeed, Lorca had communicated directly with Pirandello and Beccari in Italy and was able to announce in an interview in August, 1935 that Pirandello—"the great promoter of my

[work] in Italy" (III 644-45)—had solicited *Yerma* for an Italian production of the play. Besides the unconcealed pride in making the announcement—of an event that, unfortunately, was not realized—Lorca is by this moment fully aware that his growing authority as a dramatist also depends upon his theater's ability to reach beyond Spanish audiences alone. Although the influence of Pirandello—specifically his trilogy on theater *Six Characters in Search of an Author, Each in His Own Way*, and *Tonight We Improvise*—is evident in the experimental plays (see Vitale 54-64), an equally significant point of continuity between the avant-garde works and the commercially successful plays that immediately follow is the issue of dramatic distance, which is fundamentally similar in both the experimental theater and the commercially successful plays that follow. The strong sense of distance between stage and theater audience that pervades the early theater fully disappears in the experimental plays, which demand the spectator's total acquiescence in a metadramatic landscape not at all subservient to realist conventions. Likewise, in the "rural dramas," the idea of distance is radically diminished as the spectator's heightened consciousness and the visual dominance of the unfolding scenario not only contrasts sharply with the characters' obviously more limited range of physical and moral vigilance but actually affords the audience an inordinate, nearly omniscient visual share of the unfolding representation.

Daphna Ben Chaim has suggested that the "deliberate manipulation of distance is, to a great extent, the underlying factor that determines theatrical style in this century" (79). In relation to other European contemporaries, here may well lie one of Lorca's greatest original contributions to Modernist theater models. For Brecht the theater experience should seek to prevent the viewer's empathetic involvement with the characters, heightening the sense of distance between audience and the stage in order to increase intellectual-critical involvement so as to enable the audience to perceive alternatives to the events depicted on stage, to drop the fourth-wall convention and to address the audience directly, to emphasize the story over the characters themselves (Chaim 25-28). In a somewhat different vein, Artaud aims at establishing an encounter between actor and spectator, "a pervasive sense of urgency [that] prevent[s] the audience from assuming the role of mere spectators" (Ben Chaim 40-41). To accomplish this, Artaud bombards the spectator with violent physical images that speak directly to the spectator's mind. Although such an assault calls to mind the finale of *Play Without A Title* in which the theater is literally bombarded from above by aircraft, for Lorca, who was forced to grapple from the outset with audiences pandered to by actors and producers alike fully accustomed to having the stage reflect their own rather limited imaginative agenda, the manipulation of distance takes the form of further erasing an already tenuous line between the space of the stage and the imagination of the spectator.

The experimental plays are, in the context of the Madrid theater scene of the thirties, unstageable (III 674) precisely because all sense of distance has disappeared. For an audience to view a play like *The Public*, it must accept the play unconditionally or simply refuse to continue to watch it—that is, leave the theater. While Lorca fully understood this, he equally understood that the effective erasure of a sense of distance—in a negative sense, as a consequence of the abdication of authority over the stage to an audience unaccustomed to innovation or discipline—also fundamentally characterizes the contemporary scene. It is precisely this issue that Lorca uses to maximum advantage in the rural dramas that immediately follow his unstageable experiments. In greatly enhancing the audience's sense of presence in the performance by affording it a perspective that is all but omniscient, Lorca is indeed able to achieve the type of stage authority he envisions in *The Public*, conditions of performance "when the audience has no further recourse except to listen, full of spirit and overpowered by the action" (II 665). This is especially true in seemingly more realistic representations like *The House of Bernarda Alba* in which Lorca, in contradistinction to Brecht, uses the fourth-wall convention to include the spectator within the enclosed space of a house—to make the spectator a privileged witness to the action, only to use that very perspective to demonstrate the insufficiency of vision and ordinary consciousness in the face of the authority of the hidden force.

This extended tension between the verbal and iconic dimensions of theater is also responsible for another significant feature of Lorca's theater: its indexicality. Often ignored in literary applications of Saussurean semiotics that have focused on the verbal-symbolic sign, the indexical sign, or index, has nevertheless been significant in discussions of theater semiotics. Along with the symbol and the icon, the index is one of the three principal categories of signs identified by Charles Sanders Peirce. If the symbolic sign is characterized by the conventionality and arbitrariness with which meaning is assigned to it by the speakers in a given milieu, there being nothing inherent in the symbol to give it meaning,[9] icons, on the other hand, typically images and pictures, depend upon likeness for their status.[10] Iconism, of course, is significant and often decisive in any discussion of theater performance since "anything which permits the spectator to form an image or likeness of the represented object can be said to have fulfilled an iconic function" (Elam 25). Although the index often manifests itself in verbal and visual contexts, its function is not to represent but rather to indicate, to point toward, the real object to which it refers.[11] Thus, demonstrative pronouns are indexes because they refer to or point in the direction of the referent, understood as a real object. Weathervanes establish an indexical relationship with the object, the wind, with which they have a real connection. A knock on a door is an index in that the sound refers to the agent responsible for its production. Fingerprints, footprints, and the impressions left by glasses on tabletops are also indexes, not representations but rather traces of the actual object/agent to which they refer. In a similar manner, photographs are indexes and not icons because the photographic process is considered not to be engaging in representation but rather is establishing on a developing medium a point-to-point relationship with the actual reality that it traces.[12] As traces and not as representations, indexes occupy a position intermediate to that of a self-referential visual and/or verbal representation and the actual presence of the referent. The importance of the indexical sign-function is emphasized by Pavis: "The theater, which must constantly attract the receiver's attention, will thus have recourse to the index" (16). As Elam also maintains, although "the indexical function appears secondary to the iconic . . . there are instances where what predominates on stage is a 'pointing to' rather than an imagistic mode of signifying" (26).

Realist representational models that presuppose the easy interdependence of visual and verbal discourse—that they are "perfect, transparent media through which reality may be represented" (Mitchell 8)—have largely overlooked the role of indexicality.[13] Lorca's awareness of the authority of a hidden force guiding his understanding of reality and art is integral to a mode of consciousness and artistic production subversive of visual-verbal complementarity. Signification becomes a process rather than a finality, movement in the direction of a more significant referent excluded from the domain of the visual. As Lorca's art matures, there is a growing tendency to suggest that meaning does not fully reside in the space of the representation, that is, on a stage filled with visual and verbal signs, but also offstage in an area that has not been explicitly revealed to the audience but which nevertheless constitutes the true, or at least a truer, locus of meaning. Although present from the outset, indexicality becomes significant in the experimental plays and continues throughout the thirties. As visual-verbal complementarity diminishes, the stage ceases being a self-contained space, providing instead indications of a more authoritative offstage referent. Meaning is thus manifested "indexically," along a directional axis rather than at a stable point of hermeneutical closure, in what may be termed an extended act of pointing, to a referent that lies beyond the space of the stage.

Although it is undeniable that the Spanish theater scene was less than desirable for Lorca as he embarked upon his stage career (see Fernández Cifuentes 11–26), he nevertheless directly benefited from certain pockets of strength that had emerged. The most significant of these was his experience with the La Barraca theater group. Here Lorca gained invaluable experience as a stage director in an atmosphere in which economic considerations were not a principal concern. What emerges from accounts of Lorca's organization of the company and of specific performances, principally of Golden Age masterpieces— among which are Calderón's *auto sacramental* of *Life is a Dream* (*La vida es sueño*); Lope's *Fuenteovejuna*, *The Knight of Olmedo* (*El caballero de Olmedo*), and *The Silly Lady* (*La dama boba*); Tirso's *The Trickster of Seville* (*El burlador de Sevilla*); and numerous *entremeses*, or interact plays, by Cervantes—is the view of a "strong" stage director very much in keeping with the strong directing styles being practiced in other parts in Europe by Brecht, Pirandello, Artaud, Stanislavski, and others. If not overtly dictatorial, Lorca certainly exerted a considerable degree of control over his performances. Actors with the La Barraca group were typically assigned roles according to the character types they could best portray, and Lorca would select from among an available pool to meet his staging needs (III 595). This, of course, gave him much greater freedom than he would typically encounter on the Madrid stage where playwrights were often forced to give their scripts to acting companies in which selections for dramatic roles were made on a much less objective basis.

Although Lorca professed a great respect for the poetic texts of the classical masters, he typically took great liberties with the script. While he rarely if ever altered the actual dialog, he did make extensive cuts in the plays. For example, in the La Barraca version of Lope's *The Knight of Olmedo*, Lorca eliminates the greater part of the final act, ending the play at the moment when the Knight of Olmedo is murdered and thus deleting the eloquent call for justice on the part of the fool (*gracioso*) and the apprehension of the assassins (Byrd *Barraca* 83; see also Fox 188–91). Clearly, Lorca's interpretation makes the play a more tragic spectacle. Likewise in *Fuenteovejuna*, which modern Hispanists have generally interpreted (perhaps incorrectly) as a plea for national unity by means of an alliance between the peasants and the monarchy, Lorca eliminated all the scenes referring to the Catholic Kings (Fox 188–89), setting the stage as well with a contemporary background and putting the actors in modern dress (Byrd *Barraca* 54). Obviously, these decisions are partly influenced by the strongly anti-monarchical sentiments in Spain at the beginning of the Second Republic. However, they are also characteristic of a stage director who understands theater in a fully Modernist sense, whereby the performance, through the director's elaboration of a performance script, is a collaborative-interpretive effort between the poetic text and the director. Lorca's repeated calls for qualified stage directors who would also be interpreters of the works they staged—that is, who would become full participants in bringing a more art-centered theater to the commercial stage—is at least in part a consequence of the experience gained and freedom he enjoyed as La Barraca's principal director. By 1934 Lorca was making his message of renewed authority for the stage a frequent subject of public pronouncements:

Therefore, in order to achieve authority in the theater it is not enough simply to stage works of merit, but it is also necessary to stage them with an indispensable stage director. This is something that all theater companies should understand. What are needed are authorized and documented stage directors who will transform the works that they interpret with their own identifiable style. And I am not advocating that only masterworks be staged, because this simply cannot be, but I do affirm that with a director and enthusiasm among the actors disciplined by him, that from even a bad work the virtues and the effects of a good work can be salvaged. (III 454)

Another frequently noted aspect of Lorca's directing is his acute attention to audience response. Lorca would carefully observe each audience to which La Barraca played to determine which aspects of the performance were or were not felicitous and which groups, typically corresponding to social position, were responding favorably or unfavorably (Byrd *Barraca* 39). In many instances the audience effectively consisted of an entire village, which nevertheless had its class divisions and distinct constituencies. If a given play or aspect of a play were not well received, Lorca would make necessary changes to ensure a more favorable subsequent response. What this also reveals, in conjunction with his thoughts on the subject of stage directing in *The Public*, is a strong awareness that the director must make himself or herself responsible for making a play work before an audience. Stageability, in the dialectical sense of what a specific audience is able to tolerate, is perhaps the most important concept to emerge from Lorca's theorizing about stage direction in *The Public*—in the aftermath of initial yet ultimately less than satisfying successes with *Mariana Pineda* and *The Shoemaker's Prodigious Wife*—and in his subsequent work with La Barraca. In writing *The Public*, a play that expresses powerful truths about himself as well as his characters and his attitudes toward life, love, and theater, Lorca also realizes that the guiding authority in his life compels him to the theater with a representational agenda that under present circumstances is unstageable. As embodied in the pronouncements of the Magician (Prestidigitador) of *The Public*, Lorca is acutely aware that the contrivance of a viable scenario, even if at odds with the poetic content, is the first responsibility of all stage direction. Lorca was well aware of the importance of the visual domain of the stage director: "the problem of novelty in the theater is intertwined in great measure with the visual. Half of the production depends on the rhythm, color, and scenography" (III 627).[14] Indeed, the tension between a hidden agenda that was clearly unstageable under then current standards and the desire to impose such a program upon spectators whose typical impulse would be "immediately to arise indignant in order to prevent the representation from continuing" (III

557) constitutes perhaps the most significant dialectical tension of Lorca's mature theater.

In spite of the mediocrity that characterizes much of the Spanish theater scene during this period, Lorca was not entirely alone in his quest to reestablish theatrical authority. In Madrid, the emergence of a small cadre of professional directors, prominent among whom is Cipriano Rivas Cherif, did exert a professionalizing influence, in certain sectors of the theater, that Lorca understood as necessary for the type of reform he envisioned. This also made it easier for Lorca himself to direct some of his own plays, significant among which is *Blood Wedding* (*Bodas de sangre*), in the manner of a professional stage director. Equally significant was the emergence of theater clubs, especially the Club Anfistora—which Lorca himself named and helped to subsidize—that offered significant outlets for him to stage plays that were not commercially feasible.[15] Besides providing a vehicle for a 1933 in camara production of *Love of Don Perlimplín with Belisa in His Garden*, in the spring of 1936 the Club Anfistora was the site of rehearsals for a planned production of *As Soon As Five Years Pass*, which along with *The Public* Lorca had been terming for years his "unstageable plays" (III 674). The evidence suggests that by 1936 Lorca had attained a significant measure of the authority necessary to bring a fully avant-garde agenda before at least one sector of the Spanish theater public—a select audience of theatergoers less resistant to innovation and intellectual challenge, if not the masses necessary to sustain a long-running play (see III 521)—which had not been possible only a short time earlier.

As tragic as Lorca's assassination was in the early weeks of the Spanish Civil War, this should not detract from the fact that by 1936 he had reached a point where he could risk bringing even his most controversial plays into public view. Laffranque ("Poeta" 31) and others have noted that by the end of his life Lorca had become quite serious about bringing *The Public* to the stage. The steadfast loyalty to his experimental work suggests that Lorca understood the pivotal importance of these plays in his theatrical development, that the unresolved tensions in these works are directly related to his commercial successes. Above all, Lorca's experimental writing confirms his awareness of a new source of artistic authority that leads him through tragedy to an eventually more positive understanding of himself and the moral-educative aspects of theater. By the *Play Without A Title*, his last autonomous piece of theater, he had become much more reconciled to his mature role as the medium of a sublime force still shaping his theater and his life. The chapters which follow trace the evolution of Lorca's relationship with this more authoritative reality, the inspiration for perhaps the most original theater of the Spanish contemporary era.

2

THE EARLY THEATER

IN HIS EARLIEST theater, Lorca demonstrates a growing awareness that the viability of his productions depends upon more than simply the written word. Perhaps the greatest lesson of the initial phase of his theater that often features poets as principal characters, all of whom fare quite poorly, is the understanding that the essential function of the scriptwriter, or poet, must be more fully integrated with the other indispensable functions of theater. Lorca begins his stage career without a well-developed sense of performance dynamics, as witnessed in the early prominence of ineffectual male characters who embody the poetic function—Curianito of *The Butterfly's Spell* and the Marquis and the Coachman of *Lola, the Actress* (*Lola, la comedianta*)—followed later by stronger female representatives whose involvement with artistry and craftsmanship nevertheless places them in peril. Rosita's needlepoint in *Tragicomedy of Don Cristobal and Miss Rosita* (*Tragicomedia de Don Cristóbal y la Seña Rosita*) generates earnings insufficient to prevent her father from marrying her for money to the hideous Cristobal, while Mariana Pineda's revolutionary flag with its embroidered credo transfigures it into a type of script, which eventually destroys her. After the disastrous four-performance run of his first play, *The Butterfly's Spell* (Gibson "Estreno" 71–73), Lorca is forced to consider the limitations of his initial understanding of a script-oriented agenda that does not adequately acknowledge the circuit of reception. Lorca's early theater may thus be read in terms of its growing, but reluctant, awareness that his theater must concern itself with the issues of performance and reception, that is, the directorial function, as much as it does with an idea regarding the operant forces in the world.[1]

The Butterfly's Spell

The limitations of this approach to theater are evident in *The Butterfly's Spell*. The prominence of prologs (and similar devices) in the early plays suggests that Lorca feels it necessary to avail himself of extradramatic instruments of stage direction, their purpose becoming to establish what the script alone cannot, a reduction of the tension between a rather unorthodox theater topic and the actual stage production. The prolog to *The Butterfly's Spell* evinces an uneasiness and defensiveness about the play's likely reception because of the playwright's consciousness of the need to direct his audience to an understanding that, without the presence of the prolog, would be unlikely.[2] Paralleling Lorca's evident desire to create an original and challenging theater script is an anxiety about the inherent strength of this composition to communicate authoritatively. Offstage prompting is thus required to bridge the gap between script and performance text, the participation of a directorial function, in the form of the speaker of the prolog, being appended after the fact.

The prolog to *The Butterfly's Spell* is interpretive in that the audience is told explicitly what to think about the play's unusual form and content. The audience is also fully briefed about the origins, intellectual evolution, and destiny of its cockroach protagonist, the poet Curianito, as well as about the outcome of his unrequited love for a butterfly who falls wounded into his humble community among the dense grasses. The speaker directs his remarks to an audience he senses is already predisposed not to be sympathetic to his artistic project. Reed Anderson, in fact, has suggested that "there are really two coincident figurations of the audience here: there is one audience whose narrowly constructed sense of reality makes it incapable of forming a sympathetic relationship with the play to be performed; and there is another audience—an imagined one, perhaps immanent in the first audience—which will form the perfect relationship with the play" ("Prólogos" 215).

I would suggest, however, that this imagined or ideal audience does not embrace the theatergoing public but rather is a private audience, of one.[3] Although the speaker in the prolog is in command of the intellectual content of his theater, his role, analogous to that of stage director, is to assist in making available to the theater audience, by means of literary allusions and other intellectual reinforcements, the physical scene of a fundamentally private script from which it has been excluded. Distancing the audience is the ultimate consequence of making only an intellectual connection between the cockroach society and conventional reality. As Balboa Echevarría has commented, "the audience is situated far above the characters" (36), at a significant remove from a self-enclosed world.

Although Lorca's subsequent acknowledgment and awareness of the presence of the audience in his theater (throughout the course of his career yet perhaps most dramatically in *The Public*) allows him eventually to become a successful playwright, his attitude to the idea of the audience as suggested here does not fundamentally change. If Lorca writes *The Butterfly's Spell* without a full consciousness of or concern for how his script will play before an audience and if the play does indeed fail primarily for this reason, then it is evident that for practical purposes Lorca has written the play primarily for a private audience consisting only of himself. Indeed, in an interview some fifteen years after the premiere of *The Butterfly's Spell*, Lorca still strongly emphasizes the ontological status of his plays laboriously constructed in mental landscapes where they essentially reside until the moment that they are given over, by an act of transference, to the public domain: "A long constant, substantial period of thinking. And then, finally, the definitive transference; from my mind to the scene" (III 629). The fundamental difference between this play and his later masterpieces is that in the later works Lorca is better equipped to handle the moment of transference. The attainment of his passionately articulated goal of full dramatic authority implies that no play would ever become the subject of public censure or ridicule and also that the distinction between private truths and the public means to represent such truths would fully collapse. Throughout his later career, which he progressively equates with restoring the lost authority of the Spanish stage, Lorca repeatedly returns to the idea of the private theater—certainly in his experimental plays but also in his commercial plays, notably, among others, in *The House of Bernarda Alba*—because as he achieves fuller authority over the stage he is also making possible, and thus returning to, the essentially private idea of theater expressed in *The Butterfly's Spell*.

The practical consequence of this approach is the audience's sense of alienation from a scenario that is clearly an appendage of the script, a mental construct rather than an integral dimension of the performance. Indeed, the prevailing sentiment in both prolog and play is one of imaginative weakness. The audience is called upon to follow an intellectual argument, to consider dialog rather than to observe a parallel society. Curianito becomes a poet because he happens upon a book of romantic poetry left in the field where he lives. Likewise, the prolog's speaker reminds the audience that the inspiration for the play arose in a dialog with a character who has escaped from yet another text, Shakespeare's *A Midsummer Night's Dream*, further emphasizing the play's intellectual foundation and literariness.[4] The prolog's attempt to situate the play in the audience's imagination by verbal means is a tacit confession of the play's failure to provide a viable physical context for its poetic content. The initial visual burden of these cockroaches is compounded by the fact that they simultaneously fulfill a symbolic function which, as the spectator refers to the ideas attached to these creatures, undermines their visual autonomy. Thus, the retiring and melancholy idealist Curianito, an aggregate of romantic conventions more than an autonomous character, is obsessively attached to a butterfly, another stereotype, the symbol and personification of impossible love. Indeed, the rest of this cockroach society becomes as inwardly directed and singularly obsessed as Curianito with the mysterious presence of the butterfly. Rather than intensifying or diversifying the reality of these creatures, the scriptwriter has caricatured them by virtue of juxtaposing their physical forms with the untenable idealism that animates them. The visual denseness of the play, in fact, demonstrates similarities with later works and characters of the mid-twenties, specifically the gypsies of *Gypsy Ballads*, whose physical forms clearly serve as a shield or barrier to a more intimate private agenda that their strong visuality serves to disguise or mystify.

Still somewhat in the manner of his juvenile dialog writing,[5] Lorca concerns himself here as much with the exposition of a personal thesis about the impossibility of love as with the drama inherent in such a thesis: "there was a bug who tried to go beyond love. He got burned by a vision that was extremely distant from his life" (II 5–6). The borrowed idea for the story, communicated to the scriptwriter by the old sylph, is related to the audience as hearsay information, its reliability made even more questionable because it is "wrapped up in its own melancholy" (II 6). In a fashion similar to the way that Curianito learns of the tragic nature of love, by reading about it, the audience must also listen to a story that grows increasingly distant and self-absorbed. Not only does "Death disguise itself as Love" (II 6) but the play itself becomes an extended disguise for forces that never fully manifest themselves. The play's visual dimension thus becomes a rather significant barrier to the communication of the verbal content and to full imaginative participation with the stage.

One of the most striking aspects of this insect society with its strong sense of class consciousness is the ease with which such a source of potential division is dissipated by the mention of the office and practice of poetry. Curianito's mother, Doña Curiana, is poor and thus more than eager to arrange her son's marriage to the upper-class Curianita Silvia. Her efforts are in vain, however, because Curianito, upon becoming a poet, orients his imagination to less earthly forms of love. As he tells Silvia ("Today I don't love you, Silvia" [II 25]), love's definition has changed. Poetry, not economic inequality, prevents their marriage. Although Doña Curiana is upset by this development, she and the other cockroaches fully understand the effects that poetry has upon one so destined. In the opening scene, a discussion between Doña Curiana and Curiana Nigromántica becomes quickly diverted to the subject of poetry and its extensions in society. In the same breath that Doña Curiana asks Curiana Nigromántica, "And you are also a poet, beloved neighbor?" (II 13), she also sarcastically affirms poetry's omnipresence since "in my class all of us know how to sing / and to suck the flowers" (II 13). Silvia's entrance as "all heart" (II 15) further sharpens the focus on poetry. Her melancholy "sadness that I am having / without anyone's knowing about it" (II 15) are clearly patterned after Curianito's. Complaints about the limitations of her small world—"I've only seen this place" (II 15)—bring her to the conclusion that she will have to go to "another world / where I am loved" (II 17) or that, in a statement that to a remarkable degree prefigures the scenario ten years hence of The Public, "I will bury myself beneath the sand / to see if a good lover / with his love will exhume me" (II 17). Doña Curiana's reaction is both to observe that "here everybody is a poet" (II 16) and also to tell Silvia that if she were to act upon these longings "you would drive yourself insane" (II 17). Thus, although Curianito is absent from the first two scenes, they are dominated by talk about him and his office. All conversations in this society ultimately defer to poetry, which seems all-pervasive in the collective consciousness. The real measure of difference among individuals is not social class or wealth but simply the extent to which one is willing to dedicate himself or herself to this office.

The discourse of these characters is reflective of the state of Curianito's imagination, which measures everything in relation to a guiding vision that has little correlation with his present reality. Enthralled in the nascent intuition of "the tepid sweetness / of the fire in which my strange passion dwells" (II 23), Curianito replies to Silvia's question "And where is your star?" (II 25) that it is "in my imagination" (II 25). The play thus depicts the dilemma of an obsessive and self-centered imagination that directs him "beyond love" to an alternate reality that is nevertheless "extremely distant from his life" (II 5). Although his imagination lifts him above the base and destructive aspects of desire personified in the sinister Alacranito, a surly woodsman who delights in eating the body parts of other insects,[6] Curianito confronts a much greater danger in the unexpected advent of the wounded butterfly, who in her delirium speaks of her treasure located in a star:

> The thread goes to the star
> where my treasure lies;
> my wings are silver,
> my heart is gold;
> the thread is dreaming
> of its sonorous vibration.
>
> (II 36)

The image of a vibrant thread correlates well with the activity of Curianito's own imagination, whose objects are bound to his consciousness rather than enjoying full freedom. Likewise, the physical presence of Curianito's longed-for image of love draws him ever more deeply into his melancholy: "In what complications of love has the wind entwined me? / Why is the flower of my innocence already withered / as another flower is given birth in my mind?" (II 38). In a sense, this experience populates an empty region of his soul, yet, as suggested by the image of the withered flower, it reveals that he is also resisting an encounter that he cannot fully comprehend or accept. The movement of his imagination, like the trajectory of the play, is, again, inward rather than expansive.

Curianito's dilemma is that there seems to be no object in the experiential realm upon which to satisfy the intensity of emotions that his imagination inspires. Curianito's vision, therefore, is of little worth in the larger audience of his present society. The unexpected appearance of the wounded butterfly, the precise physical correlative for the love he seeks, only reconfirms and intensifies this impasse, for she is unable to reciprocate love in any conventional sense. In addition to belonging to a different species, which precludes any possibility of producing offspring with Curianito, the butterfly does not even possess a mouth with which to kiss him ("Ay, I have no mouth!" [II 52]). Not only is physical intimacy impossible but the physical manifestation of Curianito's ideal proves more frustrating than its absence. The butterfly herself suggests that she and Curianito are incompatible precisely because they are so much alike. She is also an introverted idealist who longs to return to a life that she is denied among the cockroaches:

> The grain of sand speaks,
> and the leaves of the trees,
> and they all have
> a different path,
> but all the voices,
> and the songs that you hear,
> are strange disguises
> for a single song. A thread
> will carry me to the forests
> where life can be seen.
>
> (II 51)

Since she is seeking to escape the present reality, love cannot become a possibility for her here ("I do not know what love is. / Why are you disturbing my dream?" [II 53]). She is too much involved in her remembrance of a more satisfying life to be able to respond to Curianito's own vision of

> a world of happiness beyond these branches,
> full of nightingales and immense meadows:
> the world of dew
> where love never ends
>
> (II 55)

that estranges him from all but the most sublime and exalted forms of love.

Significantly, Curianito contrasts his version of love with the traditional religious tenets of the community, which have taught countless generations of cockroaches that they are "superior to everything cre-

ated" (II 55).[7] Curianito's hope is that love will also bring a reconcilia-
tion, a new context in which to affirm the worth and superiority of
truly sensitive souls like himself trapped in an untenable present. Un-
like the promise of religion of a life to come, the higher order to which
Curianito aspires is ultimately a phantom projection, an understand-
ing that originates in and remains with himself. The final scene af-
firms such a trajectory as Curianito attempts to communicate with
the butterfly who faints as soon as he embraces her. When she revives,
the butterfly breaks free and begins to dance alone (again, in a manner
that is repeated subsequently by Bells and Vine Shoots in *The Public*).
Overwhelmed by the realization that his vision of love is a futile one,
Curianito restates in the form of questions the premises of an intui-
tion that has destroyed him:

> Who gave me these eyes that I don't want
> and these hands that try to
> capture a love that I don't understand?
> And that brings my life to an end!
> Who gets me lost in the shadows?
> Who makes me suffer without having wings?
>
> (II 57)

These sentiments strongly echo the warning in the prolog that pro-
claimed a "a broken play that wants to scratch the moon and scratches
instead its own heart" (II 5), that is, a drama with an idealistic trajec-
tory that affirms instead the activity of an imagination as far from its
object as it is close to its own introverted desolation. Curianito's ques-
tions reveal his true status in relation to the intuited existence of a
better reality. His questioning of the given reality is thus undertaken
at the price of his own destruction.

The Girl That Waters the Sweetbasil and the Inquisitive Prince (*La niña que riega la albahaca y el príncipe preguntón*)

The superior reality that Curianito and the butterfly associate with
the stars is hidden from their view by the grasses, a milieu of lesser
associations that the more traditional cockroaches nevertheless find
comfortable. These elements reappear in Lorca's next theater project,
the short puppet piece *The Girl That Waters the Sweetbasil and the*

Inquisitive Prince, which shares much in common with the previous play. Both the Prince and Curianito ask questions for which they receive no satisfactory reply; both suffer the unfortunate consequences of lovesickness. The Prince is spared, at least temporarily, Curianito's unkind fate because of the curative intervention of Irene, the commoner who waters the basil plants and who, despite the Prince's alienating trick, eventually agrees to marry him.

As physical symbols, the stars and plants acquire a more direct and intimate significance in the puppet play. If the grasses symbolize the givens of consciousness as well as the unconscious inheritance of the collectivity in *The Butterfly's Spell,*[8] in the puppet play Irene's activity of watering inspires the Prince's first question, "How many little leaves do the plants have?" (II 63). Although it seems less than profound, it is actually a cruder version of Irene's more pertinent and metaphysical question-response "How many little stars are in the sky?" (II 63), which the Prince interprets as mockery, an attempt to humiliate him, since he intuits that a satisfactory answer does not exist. This inspires the Prince to a prank of his own, in the guise of a grapeseller, to obtain kisses from Irene. She responds by fleeing the scene, which leaves the Prince frustrated and severely depressed. Whereas Curianito's ungrounded fantasy provides no protection from the phantoms/questions that emerge to destroy him, the Prince's own tendency toward introversion and self-absorption—which the Page and the Negro underscore by attributing the Prince's lateness to the scene to his having to attend to bodily functions (II 62)—is redirected as a consequence of his fixation upon Irene. In the symbolic context of the early theater, however, Irene's care of the basil plants, whose name means "royalty" and whose heart-shaped leaves are often a symbol of love, is emblematic of their relationship. Just as the plants depend upon Irene for their continued vitality, however, so too does the Prince.

While this short piece originally performed before an audience of children seems to suggest a happy ending, its deeper content is more ominous. Desolate after Irene refuses to see him, the Prince falls into a deep melancholy as he laments the trials that love imposes: "Ay, how much it costs me / to love you like I love you! / Because of your love I am pained by the air, / my heart and my hat!" (II 67). These verses strongly echo the sentiments expressed in "Song of the Departing Day," "How much it costs me / to leave upon your breast possible realities / of impossible minutes!" (I 390), in which the departing day assumes qualities associated with a beloved. Analogous to the passing day in "Song of the Departing Day," Irene is the inconstant medium of the Prince's desire for fulfillment. Her absence provokes intense feelings of loss and painful awareness of his dependence upon an agent who demands extraordinary efforts that are exacting a severe personal cost. Without Irene, the Prince faces a destiny of melancholic debilitation or death. Although Irene's change of heart does save the Prince, at least momentarily, like the butterfly of *The Butterfly's Spell*, Irene's presence in the physical scene is contingent at best. Her more refined mode of questioning has oriented her toward a more exalted domain— a more sublime expression of their present activities—which is the very source of the Prince's anxiety.

Inconstancy is also a prominent aspect of the staging, dominated visually and verbally by the figure of the Negro, who acts as both narrator and scene setter for scenes referred to as "engravings" or "imprints" (*estampas*). As opposed to "scene" or an equivalent term, the designation raises again the issue of the distance between audience and stage. If *estampa* is understood to refer to printing or engraving, then the stage directions suggest a scene that is the self-conscious copy of an original, that the reality of these characters originates in another medium of which they are but projections. As in *The Butterfly's Spell*, the Prince and Irene are also stand-ins for forces that they embody. Irene, in fact, is summoned to the scene only after her father, the Zapatero, and the Negro decide that the story will focus upon her and not someone else. That the Prince, the son of a king who never appears physically on the stage, enters even later emphasizes that these characters are continuing an ongoing story rather than originating it.

Estampa, however, supports other meanings that associate it with metaphors for empirical cognition and thus may also connote the directness with which an image is copied or imprinted upon the imagination, suggesting, therefore, a simultaneous diminishment of the sense of distance between actors and audience. These meanings are not contradictory but rather affirm an intuition of a theatrical space that involves both associations. The decision to formulate this story as both a self-conscious imitation—a selected excerpt of a larger story, the form of which depends upon the quantity of money paid to its narrator—and something of a spontaneous eruption, which also hinges upon the audience's willingness to summon characters to the scene,

suggests that Lorca is more conscious of the verbal and visual dy-
namics of theater in this play. Both the late-arriving Irene and the
Prince are simultaneously aspects of a story narrated by the Negro,
actors themselves during moments of that story, and embodiments of
a larger discourse, a mode of consciousness-desire whose bewildering
premises they help to frame. The further suggestion that the true locus
or referent of the representation does not lie in them or in the story
proper but in an offstage field of reference means that the stage signs
are complementary primarily at a metadramatic level. Their most im-
portant function is indexical: to indicate the direction or location, if
not the presence, of that referent.

The narrator provides vital information to the audience about the
characters by interrupting the story, which in turn serves to distance
it from the visual stage where actors are in a sense already surrogates
by virtue of their wooden constitution. The representation is thus in
constant motion between the activity of the characters and the imagi-
nation/consciousness of the narrator. The principals are forced to
share the space of the stage with a medium that interrupts them and
undermines their autonomy, the mind that has elaborated a script but
has not counterbalanced it with a stable physical scene. A story that
has not freed itself from the mind of its teller thus adds a further note
of caution to the Prince's happy ending. Although the directorial func-
tion here is more integrated into the puppet play than in *The Butter-
fly's Spell*, it is still clearly a puppet of the script. More prominent than
the characters are the questions they ask, the answers for which, if
they exist at all, clearly lie beyond the space and scope of the stage
representation. Notwithstanding the fact that the narrator performs a
directorial function by announcing the scenario, narrator and scenario
ultimately reflect a continuing dependence upon the symbolic-poetic
discourse to which the play ultimately defers. The unanswerable ques-
tions obsessing the Prince become the play's real protagonist and a fur-
ther indication of the contentiousness between word and image in
Lorca's early theater.

Lola, the Actress

Contentiousness and inconstancy are also the principal themes of
the incomplete libretto *Lola, the Actress* which depicts a *burla*[9] by the
actress Lola, married for only four days to a scriptwriter whom she

obliges to play the role of her coachman in a ruse (a play within the present play) expressly staged to even the score for his earlier flirtations. Lola's victim is the Marquis, yet another poet who recalls both Curianito and the Prince, an aristocratic romantic returning home from a long exile. The Marquis immediately falls in love with Lola and unwittingly enlists the husband, greatly pained by his role, to find out more about her, especially her name. Although Lola accomplishes her hoax, which leaves the Marquis "slumped over in a chair" (II 94) as she rides off in her horse-drawn carriage, it is evident that the charade exacts a severe price on both "poets." The humiliation of two poets by an actress portrays in literal terms, a now familiar pattern of contentiousness that is directly reflected in the relationships among the theater functions. The failure of the scriptwriter-coachman-husband to direct Lola's energies on a productive path leads to his victimization as well as that of the Marquis who, like Curianito, suffers greatly for his belief in a love that from the outset was impossible. The actor and not the poet dominates, creating as a consequence a new and more sinister variation of the audience-of-one phenomenon while offering an indirect commentary on the inadequacy of the poetic function to serve as a stabilizing force for theater.

Lola so obsesses the Marquis that he offers "twenty ounces of gold and all my jeweled rings" (II 80) for information about her. Although money is first introduced in the puppet play by the Negro, who offers his stories for sale to an audience, it now becomes more closely identified here with the personal costs of theater production. The deception costs the Marquis both his money and his poetry, which he offers to Lola in its entirety: "This book and my life, / madam, are all yours" (II 90). After Lola copies the poems, they become part of her theatrical repertoire. The Marquis is thus also dispossessed of a more valuable capital that had sustained his imagination. Although her deception is performed before the Marquis, Lola is the true audience since the value of her performance resides in the gratification it brings to her alone. The ruse through which she also gains control of a theater company is, in fact, simply an imitation of, a response in kind to, her husband's earlier indiscretion, not a solid basis for a sustained theatrical repertoire. Lola's lack of imagination is confirmed by the fact that she copies poems from the Marquis—of questionable value regardless, considering their source—in order to use them in later productions.

Lola's victory over her husband and the nobleman is thus a hollow one, for she is becoming a theater person as a consequence of exploiting and appropriating the weaknesses and vulnerabilities of victims who will likely not provide sufficient material upon which to sustain a theater. Although Lola seems triumphant at the conclusion as she departs for the next adventure, her company may well be destined for failure rather than success since her theatrical inventory consists almost exclusively of stolen artifacts.

The poem that Lola recites in the play, in fact, is almost identical to Lorca's "Grove" ("Arbolé arbolé") from *Songs* (*Canciones*), perhaps to emphasize by use of a poem originally written for a different context that, rather than producing something original, the script is merely continuing, or even duplicating, a preexisting agenda. Lorca also draws attention by this to himself as poet in the dual aspect in which that office is represented in the play, lyric poet and scriptwriter. The close association of the play's two victims additionally suggests a consciousness that the present equation for theater dominated by the poetic function may be in need of revision. An occasion for theater conceived of in purely personal terms as a rather cruel hoax diminishes everyone involved, including the theater audience, whose expectations of involvement with a story are also shortchanged as a consequence of the play's strong orientation to self-entertainment. The play's final scene physically underscores the introversion typical of the early theater: Lola abandons not only the Marquis but also the theater audience that her ruse has kept at a distance. The four horses that Lola uses to depart the scene will reappear in different contexts in later plays, and significantly so in *The Public*. Even here, however, it is obvious that the strength and vitality embodied in the horses is misdirected. As his meditation on theater grows more intense, Lorca understands that an idea of a theater dominated by the poet function requires more stable scenarios capable of affirming *veras* ("truths") as well as *burlas* ("tricks").

Tragicomedy of Don Cristobal and Miss Rosita

That Lorca chooses one of the names the Marquis imagined that Lola might be called (II 80) for the heroine of *Tragicomedy of Don Cristobal and Miss Rosita* suggests that it offers a further exposition on the direction in which Lola's theatrical intuitions have taken his theater. Rosita's embroidery cannot generate enough income to support her household, which motivates her father to marry her off to Don Cristobal. While the insolvency of her craft provides the basis for the story, it also affords Lorca a further occasion to examine the deficiencies of the early theater. The shift from poetically conceived characters makes it more difficult, however, to sustain the repressive equilibrium that, while it preserved the independence of the poetic vision, also gave rise to suffocating conditions for theater. No longer able to repress a more serious underside, the *Tragicomedy of Don Cristobal and Miss Rosita* dramatizes the insufficiencies implicit in the earlier theater as it encounters new issues to confront, the need to extend the theater equation.

In the context of the earlier script-oriented plays in which female characters dominate their idealistic male counterparts strongly identified with poetry, Rosita, only marginally involved in artistic endeavor via the craft of embroidery, occupies a rather different situation. Unable to maintain her autonomy through her private craftsmanship, she is forced into the public marketplace where her worth is determined by different criteria. If the poetry-obsessed theater culminates in Lola, who steals poetry in order to create *burlas* rather than high art, Rosita's failure to sustain herself through her craft reflects a further deterioration of an autonomous conception of such a function. Rather than dominating the scene, the female characters will themselves be dominated, which in Rosita's case is expressed in the language and functions of the stage. When Rosita's father declares that "I give orders here, I am the father" (II 114), he is not only affirming his superior will but is also behaving like a theater impresario or stage director whose business decision creates a new and fuller scenario which his daughter is now forced to occupy.

The father, however, only facilitates the manifestation of this function which is embodied in the physically repugnant Cristobita, whose money is exclusively responsible for the creation of the new scene. The least human-seeming of all the puppet characters, his wealth nevertheless makes him the most powerful. Indeed, money is the sole catalyst for a production that for all intents and purposes is directed by Cristobita. In the end, however, Cristobita does not triumph. Mosquito[10] intervenes in the scene to awaken the sleeping Cristobita by sounding "a loud trumpet blast in his head" (II 156) at the very moment that Rosita is extracting her former and present lovers, Currito and Cocoliche, from her armoire. Although the lovers physically triumph over the negative power of Cristobita's money, they also expose their fundamental incapacity to direct the course of their own lives. As in the cases of Curianito and the Marquis before him, Cristobita succumbs because he realizes that the love he had imagined, and also paid for, is impossible. His death, however, does not comfort the lovers, for it becomes the occasion for the additional discovery that Cristobita was not a man of flesh and blood but rather a wooden puppet, as Cocoliche screams: "Cristobita was not a person!" (II 159).[11] More than a dramatic role, Cristobita has fulfilled a theatrical function. Ironically, his departure from the scene he creates for Rosita emphasizes the authority and the inescapable demands of his function. The characters who survive him are left desolate and confused with the terrible knowledge that they share his destiny. Disappearing along with Cristobita is also the illusion of the characters that they are persons. They become, in effect, themselves, puppets conscious of their untenability and theatricality now that the pretext for their presence in the scene has disappeared.

Mosquito's final interruption with a group of puppets to bury Cristobita and to reiterate that "he shall not return" (II 161) does not diminish the tragic insights of Cocoliche and Rosita or the continuing influence of Cristobita, who has forced everyone to acknowledge the inevitability of his function. Mosquito's subversive presence in the representation underscores, however, a conscious intensification of the tense imbalance between the values of script and scenario that progressively dominates the early theater. While provoking a climax by awakening Cristobita, Mosquito also indirectly suggests that tragicomedy is ultimately a reference to the combative juxtaposition of antagonists. Comedy and tragedy—like Mosquito and Cristobita and the values of script and scenario which they embody—represent conceptual extensions of what will remain an ongoing dialectic between necessary, coexisting yet antagonistic aspects of the process of playmaking. In his first truly legitimate theater production, *Mariana Pineda*, Lorca acknowledges that struggle in fully serious terms.

Lorca's Early Theater and Brechtian Distance

Before turning to *Mariana Pineda*, however, I should like briefly to discuss these early pieces in relation to the theater of Bertold Brecht, which—along with that of Pirandello in Italy, Stanislavsky in Russia, and, slightly later, Artaud in France—had already made its presence well-known by this time in Modernist Europe. The object of my digression is not to suggest that Lorca's early theater was directly influenced by Brecht. Indeed, Lorca's early theater seems clearly to emerge from a private rather than a social vision and, at least at this stage in his development, from his largely personal intuitions about theater rather than from a fully articulated theoretical position. Nevertheless, there is a certain overlap as regards the practical effects of the early productions of the two playwrights, which in both results in the creation of an appreciable sense of distance between the activities depicted on the stage and the audience called upon to react and interpret such action. Brecht's conscious goal in his productions was to create an alienation effect, to make spectators adopt an attitude of inquiry and criticism in their approach to the action depicted onstage. This was accomplished in part by a strict control over the actors, to ensure that they would only minimally empathize with their roles by virtue of their refraining from "living the part" or becoming completely transformed by the role (Brecht 136–38).

In Lorca's early theater, there is also a strong sense of distance not because the productions themselves aim to disrupt the illusion that the actor and his situation occupy an autonomous space but because such a disruption already exists in the character as conceived and drawn. The disruption or incompleteness of the illusion is thus a consequence of something more fundamental than the conscious interventions of stage director and actor in the elaboration of the performance text. Lorca's characters, therefore, lack autonomy as a direct consequence of the informing vision of the script and not because of something added during the performance. Indeed, an important feature of the early theater—and it persists in some manner throughout Lorca's theater—is a refusal, or incapacity, to draw definitive boundary lines between characters as full human beings and as puppets, caricatures, or self-conscious parodies of characters from the Spanish theater tradition. As Robert Lima has observed about *Tragicomedy of Don*

Cristobal and Miss Rosita, Lorca originally intended the play as a farce and not as a puppet play, to be entertaining but "also a satirical study of the modern Spanish stage with its thin plots disguised by ornamentation and its contrived 'happy endings' " (86).

What this also suggests, however, is a dramatist constrained both by the limitations of the conventions of his craft in his specific historical and national moment and by a growing sense of frustration at his inability to express existential-dramatic intuitions that presently surpass the theater's capacity to accept them. Thus while Brecht's innovations fully dismantle the fourth-wall convention of the realist tradition from a position of growing strength, Lorca's theater, although it evinces numerous manifestations of Brechtian distance, must respond via the minor genres of puppet theater and farce. If dramatic distance proves to be a powerful expressive weapon for Brecht, for Lorca it becomes rather an index of his defensiveness and lack of stage authority. The unconventional settings of the early plays actually reflect a strong desire for a greater directness in the act of theater, that is, a desire to transcend the very sense of distance in which his early theater is framed. Such a desire is made problematical, however, by the equal realization that greater directness portends strongly negative consequences, the likelihood of public exposure, ridicule, and thus the destruction of his theater. *Mariana Pineda,* Lorca's first significant theater success, gains much of its expressive power as a consequence of its willingness to confront this issue more seriously.

Mariana Pineda

Mariana Pineda offers a liberally adapted portrait of one of Spain's most famous heroines[12] as it simultaneously explores Lorca's evolving attitudes toward the public requirements of theater and toward the directorial function. Lorca himself had commented on the fact that the play can be appreciated on more than one level (III 492–95), suggesting perhaps that the dubious value of his play as a history is outweighed by the continuing exploration of the demands of his private world in relation to the requirements of the circuit of reception. Continuing to emphasize that theater is the public extension of an essentially private understanding and inspiration, Lorca introduces in the prolog a young girl who, as she returns home, lingers to ponder the meaning of the popular song about Mariana Pineda sung by a group of children. As Sumner Greenfield ("Problem" 762) and others have suggested, the action of the play proper may be understood to take place in the girl's imagination and thus to represent the impressions of an innocent consciousness rather than being a faithful recreation of an historical moment.

Although the girl is a convenient vehicle through which to justify the considerable melodrama of the play and its many imaginative departures from the historical facts, it more importantly establishes that a private dramatic-imaginative space overlaps the entire performance. That the play ends as it begins, with the same popular song sung by a group of children in the background, more explicitly situates the play between history and popular legend and suggests that the most significant truth of Mariana Pineda lies in her capacity to stir the imagination. Referring again to the scenes as *estampas*—that is, evocations of old engravings from a bygone era yet brought vividly to life in the child's innocent imagination—Lorca is simultaneously emphasizing both the great distance of such a vision from Mariana Pineda's actual history and its immediacy, as spontaneous impressions upon the imagination of a living consciousness. He thus creates the conditions for a double theatrical space in which intimate dramatic contents, a young girl's daydreams, are given over to an audience that, while it remains distant from the historical Mariana Pineda, simultaneously intrudes upon a private scene of the imagination. This is also how Lorca characterizes the two men in Mariana's life, her beloved don Pedro and Pedrosa, her pursuer, as intruders upon Mariana's previously tranquil and decidedly private life.

Those familiar with the actual facts of Mariana Pineda's life would identify Pedrosa as an historical character and don Pedro as a fictionalized supplement (Havard *Pineda* 1–12). In the play, however, both characters function almost identically in that they oblige or attempt to coerce Mariana into taking public stands on issues that she would have preferred to remain private. In having her sew for the revolutionaries a flag that features, on a crimson background, a script of green letters which spell "liberty," Pedro makes Mariana vulnerable to Pedrosa, who subsequently demands that she reveal other names, those of the conspirators, in exchange for her life. As much as portraying the life of an historical character, Lorca's Mariana also dramatizes the conflict between the private and public aspects of playmaking. Although initially associated with weaker male characters, the values of the poet, or script, have also been echoed in the early theater by female characters such as the aloof and introverted butterfly of *The Butterfly's Spell*, who chooses to remain in her private world rather than to respond to a milieu with which she feels no connection. By *Lola, The Actress*, the insufficiencies of such introversion are exposed in Lola's self-indulgent practical jokes. With the *Tragicomedy of Don Cristobal and Miss Rosita*, the poet's unsuitability as an exclusive medium for theater is symbolized in the failure of Rosita's craftsmanship to protect her from the encroachment of outside forces. If Cristobita embodies the ugliness associated with the public domain, that grotesque unpleasantness intensifies into the fully destructive power of Pedrosa in *Mariana Pineda*. Like Rosita before her, Mariana embroiders, at another's insistence, a flag-text that, although never publicly unfurled, is responsible for her destruction. Mariana's most important role is thus to embody the continuing impetus to an essentially private understanding and to resist the incursion of public demands.

From the outset Mariana is extremely fearful of anything that would bring public exposure upon her clandestine activity: "I feel myself dressed in trembling and lament" (II 190). Her servant Clavela takes note of the emotional and physical price Mariana is paying as a consequence:

> Ay, doña Mariana, how ill you look!
> Since you placed your precious hands
> on that flag of the liberals,
> the colors of the pomegranate flower
> have disappeared from your face.
>
> (II 189)

In the context of the earlier plays, these words underscore a now familiar theme: artistry intended for a public context exacts a steep price. In this case the suggestion is that the embroidery project has drained Mariana's vitality and thus, like the other Lorca protagonists who involve themselves in art and love, she has become debilitated and vulnerable.

Pedrosa's discovery of the rebel flag, Mariana's imaginative response to the ill-defined public cause of liberty, brings the ultimate loss, losing Don Pedro, the bittersweet inspiration for an unconventional idea of freedom that bears little resemblance to its public counterpart:

> [Pedro] loves liberty
> and I love it more than he.
> What he says is my bitter
> truth, that tastes to me like honey.
>
> (II 196)

Freedom for Mariana means the power to live and love without the intrusion of the outside world, an audience of onlookers. After her exposure and condemnation, Mariana intensifies her loyalties to this private idea of freedom with which, by the play's conclusion, she completely identifies herself:

> . . . I am Freedom herself. I give my blood,
> that is your blood and the blood of all creatures.
> . . . .
> Man is a prisoner and cannot free himself.
> Highest Freedom! True Freedom,
> light for me your distant stars.
>
> (II 271)

As indifferent and distant in its public manifestations as it is intimate and all-pervasive in Mariana's private understanding, this unconventional form of freedom offers the real reason why she joined Pedro's conspiracy: "I embroidered the flag for him. I have conspired / in order to live and to love his very thought" (II 266). For Mariana, Pedro's devotion to a conventional, public freedom means condemnation, disgrace, and destruction. Love is possible only for as long as it remains private, for outside her house awaits Pedrosa: "Fixed, behind the balcony, / his gaze is placed on me" (II 193). Her only consolation is that her special understanding of freedom and love may survive her, in innocent imaginations: "Sing my sad story to the children that pass by" (II 271). This is, of course, the very context of the present scenario in which the story has acquired additional intimacy and innocence since the freedom to love can only flourish in privacy and silence. Pedrosa's offer to spare Mariana's life if she will expose the conspirators thus affords her a means to demonstrate her allegiance to these principles by refusing to speak.[13] Silence is the final defense and resistance against encroachments upon the intimacy and privacy of the imagination.

Mariana's transformation into a public figure as a consequence of her role as scripter for the cause of freedom parallels the transformation that theater scripts must undergo in order to become available to audiences. Mariana is identified throughout the play with the production of a type of script, the rebel flag using writing rather than colors or other symbols to communicate its message. Accompanying Mariana in this endeavor is an intense fear of public exposure, which is fully confirmed almost immediately after the flag is taken from her house. It is also at this point that political activity becomes consciously associated with the activity of making theater. When Pedro reveals to Mariana his military and political claims to have "fooled Pedrosa in the countryside" (II 213), he is also recalling the ineffective theatrical strategy, the *burla*, so prominent in Lorca's earlier plays. When he takes Mariana prisoner, Pedrosa repays this trick and introduces a new dimension to the art of orchestrating strategies, his personal authority, which intervenes to establish dominion over Mariana's life, to move her from the benign enclosure of her house to prison:

> You know that, with my signature
> I can erase the light of your eyes.
> With a pen and a bit of ink
> I can make you sleep a long dream.
>
> (II 257)

Both Pedro and Pedrosa fulfill a directorial function in that they become the means by which the retiring Mariana is brought into the public consciousness, if not fully into public view.[14] Indeed, Mariana's only public act, not actually represented in the play, is her sacrifice upon the executioner's stage. The suggestion is obvious: full public exposure is synonymous with destruction.

The source of Mariana's strength during her imprisonment is precisely her refusal to speak, a steadfast resistance that becomes her only recourse against Pedrosa's absolute authority over her. Although the tangible evidence of her involvement with the conspiracy, the flag, does not represent her true intention for crafting it, in the end Mariana embraces a role that reconciles public and private motivations by associating her person with the concept for which she is sacrificed. Private and public intentions fuse as Mariana cries out to her beloved for the final time:

> I am Freedom because love wanted it that way!
> Pedro! The Freedom for which you abandoned me.
> I am Freedom, wounded by men!
> Love, love, love, and eternal solitude!
>
> (II 272)

By collapsing the distinction between the incompatible demands of love and ideology, Mariana recreates in public terms the unspoken premises of her love for Pedro as she transforms herself into the physical locus of both. In asking that her story be told to children, she acknowledges that it will have meaning only in the privacy of an innocent imagination and not as a fully public spectacle. Likewise, only by presenting Mariana's story through such a filter can Lorca reconcile his growing awareness of the untenability of his theatrical intuitions, the incompatible demands upon a fundamentally private vision fully conscious of its vulnerability in a public context.

Paralleling Mariana's apprehension at the possibility of her public exposure are Lorca's own anxieties at the level of pure theater. What Pedrosa has to say about Mariana's countrymen, whom he knows will watch passively as Mariana goes to her execution ("There will be nobody in Granada to come out / when you pass by with your procession. / Andalusians talk a lot; but later . . . " [II 257]), is also the type of indifferent response that contemporary audiences may well have to Mariana's story.[15] The genuine if nevertheless modest success of this play, in which Lorca for the first time reluctantly acknowledges not only the unavoidability but also the dangers of representing publicly a fundamentally private vision, underscores for him that his authority as a dramatist will depend upon how well he can continue to adapt an essentially private theater model to new contexts. While enacting the drama of a public figure, Lorca nevertheless incorporates his own theatrical commentary grafted upon the backdrop of Spanish history and politics. Mariana is more than a poetic vision. She is poetry itself, as Lorca has conceived it in relation to his theater, besieged by the exigencies of time and space, and the even more pressing need to make it palatable for the theater public. The framing devices and the *estampa* format suggest that, although he understands the demands of theater, Lorca is still unwilling to abandon an orientation to playmaking that is antagonistic to constraints associated with a "strong" directorial component. Lorca is thus at the point where he understands that he will be required to make further concessions to his audiences or else resign himself to the same silence that sealed the fate of his protagonist. As exemplified in the tragedy of Mariana, he also clearly understands that the consequences of inopportune adventures in the public eye are public exposure and destruction.

3

THE FARCES

Dᴜʀɪɴɢ ᴛʜᴇ ᴛɪᴍᴇ of his bringing *Mariana Pineda* to the stage and embarking upon the next phase of his early work, which produces *The Shoemaker's Prodigious Wife* and *Love of Don Perlimplín with Belisa in His Garden* (referred to as *Perlimplín*), Lorca writes a number of short quasidramatic dialogs, among which is the "Dialog with Luis Buñuel."[1] These innovative pieces reveal an intensifying interest in experimentation at the very moment of *Mariana Pineda*'s favorable reception as a work of traditional theater.[2] The dialogs precede the acclaim of *The Shoemaker's Prodigious Wife* and the censure of *Perlimplín*,[3] the latter ridiculed privately as well by Buñuel and Dalí.[4] Lorca's acknowledgment in the "Dialog with Luis Buñuel" of a divergence in artistic positions between himself and his avant-garde friends is reflected in these farces in his maturing appreciation of the unavoidability of schism and scandal, further extending his exploration of the unresolved tensions of his theater.

The Shoemaker's Prodigious Wife

One of the significant issues in *Mariana Pineda* is its heroine's deep and well-founded fear of public exposure as a consequence of the artifact she produces in private. The prolog to *The Shoemaker's Prodigious Wife*, presided over by a complex yet ambiguous character identified as the *autor*, also begins with the question of the dramatist's fear in the public gaze. Voicing Lorca's deepening intuition of the need for a greater integration of the principal theater functions, the *autor* speaks in the capacity of both stage director and scriptwriter. For the first time as well, the authority of the theater audience is openly acknowledged, authority to which those involved in theater have all too willingly responded in obsequiousness and fear, "a delicate fearful trem-

48

bling and a type of supplication so that the audience will be generous with the efforts of the actors and the art of the playwright" (II 307). This fear, in part, is also the poet's fear of exposure to ridicule and censure as the dramatic script, conceived and written in private and perhaps motivated by intentions that may bear little relation to the artifact's actual content, is given over to the theater public. The *autor*, however, insists on a new attitude toward the audience: it should not be called "respected audience" but rather "audience and nothing else" (II 307). Hidden behind "respected" is the fear that occasions deference to conventional tastes, which results in safe and timid productions. Immediately following, the *autor* asserts the poet's fundamental demand. The audience must hear and acknowledge the words of the script: "the poet does not ask for benevolence, but rather attention, once he has transcended the thorny bar of fear that playwrights have of the theater" (II 307).

If the *autor's* acknowledgment of the involved dynamics of the circuit of reception heralds a stronger and more hopeful focus within an ongoing internal dialog, the goal of which is greater stage authority, a long Spanish tradition of lesser associations with the term *autor* also affiliates it with other stage figures or interests: the leading actors, whose pandering to applause has diminished that authority, and the theatrical producer, whose principal interest in theater is a profitable return on a financial investment.[5] In actual practice, stage authority does not reside in a strong stage director but rather in an untenable theatrical arrangement which has allowed the influence of the theater audience to extend into the space of the stage. Added to the obstacles that the poet must face in order to be heard, therefore, is the "fear that playwrights have of the theater," their trepidation of those charged with staging the script. The appreciation that theater is "in many instances a matter of finances" (II 307), prospective income often being decisive in the determination of which scripts will become actual theater productions and which will not, has weighed against a poetic, script-oriented conception of theater. As the *autor* confesses, "poetry retreats from the stage in search of other surroundings where people will not become fearful" (II 307–8).[6] When the *autor* announces that he "has preferred to situate the dramatic example in the living rhythm of a common shoeshop" (II 308), he is confessing his acquiescence in audience and theatrical producer preferences for nonthreatening scenarios. Financial consideration for a similar script set less conventionally would be much less likely.[7]

While not abandoning earlier positions, the prolog more fully acknowledges the external demands for a commercially viable scenario and thus the requirement to collaborate more closely with the visual domain of the stage director. The controlled poetry that dominated the earlier plays becomes a more energetic, yet also turbulent, prose:

> Everywhere there pulsates and comes to life the poetic creature that the playwright has dressed as the wife of a shoemaker with the air of a refrain or simple little ballad, and the audience should not find it strange if she seems violent or takes bitter postures, because she always fights, fights the reality that encircles her and fights fantasy when it becomes a visible reality. (II 308)

If *Mariana Pineda* presents a passive, fearful, yet also uncompromising heroine, *The Shoemaker's Prodigious Wife* offers an active, resistive, and even outwardly defiant character who nevertheless more readily acquiesces in the demands of the physical scene.[8] Lorca emphasizes the Wife's relationship to his ongoing metatheatrical dialog by bringing her to the stage to interrupt the prolog and to demand that her story begin immediately. This "poetic creature"—whose strong desire to express herself, in or out of her appointed social context, aligns her with the values of the poet—is already conscious of the limitations placed upon her by the scenario. Although the *autor* professes an admiration for the Wife's prodigious capacity and proclivity to public expression, he nevertheless becomes the first to demand her silence.[9] This explicit acknowledgment of the growing prominence of the demands of the scenario in relation to the expressive desires of the script exposes the *autor's* conflicting loyalties and responsibilities. Although he promotes the values of the poet, he is also required to be equally attentive to the demands of the receptive circuit and thus to the necessity for fully contextualized scenarios. Rather than mediating script-scene antagonisms with authoritativeness, the *autor* allows the stage to become a gathering site for irreconcilable forces, the ultimate consequences of which portend the interruption of the production.[10]

A multiple personality more than a substantive reflection of stage authority, the *autor* confesses that the demands of staging have made it necessary to disguise the truth, "the poetic creature that the playwright has dressed as a the wife of a shoemaker" (II 308). Lorca's calling his play a violent farce (*farsa violenta*) accentuates the immanence of violence, even in a genre that normally requires it (J. M. Aguirre 244), because of the growing antagonisms of the theater functions. The Wife's character and context are responses to a more subtle form of violence, by the audience, whose prevailing viewing conventions have precluded other less conventional possibilities, for example, the Wife in a "costume with a long tail and inverisimilar feathers" (II 308). If the requirements of the scene weigh heavily on the "poetic creature," so too the *autor* brings little positive authority to the director function in a scenario cloaked in the entertainment of farce. At the prolog's conclusion, when the *autor* takes off his hat to reveal inside a green light from which water eventually spurts, he also exposes his true status. A figure who has pretended to be an authoritative spokesperson for theater at this moment looks very much like a vaudeville magician who has just performed a trick.[11]

The Wife's verbal intrusion into the prolog by means of her reiterated declaration of "I want to enter!" (II 308) demonstrates her impatience with the *autor* and with what she already understands to be a tenuous situation. As a character who lives primarily in a private world of the imagination, who "fights the reality that encircles her and fights fantasy when it becomes a visible reality" (II 308), the Wife's primary function is to resist conventional visible reality by means of her verbal presence. The *autor*, however, cautions her not to exceed the limitations of her role since her personal authority in the scene and society she is about to enter is minimal. She has been given "a torn costume, do you hear? the costume of a shoemaker's wife" (II 308), and it is from this narrow context that she must operate, be scrutinized, and be accepted or rejected by others. The Wife is thus expected to emulate the theater audience's custom of suppressing its "half-world of dream" (II 308), its private imaginative world, in order to enter into practical dealings with her scene. Again, it is the *autor* himself who first invokes this requirement by demanding her attentiveness to his instructions.

In the play, the Wife's demands to be heard arise within the context of a wifely role that renders her articulations progressively more inappropriate and that constantly reemphasizes to her that she is living with someone whose most fervent desire is that she refrain entirely from speaking in public. The Wife's marriage of necessity thus reflects the views implicit in the prolog, understanding theater to be a necessary, if unstable, marriage between the desire to express the unadorned truth and the practical requirement not to transgress against the viewing conventions of the theater audience. The *autor* thus becomes the spokesperson for a theater that has become aware of its shortcomings as well as any strengths it may now possess. As the Shoemaker quickly realizes as an unhappy partner in a marriage entered into for the wrong reasons, that authority cannot be manufactured; the lesson for theater is that neither can stage authority be summoned in a forced alliance between script and scenario. More significant for this play is a force more impatient than even the Wife—the paying customers whose desire for entertainment places further limits on the possibilities for theater. The *autor*, therefore, ultimately becomes a reminder, to Lorca himself if to no one else,[12] of the distance that presently lies between a truly dignified and secure stage authority and the vaudeville subterfuge with which the prolog concludes. In the aftermath of the discomforting lessons of his earlier theater, Lorca begins now to explore the implications of this forced union to the circuit of reception, and, indirectly, to explore his stage authority, through the vehicle of the unhappily married couple around whom the play turns.

Like *Mariana Pineda, The Shoemaker's Prodigious Wife* prominently features the themes of public exposure and disgrace within a context of violence. Threatened with scandal, humiliation, and physical harm, the Wife nevertheless remains fearless: "I have the whole town on top of me, they want to come and kill me, yet I am not afraid" (II 368). If Mariana Pineda's dignity lies in her refusal to make public utterances, the Wife is equally determined to express herself and to be heard. Her first statement in the play, "Shut up" (II 309), directed to a neighbor offstage with whom she is quarreling about the worth of their husbands, strongly recalls the *autor*'s earlier admonition to silence to the Wife. It thus calls attention to the most significant issue of the play: what authority does the Wife possess to express herself in her scene and to resist the assaults upon her private world?[13] The Shoemaker is motivated by exactly the opposite consideration: "a true obsession with avoiding scandal" occasioned by "the fear of seeing myself encircled by all sorts of people, carried out and dragged about by women and other idle folk" (II 318). Indeed, he perceives that his standing in the community is being jeopardized as a consequence of "this shouting and being the topic of everybody's conversation" (II 323), the critical response to the Wife's exercise of her "sacred will" (II 319). More than to conform to his expectations, the Shoemaker wants the Wife to accept the collective authority of a disapproving audience of townspeople. Unable to restrict her physical activity or to control her verbal outbursts, he abruptly departs the scene.

A less threatening but much less effective manifestation of the director function, the Shoemaker abdicates any positive authority he may possess when he abandons his wife. Although superficially more sympathetic than his immediate counterpart Pedrosa, the Shoemaker is no less attentive to the requirements of public conformity. That he feels an obligation to the townspeople to keep his wife quiet emphasizes that the negative associations of directorial authority have not diminished. Indeed, the discord between script and scenario is as ongoing as is the distress of the partners in this unhappy marriage. Lorca's more explicit association of these characters with the functions of theater exemplifies his maturing awareness of the significant constraints of the receptive circuit that threaten the viability of the space of the stage.

The Shoemaker's abandonment of his primary function brings even more severe consequences as the townspeople collectively assume his function in act II. The vulnerability of a much more subdued Wife underscores the necessity of reaffiliation in a partnership in which the only affirmative feature was the union itself. Like the Shoemaker, who admits that "I am not in love with my wife" (II 320), the Wife is from the outset deeply ambivalent about her marriage and her obligations to it: "But the blame is mine, mine, mine . . . , because I should be at home with . . . , I almost don't want to believe it, with my husband. Who would have told me, a black-eyed blond, that one must see the merit that lies in this, with this body and these most beautiful colors, that I would see myself married to . . . I would tear out my hair!" (II 309). The Wife's consolation for lack of amorous interest in the house is her vivid imaginings, the very catalysts for the confrontations with her neighbors which in turn provoked the gossip that so dismayed the

Shoemaker, prompting his departure. The absence of a real bond between the couple allows the townspeople to intrude more directly into their private lives.

Although the Wife is represented as protagonist, the much weaker Shoemaker is equally important. What the Wife does not understand until after he leaves her is that her public comments had been tolerated only because of his own legitimizing presence. As long as he was part of the scene, she was shielded by the authority of his function and was able to address the gossipy female neighbors and lecherous men with relative impunity. She was also able to act as the Shoemaker's business manager and accountant by reminding him, and demanding from others, that they pay a just sum of money for services rendered. Even more so than in the earlier dramas, money plays a significant role. In contrast to the retiring Mariana Pineda whose craftsmanship entangles her in a dangerous public cause, the Wife's association with craft arises solely as a consequence of her marriage. Her interest is not in craftsmanship but in the money that the Shoemaker charges, or undercharges, for his services.[14] As the townspeople themselves suggest, money is the reason that the Wife has married an impotent old man.[15] Money (finanza) is also the go-between that makes theater a wedding of necessity. When at one point the Wife denounces one whom she projects as money's inventor, wishing that "the loss of hands and eyes should have been the fate of the one that invented you" (II 312), she is also condemning the very force that has defined her role in this production. In the absence of the hands and eyes of a strong stage director, that function largely resides with the will of the paying customers. The Wife's ambivalence toward money is identical to her ambivalence toward her marriage. While coveting neither, lacking either means that she loses her status in the scene.

It is only after the Shoemaker leaves that the Wife begins to consider that "he was my happiness, my defense" (II 359). "Defense" is well chosen. More important for the Wife than her husband's active participation in the scene is the stability of his function, a cushion against the criticisms of the townspeople, which remained rather muted until his departure. The Wife thereafter becomes fully aware of their threatening reality: "Everybody is besieging me, everybody criticizes me" (II 361).[16] Indeed, the Shoemaker's absence forces the Wife to adopt a public posture similar in many respects to the one he had previously desired for her. Although she converts the shoeshop into a tavern, she does so as "a married woman [who] should be in her place like God wills" (II 338), which requires that she restrict her range of movement to the confines of her house.[17] This only further incites the growing chorus of female critics, who become even more upset because the men linger there for extended periods simply to watch the Wife.

His failure to channel his wife's expansive imaginings in a productive direction chases the Shoemaker from the scene and forces him to assume a new identity, as puppetmaster, which in relation to the evolution of theater functions is clearly a throwback to an earlier time when Lorca considered theater in more unified yet private terms, free from the impositions of the receptive circuit. A reluctant husband from the outset, the Shoemaker has been even more unwilling to affirm the positive authority inherent in his role in order to move the Wife toward a more viable social identity. Rather than becoming a stronger force within his household, he abandons the exclusive domain of his authority, only to return in apparent dictatorial command of a puppet theater that in reality further exposes his loss of status. The script of the puppet play is clearly inspired by the Shoemaker's earlier life with the Wife, as she alone among the audience of townspeople tacitly acknowledges, by her tears. It also reveals the limits of an imagination that remains fettered to a particular social circumstance no matter how reduced its possibilities or how much humiliation it requires him to endure.

As communicated through the Shoemaker's story about the life of the character he now plays, who hails from the Philippine Islands where "almost all of them are shoemakers" (II 350), his imagination has been obsessed with reenacting the circumstances of his former role.[18] In the most important sense, therefore, the Shoemaker never really leaves home because he continues to carry the ill will that provoked his departure. What the theater audience, if not the townspeople, can easily recognize from the puppet play is the agenda of the Shoemaker's imagination during his absence. His play-within-a-play is clearly an attempt to justify, primarily to himself, his abandonment of the Wife. The significant change in the facts of his version of the story, that it is the wife and not the husband who leaves, again underscores the Shoemaker's stronger bond with the social scene than with his wife. He remains consumed with repeating a story that, in a circular trajectory, returns him to the site of his original disempowerment. Indeed, his full return to his former identity is actually hastened by his own incitement of the townspeople during his awkward attempt to reenact theatrically his motives for leaving.

The most telling moment of the Shoemaker's performance, however, occurs at the beginning when he addresses his audience with the words "respected audience" (II 352), which repeat the *autor*'s words in the prolog signifying fear in the face of the audience. The Shoemaker's salutation is thus suggestive of the inherent weakness of his position as a one-personality theater that also depends upon deferring respectfully to his audience. The Shoemaker's borrowed script, however, features a female protagonist who is disrespectful of convention. Even in the deferential and conforming context in which he attempts to frame his own character, the Shoemaker nevertheless upsets his audience and thus recreates conditions identical to those of his original humiliation. This, of course, testifies to the latent authority of the poet function. An important embellishment to the Shoemaker's play, however, is the knife fight between two jealous rivals for the woman's affection. When a similar occurrence of real-life violence interrupts the puppet play, art helps to incite the townspeople to the serious contemplation of violence against the Wife. By this point, the consequences of the couple's separation have become evident: the Wife's outspokenness carries no authority in the community without the Shoemaker's sanctioning presence. In the face of this potentially violent turn, however, the Shoemaker's desertion now seems more than simply misguided. His failure to exercise his role in a positive fashion has created a dangerous situation in which the Wife is indeed defenseless.

Although it is possible that the return of the Shoemaker as head of his household will frustrate the violence that the townspeople are contemplating against the Wife, there is also the distinct possibility that the Shoemaker may no longer possess sufficient personal authority to guarantee a "happy ending."[19] His own puppet play has strongly reinforced the negative opinions of the townspeople regarding outspoken women like the Wife and has actually incited threats of violence against her. Further, the Shoemaker's obsessive yet limited imagination has not accommodated itself in any significant sense to the Wife's penchant for irreverent flights of fantasy. Internally, nothing has changed while externally, even though the Shoemaker reveals his identity and the couple reunite, both are clearly in a much weaker position. Although the Wife gives every indication that she will continue bravely to resist her detractors and although the Shoemaker seems now to be more accepting of his married role, the earlier if somewhat tenuous balance of authority between domestic and public domains has shifted decisively in favor of the townspeople. The generic subtitle "violent farce" clearly refers to the Wife's relationship, potential and actual, to the townspeople, whom she consciously likens to an audience of critics. By the play's conclusion, it is most uncertain if the Shoemaker can reestablish the authority of his household.[20]

Even once she is reunited with her "scoundrel, with this rogue" (II 372), the situation has so deteriorated that the final outcome is quite open. While it is possible that the Wife will be spared the full wrath of the townspeople, it is also likely that she will never regain her license to speak fully and publicly as before. Likewise, the Shoemaker's fears of being denied a life of quiet respectability have now been fully realized. His abandonment of the scene has made him a cuckold, if not in reality, certainly in the imaginations of the townspeople. As much as extolling the indomitable poetic imagination embodied in the Wife, the play also portrays a violent encroachment upon a "poetic creature that the playwright has dressed as the wife of a shoemaker" (II 308). The townspeople act as members of a society but also, in the aftermath of the Shoemaker's puppet play, as an angry theater audience for whom the boundaries between theater and life have become blurred. The violence that threatens this reunion is also manifested metadramatically, as a disruption of the circuit of reception. The brilliant colors in which the neighbor ladies are dressed underscore a deeper conflict between the visual authority of theater as a commercial spectacle and the "attention" to the words of the script demanded by the poet. If in his earlier theater Lorca was loath to affirm the marriage of script and scenario as necessary, here he represents the consequences inherent in the failure of such a marriage to be productive. The absence of an authoritative presence to defend the space of the stage means that, like the townspeople in relation to the puppet theater, the actual theater audience is in a similar position to usurp authority from the dramatist, who "because of this absurd fear" allows "poetry to retreat from the

stage in search of other surroundings." A union beset by so many in-
herent defects and such intense criticism is indeed vulnerable. Like
the *autor's* final gesture in the prolog, it is overthrowable at the tip of
a hat.

Love of Don Perlimplín with Belisa in His Garden

One of the more interesting comments by the Shoemaker as puppet-
master is his claim that what he presents to his audiences are *aleluyas*
meant to represent "life from within" (II 351). While such claims may
be exaggerated in relation to the truth of his life with the Wife, they
offer an excellent description of the form, and content, of *Love of Don
Perlimplín with Belisa in His Garden*, the subtitle of which identifies
it as an "erotic" *aleluya*. The character Perlimplín originates in the
popular tradition of the *aleluya*, which began in the form of booklets
thrown from the religious processions during Holy Week in order to
express jubilation at the resurrection of Christ (Ucelay "Aleluyas" 95).
Often associated with the satirical tradition of the pamphlet and
broadsheet (Grant 104–5) as well as with popular literature about he-
roes, the *aleluya's* final evolution, toward the end of the nineteenth
century, took the form of children's literature, illustrated newsprint
storybooks (perhaps a predecessor of the modern-day comic strip or
comic book [Allen 37]), sold like newspapers on street corners at a very
cheap price (Ucelay "Aleluyas" 96). The typical format of these edi-
tions is a series of drawings accompanied by a separate poetic script
(Ucelay *Perlimplín* 22–23), which, indeed, correlates well with Lorca's
proclivity to oppose the visual and verbal aspects of his theater. Al-
though by the time of Lorca's youth, the *aleluya* had largely disap-
peared, it is nevertheless likely that the average theatergoer would still
recall both the genre and its primary audience, which makes the ac-
companying adjective *erótica* all the more provocative.[21]

The intended effect of Lorca's adaptation of this once popular phe-
nomenon is, I believe, similar to that of the *estampas* of *Mariana
Pineda*, which bring a distant past to life by means of the innocent
imagination of a young girl who fashions her own interpretation of
that past from old engravings. Lorca's aim is, again, not to imitate the
past but to resurrect it on more intimate terms. In *Mariana Pineda* the
audience sees the past that the girl imagines, thus producing a hybrid

image clearly at odds with actual history yet nevertheless much more immediate and present than a mimetic evocation. Like the *estampa*, the *aleluya*, in the figure of Perlimplín, offers an opportunity to bring back to life a tradition of caricature that simultaneously refers to something much more immediate, "life from within." A hybrid creature whose only existence has been in newsprint yet whose visuality affords the exclusive vehicle for the contextualization of the accompanying script of his adventures, Perlimplín nevertheless provides the stabilizing setting that *The Shoemaker's Prodigious Wife* lacked. The necessity for *Perlimplín* becomes apparent in relation to the Shoemaker's imaginative insufficiencies. The Shoemaker's *aleluya* fails because it becomes obsessed with exposing private shortcomings in public, thereby simply recreating in his theater a scenario very nearly identical to his original experience. The resurrection of the imagination in Perlimplín becomes a necessary antidote to the Shoemaker's inability to maintain a setting in which, regardless of content, fantasy can flourish. This in turn raises again the question of the relationship between script and scenario in the theater equation.

For the first time in earnest, Lorca's stage images begin to distance themselves from what might be called the activity of mimesis. Perlimplín is different from even the puppet tradition in that his only existence is as a detached image separate and distinct from the words that describe and explain his activities. As a stage figure who dedicates himself to effecting a positive change in his wife's uncentered imagination, he acquires the mission of enhancement of "life from within." His stage identity, therefore, is a transitional one, flanked by the two-dimensional image taken from a children's tradition and a Perlimplín who becomes transformed, on the plane of Belisa's imagination, into an irresistible erotic image. At no time a stable icon, Perlimplín's significance lies in the fact that he becomes progressively conscious of his role as a facilitator of "life from within," of things that cannot be represented in public or on stage. As the incompatibility between script and scene, word and image, intensifies in Lorca's theater, Perlimplín's indexical role becomes progressively apparent. His visuality becomes simply the point of departure toward a more significant, if incorporeal, referent. The stability Perlimplín provides is as a direction, a pathway toward an new affirmation impossible under strictly mimetic models of consciousness and social comportment. Perlimplín's rejection of conventional morality is paralleled by Lorca's own rejection of traditional models of signification premised upon the weddedness of symbol and icon.

The play's dominant metadramatic dimension manifests itself initially with a reference to what may well have been the logical, and violent, conclusion of *The Shoemaker's Prodigious Wife*, as Perlimplín relates: "When I was a child a woman strangled her husband. He was a shoemaker. This cannot be forgotten. I have always had it in my mind not to get married" (II 461). As the living referent of a dead tradition, Perlimplín resurrects himself in full consciousness of his theatricality. Indeed, his most important function is to impart this consciousness to others, especially the instinctive and spontaneous Belisa, whom he endeavors to convince "that you live in a drama" (II 483). Progressively more conscious that he embodies the role of a stage director (Balboa Echevarría 97–100), he perceives his role as that of providing a compelling visual spectacle for Belisa upon which to anchor her restless imagination. Perlimplín thus brings a new dimension to a function represented in the early theater by unattractive male characters, culminating in the Shoemaker,[22] who fail to inspire their female counterparts.

By *The Shoemaker's Prodigious Wife*, Lorca's thinking about the director function has reached a critical—indeed, a self-critical—point. The Shoemaker's becoming a puppeteer alludes to the earlier theater's unwillingness to acknowledge that, for better or for worse, the domain of the dramatic scene necessarily extends into the theater audience. By the conclusion, the physical scene is dominated by the townspeople, who reflect the visual hegemony of the theater audience that has relegated the poet's imagination, the determination to be heard, to the lesser context of farce. *Perlimplín* is perhaps best understood as a systematic response to the shortcomings of *The Shoemaker's Prodigious Wife* and the inability or reluctance to assert greater authority over the stage. The lengthy enactment in the prolog[23] of the reasons for, requests about, and reactions to the prospect of Perlimplín's marrying Belisa places this marriage in sharp contrast to the marriages in earlier plays. Belisa's mother agrees to the marriage specifically for "aesthetic," not economic reasons ("the grace and manners of that great lady who was your mother, whom I never had the fortune to meet" [II 464]), thus underscoring what was left unsaid in the prolog to *The*

Shoemaker's Prodigious Wife: the conditions under which one enters marriage—and the theater performance—make all the difference. Although Belisa is obliged to marry Perlimplín, the marriage actually intensifies Belisa's detached imaginative obsession with love and sexual desire, an edifice that has precious little grounding in social reality. To Perlimplín, as the successor to a long line of significantly deficient male characters in Lorca's early theater, it now falls to redeem his role and function by providing what his predecessors could not, a purpose and direction for the imagination.

Perlimplín is pivotal for the evolution of male-female relationships that have embodied Lorca's ongoing dialog with the theater functions and the need to situate the insights of the dramatic imagination in a more authoritative performance context. In certain respects, Belisa's and Perlimplín's characters are more fully drawn than their counterparts in *The Shoemaker's Prodigious Wife,* as Lorca may subtlely have implied by making Perlimplín younger than the Shoemaker.[24] Perlimplín is more cerebral, preferring the company of books to extensive contact with others. As introverted as the Wife is extroverted, Belisa is openly obsessed with satisfying her desire for love, without regard for the social consequences: "He who seeks me with passion will find me. My thirst never ends, just like thirst never ends for the figureheads that spurt water from the fountains" (II 469). Inspired by her example and her body, which he could not picture in his imagination until after the marriage—("I was not able to imagine your body until I saw it through the keyhole when you were dressing as a bride" [II 471])—Perlimplín becomes equally obsessed, at an intellectual level, with the same questions of love and desire. As the immediate and ostentatious infidelity of Belisa underscores, he also begins to understand himself in relation to a wider and uncontrollable predicament which must be confronted.

Perlimplín discovers that marriage involves a more significant commitment than passive conformity to societal expectations of fidelity and family: "now I am outside the world and outside of the ridiculous morality of the people" (II 487).[25] Consciously ignoring his social standing and norms of personal honor ("Don Perlimplín has no honor and wants to amuse himself" [II 489]), he dedicates himself instead to forging the type of union that will withstand commentary and criticism from outside parties. If in *The Shoemaker's Prodigious Wife* that audience was closely identified with the townspeople, the public in *Perlimplín* coincides with the actual theater audience, which is made privy to all intimate moments.

A significant disruption of such intimacy, however, occurs, at approximately the midpoint of the play, during the couple's wedding night as Perlimplín and Belisa prepare to go to bed. Lorca introduces a fantastic element at this precise moment with the entry upon the scene of a pair of daimonic spirits, or *duendes* (from the Spanish folkloric tradition), who shield the couple's activities—the stage directions indicate that they enter "from opposite sides of the scene [and] extend a gray colored curtain" (II 473)—and engage in commentary as the newlyweds attempt to consummate their marriage. At this moment the lights dim and the spirits, "who should be cast as two children . . . sit on top of the prompter's box, facing the audience" (III 473). In addition to disrupting the realist illusion of the invisible fourth wall that, despite the unusualness of the characters, has been fully maintained up to this point—indeed, the effect has been to diminish strongly the sense of distance between stage and audience—the spirits effectively address the audience as they comment on the issue of distance itself, that is, on what is or can or should be revealed, and under what conditions, to an audience.

Undoubtedly the most significant metadramatic moment of all of Lorca's early theater, this scene also physically embodies many of the tensions that lie at the heart of his thinking about theater up to this point, centered increasingly on the question of aesthetic distance and, more specifically, on the presence and visual authority of the audience in the creation and elaboration of the space of the representation (for a related discussion, see Felman). Up until this moment, Perlimplín and Belisa's space has also been effectively occupied by the imagination of the theater audience. Indeed, as the *duendes* comment to each other regarding the need to "conceal the faults of others" (II 473)—uttered at this moment presumably in reference to Perlimplín's failure to consummate his marriage—they are aware of such a responsibility because "the public makes it its responsibility to expose them" (II 473); that is, not only this moment but literally everything that could be considered private. Life itself, therefore, is understood as an unending process of masking and unmasking in which the individual, or the family unit, is constantly engaged in order to create and to keep secrets from outside parties, audiences that in turn attempt to discover and to expose them, and so on.

Situated on the prompter's box, between the space of the stage proper and the theater audience, the *duendes* are reinforcing a fundamental tension of the early theater: the confrontation between private and public worlds. More important than the "erotic" content of the scene concealed by an "efficient and most social screen" (II 475) is the issue of the inevitable exchanges between public and private domains that lie at the core of all of Lorca's early theater stories. Here, however, the process becomes self-conscious as the actual theater audience is called upon to participate in both the happenings on stage, the *duendes'* discourse, and the activity behind the curtain. The disruption of the stability of the relationship between the theater audience and the physical scene is accompanied by the emergence of another space, from which the audience is effectively excluded. This provides the model for the type of relationships that prevail subsequent to this moment as Perlimplín begins to enact, through the medium of Belisa's imagination, his own more intimate scenario. A "hidden moment" that by conventional standards is among the most humiliating a man can endure instead becomes pivotal in Perlimplín's development; he uses it to demonstrate just how unimportant such an issue is to him. Indeed, it actually marks the end of his spiritual-imaginative impotence, a role reversal that heralds the onset of "impotence," the loss of authority, with regard to the audience's position. As a consequence of this moment that was kept from the full view of the audience, Perlimplín ceases to exist for the approval of an audience of onlookers but instead begins to fulfill his role and function, in which he invokes a different authority, his own dormant imagination that now emerges in order consciously to exclude the idea and reality of the audience. In this sense, the *duendes* are actually the physical embodiments of the truest expression of Perlimplín's desire, to reaffirm a private space free from the unwanted intrusions of the public. The attitude that Perlimplín adopts toward all audiences, whether societal or theatrical (both are by now fully conflated in his consciousness) is that although audiences may have the power to watch him in the fulfillment of his role, that is now the extent of their authority. The fundamental difference between Perlimplín and the Shoemaker is Perlimplín's unconcern with audience approval. He senses the emergence of a higher authority, expressed in terms of his own vision rather than in his being viewed by others. He thus becomes determined not to allow fear, in the form of societal conventions and expectations, dictate the terms of his public or private comportment.[26]

Although it is not apparent to Belisa, Perlimplín understands quite early that she has awakened his imagination. Refusing to respond in a conventional manner to Belisa's infidelities, Perlimplín now contemplates different possibilities: "I have learned many things, and above all I can imagine them" (II 481). Understanding that his impotence prevents him from fulfilling the more conventional responsibilities to Belisa as a husband, his imagination, impelled by a desire to possess Belisa at some level, inspires him to the idea of self-sacrifice (II 486). This takes the form of the fashioning of the image of a more appropriate counterpart for Belisa, a "beautiful adolescent" (II 496) whom Perlimplín hopes she will love "more than her own body" (II 489) so that, via this proxy, she will come to love him as well. Perlimplín's desire is thus doubly motivated: selfishly, to place limits on Belisa's imagination by creating an image so intense that she will never be free of it, but also unselfishly, to unburden her from an imagination not of this world that wastes itself on thoughts of "ideal lands, of dreams and wounded hearts" (II 485), and thereby to direct her to a more intense and worthwhile, if no less unreal, object of desire.

Abandoning all notions that his body or that the physical comforts and stability of his position in society could ever be attractive to Belisa, Perlimplín dedicates himself instead to the production of a superior image, the Youth of the Red Cape (Joven de la Capa Roja), who at the cost of Perlimplín's reputation in society and eventually of his life, succeeds in captivating Belisa's frenetic yet aimless imagination. With the revelation that the Youth and Perlimplín are inseparable aspects of each other, the old man is able to proclaim "the triumph of my imagination" (II 492). Belisa is forever changed. She will never be able to imagine in the same way upon accepting the Youth as her beloved. The Youth's configuration, however, parallels closely Lorca's own crafting, from an image, of Perlimplín. A creature whose only previous existence has been as a caricature in the two-dimensional medium of newsprint, he assumes a physical presence onstage in order to set a scene in Belisa's imagination, that is, in order to return to a realm where he can continue to exist as an image, which no audience can see.

Indeed, throughout the latter part of the play the audience is relegated simply to imagining something that Belisa and Perlimplín are experiencing as an intense and immediate presence. The most intense moments of the play thus take place in private as the theater audience is relegated to the rather impotent role of mere spectator, at a significant remove from what emerges as the true center and scene of this play, Perlimplín's imagination.

If the revelations at the play's conclusion underscore the untenability of this pair as a conventional couple, the unconventional ending nevertheless portends significant consequences for Lorca's ongoing dialog with theater. More so than any of Lorca's strong female characters, Belisa embodies attitudes long identified with the poetic function. Indeed, Belisa's costume in the first tableau, a lace dressing gown and an enormous bonnet from which a rush of needlework extends to her feet, strongly recalls the activity of embroidery and needlework of Lorca's earlier heroines also associated with the elaboration of the poetic script, that is, the interweaving of the threads of a dramatic plot. Perhaps even more strongly than some of the other early characters, the poets like Curianito and the Marquis, she is quite detached from the social scene or concerns about her place within that larger milieu. At the moment that Belisa learns that she is to marry Perlimplín, she responds by leaving the scene.[27] When she returns, she is reciting a song about love and desire ("Love . . . / Cock, the night departs! / Do not leave, no" [II 467]) that excludes Perlimplín. Independent of her husband from the outset, Belisa does nothing to affirm any of the traditional expectations of married life. As Perlimplín comes to understand, however, her independence is ultimately a consequence of her intense if unfocused and self-absorbed imagination.[28] As undirected as she is directionless, Belisa is nevertheless the character least affected by the physical scene. That she frequently recites her lines in poetry only enhances her association with the poetic function. Her effect on Perlimplín, his abandonment of social conventions in order to remain associated with her, underscores her subversive power. She resists direction of any sort as regards her activities within a physical scene to which she is always only nominally associated.

Perlimplín's creation, an image that implies a world, the youth whose direction Belisa accepts even though she knows that she can never possess him physically, provides her with a scenario she can accept, in her imagination. Whereas in *The Shoemaker's Prodigious Wife* the stage audience of townspeople encroached upon the Wife's physical space in order to silence her, here there is no onstage force—except possibly the servant Marcolfa[29]—to impede the couple from choosing highly unconventional responses to a rather familiar marital dilemma in which one of the marriage partners loves someone else. Perlimplín's creating the image of a youth Belisa will never see except in the privacy of her imagination stabilizes the scene of a desire that, impossible to satisfy, now begins to ring tragic rather than farcical. Imagination weds desire in the hope of embracing a directing agent whose absence only intensifies desire as it also frustrates movement in his direction.

This also signals a qualitative shift in a formula for theater that has visualized the theater functions as a forced marriage of script and scenario. As the play's title framed by "love" and "garden" suggests, here the public circumstances are largely eliminated in order to emphasize that private causes have provided direction to the script. Perlimplín's *burla* of Belisa is different from those of the early theater because it exposes rather than disguises the tragic underpinning to Lorca's theater. A newsprint image taken from a defunct tradition at the margins of art, Perlimplín brings Belisa to the deeper affirmation that she can never separate the creature of Perlimplín's imagination from his creator, to whom she is also inseparably bound. The external impediments of the earlier plays are replaced by an internal dimension that intensifies their dilemma as it also confers greater authority to their functions. Belisa and Perlimplín transcend the restrictions of society in a way that the Wife and Shoemaker could not imagine, yet at a terrible cost to themselves.

Perlimplín fundamentally alters the nature of the scenario by displacing the effects of the external social milieu with a force that resides in an elusive locale at a conscious remove from the nominal physical scene. The force of desire, which destroys as well as inspires, heralds a more profound and authoritative vision for theater. Perlimplín is the first authority figure of the early theater who refuses to acquiesce in conventional expectations. His renunciation signals that Lorca has also realized the need to reveal more of the dramatic potential hidden beneath these masks in order to take his theater in a new direction. Perlimplín and Belisa's ordeal also becomes Lorca's opportunity to rededicate himself, in *As Soon As Five Years Pass* and *The*

Public, to the exploration of a less disguised version of the inspirational image that sustains and consumes both Perlimplín and Belisa. The private scenarios inspired by the "beautiful adolescent" offer as well eloquent replies to the criticisms advanced against *Perlimplín* by Buñuel and Dalí. Even though it may not have been apparent to his friends, *Love of Don Perlimplín with Belisa in His Garden* marks Lorca's serious entry into Modernist theater, bringing with it a new understanding that stage authority derives from the willingness to engage the creative and destructive forces that reside beyond its visible margins.

4

EXPERIMENTAL THEATER

CRITICAL DISCUSSION OF *As Soon As Five Years Pass* and *The Public*
has tended to isolate these plays from earlier and subsequent phases
of Lorca's career.[1] As a consequence of the long delay in their critical
scrutiny, the experimental plays have generally not been considered
integral to the development of Lorca's mature theater.[2] Rather than as
a radical departure, however, the experimental theater emerges as a
logical progression of the desire to direct the scene of a fresh begin-
ning, expressed initially in *Perlimplín* in the rejection of audience ap-
proval, "the ridiculous morality of the people," but also in the affirma-
tion of the more sublime authority of desire, in the powerful yet
completely private image of the "beautiful adolescent." As these plays
intensify the implications of such a vision, they also allow Lorca to
bridge a rather formidable gap between his private world and the pub-
lic-commercial demands that have forced him to make compromises
with its authority.

In the prolog to the unfinished *Dragon* (*Dragón* [1929]), Lorca ex-
presses again his acute awareness that the director function encom-
passes, and is encompassed by, the theater audience. Explicitly identi-
fying himself as a stage director, the speaker reintroduces the theme of
fear prominent in the prolog to *The Shoemaker's Prodigious Wife*, re-
locating it, however, in the audience: "I could tell you some things that
would produce disgust in you, and fear, yes, fear" (*Inconcluso* 116).
Intimating that he is privy to a more imposing private agenda, he de-
mands "that the playwright distance himself a bit from his presence
in the playhouse, that he dare to go with his muse through places
where he will not be in the company of spectators grabbing at him by
little threads to dash him to pieces" (*Inconcluso* 115), to move, as in
Perlimplín, to a space where the audience cannot follow. This un-
finished "new play of magical love" (*Inconcluso* 115) about love's im-
pediments, embodied in the fabled dragon who guards the damsel, may

have been conceived as a commercially feasible version of *As Soon As Five Years Pass*, in which the Youth (Joven) is rejected by the Bride (Novia) in favor of a rugby player whom she calls "my dragon" (II 533; see Fernández Cifuentes 270; Vitale 27). The focus in the experimental plays is, indeed, the "dragon" of desire that moves Lorca in the direction of the more authoritative stage proclaimed here. The experimental plays witness a significant realignment of the theater functions by means of a strategic retreat to a private theater that makes no concessions to the "horizon of expectations" of public audiences. Quite simply, the audience must either accept the premises of these plays or refuse to participate in the representation.

As Soon As Five Years Pass

A nearly unanimous critical opinion has insisted that *As Soon As Five Years Pass* is physically set in the dream, or reverie, of the Youth, considered the play's protagonist.[3] His supporting cast of characters has been generally thought to reflect some aspect of his experience or life choices that he has not embraced, for example, the sexual inclinations, respectively underdeveloped and excessive, of First Friend and Second Friend. My interpretation recognizes an older protagonist, a mature adult who—in the manner of Perlimplín—imagines the Youth. Beginning with a conversation between the Youth and the Old Man, the dream moves simultaneously and ambivalently in two directions: toward the past and the time of youth that forcefully persists in the dreamer's imagination yet also toward present and future embodied in the Old Man who, in the pattern of the old men of earlier plays, presages the advent of a more conventional existence. An offstage presence and not the Youth's phantom projections, therefore, provides script and scenario for a dream representation produced by desire. The phenomenon of hybrid image production in *Mariana Pineda* and *Perlimplín* is significantly intensified in the dreamscape. The Youth is not a self-referential icon but rather the unmediated projection of a living presence, a "photographic" trace in a one-to-one relationship with his dreaming referent. Accompanied by the Old Man and others who attempt to sway him in a specific direction, the Youth embodies but one of the play's competing crosscurrents of desire. He is the most prominent effect, but not the cause, in someone else's dream.[4]

Alternating its focus between the Youth's amorous dilemma and the more philosophical question of time, the play evinces as well frequent temporal and spatial shifts. The initial dialog between the Old Man and the Youth moves immediately toward the past, the true ground of the Youth's personality and the explanation for his compulsion to postpone gratification. The Old Man advocates a different course by proposing what seems to be an unorthodox possibility: "it is necessary to remember toward tomorrow" (II 501). While it is impossible to remember a phenomenon yet to be experienced, these words make perfect, and conventional, sense if the Youth is understood to belong to a larger continuum extending beyond adolescence. Remembering "toward tomorrow" is an exhortation to adopt a more appropriate role in a scenario relentlessly undermining this earlier identity.[5] A more authoritative protagonist whose mission can no longer be postponed is thus intensifying the focus on issues left unresolved from the earlier theater symbolized in Perlimplín's "beautiful adolescent," the very image of resistance to a conventional destiny. The relationship between the Old Man and the Youth thus reveals a hidden struggle to compel the Youth to resolve an impasse.

The Old Man believes that such a pathway lies in the Youth's marriage to the Bride, which requires that he adapt his image of her. The Old Man considers the five-year postponement of marriage plans in a positive light, a prelude to remembering the future and the affirmation of a more appropriate image of the Bride.[6] This may also be why, when speaking of the Bride's chronological age, fifteen, the Old Man redefines it as "fifteen roses, fifteen wings, fifteen little grains of sand" (II 503) since to accept a more mature image of the Bride, the Youth must abandon his established frame of temporal reference strongly resistive of change. The Youth fully understands that the Old Man is attempting by this to dislodge him from a secure site which the Youth has defined in relation to a much younger Bride: "You want to separate me from her" (II 503). Their positions become clearer in the subsequent discussion about the Bride's physical appearance. Both acknowledge that things change more slowly in the present context, an unconventional realm of dream space "without distance beneath your face" (II 505).[7] This is why the Youth prefers "the inside even though it also changes" (II 506), for it is here where the image he carries of the Bride has also resisted precise formulation. Resistance, in fact, constitutes the Youth's very essence.[8]

When at this moment the Typist appears—prompting the Youth to ask her, "Did you finish writing the letters [*cartas*]?" (II 507)—she confesses both her love for him and a strong desire to abandon his employ. The Old Man considers that "that woman is dangerous" (II 507) since as guardian of the written medium through which the Youth continues to express his ambivalence, the Typist is serving to prolong his resistance to a more mature Bride. The Bride has been a pretext for the Youth to delay the demands of a conventional destiny that he now must confront. She exists in multiple aspects that embody both the Youth's unfocused "love without an object" and the more mature face of desire that has emerged in the interim. By the time the Youth is ready to declare himself, the scenario has changed decisively. The Bride's reality exceeds his ability to imagine her, and thus she finds him unsuitable. Emptied of all illusions associated with the Bride's image, the Youth feels utterly forsaken: "even the letters have forgotten me" (II 549). His loss thus reveals, and also parodies, the more imposing requirements of this relationship: to remember who he is by awakening from this dream.

At precisely this point the Youth looks to the "other woman" in his life, "the woman that loves me" (II 558), the Typist. Earlier the submissive conduit and transcriber of the Youth's thoughts, the Typist now acquires all of the aggressive traits displayed by the Bride. The Bride and the Typist embody, respectively, the decisive image of the Youth's life and his impotent epistemological means of closure regarding this issue. As such they also embody and parody empirical cognition and mimesis which are premised upon the easy translatability and interchangeability of visual and verbal signs. In *As Soon As Five Years Pass*, images overwhelm and words fail the Youth. Reminiscent of Perlimplín's inability to "decipher" Belisa's body, the Youth's ultimate reliance on a Romantic model of consciousness in a realm premised on a different set of assumptions makes it impossible for him to stabilize either his scene or the medium of signification embodied in the Bride and the Typist. The Youth persists in understanding his scene as an autonomous finality, yet the signs of his immediate milieu do not display the characteristics of conventional referentiality. They refer instead toward the dreaming entity in and through whom the Youth's drama transpires.

This becomes more explicit at the beginning of act III, which, in the context of the earlier self-conscious commentary on theater relationships in the intervention of the daimons/*duendes* in *Perlimplín*, offers another significant metadramatic assessment of the issues regarding the evolution of Lorca's theater. As the stage directions indicate, the physical setting is self-consciously evocative, in a symbolic sense, of the play's psychic scenario:

> A forest. Large trunks. In the center, a theater surrounded by baroque curtains with the stage curtain lowered. A small stairway unites the small stage with the larger stage. As the curtain rises two figures dressed in black cross among the trunks, their faces as well as their hands white with plaster. A far-away music sounds. The Harlequin enters. He is dressed in black and green. He caries two masks hidden behind his back, one in each hand. He moves in an evocative fashion, as would a ballet dancer. (II 560)

In the context of early plays like *The Butterfly's Spell*, which featured the activity of the principals set among dense grasses, the forest is evocative of a paradoxical "deeper" level within the dream landscape that is said to exist "without distance beneath your face." At this level, where form itself is threatened with dissolution and destruction by unconscious forces, emerges a clearing where the issues inherent in this unorthodox representational medium expose their conflicting and contradictory dimensions. The principal actor in this "open-air" theater[9] is the Harlequin, accompanied by a Girl dressed in a black Greek tunic and later by a guffawing Clown costumed in sequins. The Harlequin begins by offering observations about three distinct modes of understanding, that is, three different alternate configurations that in fact disrupt standard empirical accounts of the epistemological process. In the first, "the dream goes on upon time / floating like a weathervane" (II 560). When the dream state dominates time, empirical understanding, premised upon the orderly progression of time, is rendered effectively inoperative. This arrangement is unproductive since "no one can open seeds / in the heart of the dream" (II 560). Nevertheless, as the association with the weathervane underscores, the salient characteristic of the functioning of signs in the dream state is their indexicality. The dream of desire moves in a constant, yet uncomprehended, direction.

The second possibility, in which "time goes on upon the dream" (II 561), corresponds to the dominion of time in an empirical context. This mode is also unsatisfying since desire's dream is overwhelmed by the consciousness of time's destruction as "yesterday and tomorrow devour / dark flowers of grief" (II 561). Although the debilitating effects of this mode of consciousness are articulated by the Youth's growing awareness that "I do not belong to myself" (II 509), its most succinct articulation is offered in the Old Man's invocation to remember "toward tomorrow," an implicit demand that the past be surpassed or forgotten.

The final possibility, and the one upon which the play turns, is an epistemological and representational framework recognizing that "upon the same column, / dream and time embraced, / intersect the cry of the child, / the broken tongue of the old man" (II 561). The largely atemporal-spatial values of the dream state and the temporal-directional movement (past–present–future) inherent in realist empirical models combine to create a hybrid mode of representation in which the visual-verbal building blocks of empirico-mimetic discourse become indexical points of reference for the primary agency, the directing authority of desire. That is to say, desire reveals its presence and authority along a temporal continuum rather than in a stable point or moment, in a direction and not in self-referential visual-verbal signs. The characters, including the Youth, are secondary aspects of a larger scene provided by both the dream and time. Unifying the play's diverse stories and scenes is desire's intention to manifest itself more fully while resisting an arbitrary point of closure. Thus, for example, the Dead Child's story is not separate from the Youth's but part of an ongoing continuum. Although corresponding to different moments in the dream saga, both are similar in their resistance to the closure that circumstances, of an empirical nature, attempt to impose. The Dead Child resists the disintegration that death imposes just as the Youth resists a conventional image of love. While resistance explains the Youth's conduct, it also explains the workings of desire, which supersedes the Youth's resistance with its own more authoritative dimension.

Interspliced with the Harlequin's pronouncements is a second movement, the laments of the Girl, who, in a fashion that closely parallels the dilemma of the Youth, finds herself in a state of psychic disarray at the loss of her Bridegroom. Yet her lamentations are exposed by the Harlequin as so much facade when he imitates the voice of her Bridegroom, only to have the Girl reply, "No thank you" (II 565)— again a response that fully reduplicates the significant events in the Youth's story characterized by resistance. Although she professes a desire to encounter her lover at a deeper level, expressed here as the depths of the ocean, the Harlequin does not allow her the consolation of this obviously false illusion. When he laughingly confronts her, the Girl is forced to admit the truth, ending her presence in the scene in the manner in which she entered, lamenting her loss—"I lost my crown, / I lost my thimble" (II 565)—in terms fully reminiscent of the sewing-embroidering metaphors that have characterized the activities of the poetic function of theater throughout Lorca's plays. The Girl, therefore, reenacts the Harlequin's speech outlining the unconventional directions for theater that emerge from the confrontation of empirical and dream realms.

The ultimate consequence of this hybrid order is a complete theatricalization, the consciousness that instead of being an individuated personality-consciousness one occupies a role, or rather roles, as the Clown also underscores later in this scene when he is asked to reveal his destination:

To represent.
A small child
who wants to change
his bit of bread
into flowers of steel.
   (II 566)[10]

Rather than to a point in space and time, the Clown returns to an ongoing role, that of the Dead Child, who, ironically, symbolizes resistance to just this type of subjective displacement and transformation. Rather than to become substantial temporal/spatial subjects, these characters function as directions in a hybrid dream/time medium. Recalling the forced marriages of Lorca's earlier plays, this juxtaposition of realities creates an unstable scene yet one in which there is a continual exchange of identities, or masks, all moving in an inexorable direction but not to a point of closure. Directionality, a continuum of movement through an unconventional space/time, strongly underlies the content of *As Soon As Five Years Pass*. The visual-verbal signs from which audiences traditionally produce meaning acquire in the dream/ time scenario an indexical dimension that serves to situate the play's locus offstage with a referent not physically part of the scene. The Harlequin describes the dream state unhindered by time in terms of pure indexicality: "The dream goes on above time / floating like a weathervane." The weathervane is the index of the invisible force that moves it, the trace of its presence that indicates the direction of its referent. Pure indexicality, however, is also directionless floating. In the play, therefore, dream and time affiliate to provide a more orderly sense of direction which nevertheless strongly resists closure: "upon the same column, / dream and time embraced, / intersect the cry of the child, / the broken tongue of the old man." The character-masks on stage refer, and defer, to a directing force whose strategy is neither definitive closure nor surrealistic chaos.

Directionality progressively becomes a dominant theme as the play moves toward its climax. When the Typist asks, in a song,

Where are you going, my love,
my love,
with the air in a bottle
and the sea in a glass?

(II 572)

the Youth answers with an exact repetition of these words, which underscores both his estrangement from desire and his displacement from the protagonist's role. He has had the task of containing a force as vast as the sea in a medium likened to a fragile glass. Therefore, not only is he rejected by the Bride but he is abandoned by "my love," the force that has sustained him. In a parody of the Bride's earlier forsaking, the Typist's subsequent rejection scorns the very trajectory of the Youth's existence as she utters the phrase that is itself an index of his ambivalent progression through time under untenable epistemological premises: "As soon as five years pass" (II 581). Love remains always at a distance, measured in time. The fundamental contradiction of the Youth's life is more succinctly addressed in the final tableau where he asks the Servant: "Is a weathervane all right when it turns in the direction that the wind moves it?" (II 584), to which the Servant replies that the better question should be, "Is the wind all right?" (II 585). That is to say, the index of the wind, the weathervane, is merely the visible symptom of a more authoritative invisible agent directing its movement. This also describes the dynamic in the play, in which the visible entities progressively lose self-referentiality in order to indicate the direction of the offstage center from which they are projected.

As Soon As Five Years Pass thus depicts a convergence of realities where the effects of causes originating outside the Youth's visible scene are more fully acknowledged. The Youth, however, is the victim of another aspect prominent in the representational equation: an account of phenomena that understands everything, including the unconscious, as being subject to temporal laws. The Youth resists change in a medium that is undergoing its own inexorable temporal transformation. Indeed, the dream is ultimately a response to the challenge of yet another unrepresented force, the public demands of consciousness, the audience in front of whom the Youth must wear his masks. The agents of his destruction, the three Card Players—young gentlemen (*señoritos*) quite similar to himself, invited for a game of cards (*cartas*) augured perhaps in the earlier query to the Typist, "Did you mail the letters [*cartas*]?"—arise from the remnants of the Youth's dream in order to fulfill the logical consequences of an inexorable process.[11]

The means of the Youth's assassination is again exemplary of the unorthodox nature of the representation. Rather than the Youth being physically assaulted by the Card Players, the First Card Player shoots an arrow from a noiseless gun into the illuminated image of the ace of hearts, at which point the Youth "brings his hands to his heart" (II 594). The act of assassination underscores again that the primary content of the play is the tracing of a trajectory, a direction that has proceeded through various mediums in a constant evolution. Emblematic of indexicality, the arrow, like the weathervane, signals the final moment of the epistemological displacement that has undermined autoreferentiality in this play. Consistent with the emphasis on the direction and evolution of desire, the Youth's death does not definitively conclude a story, only his centrality in an ongoing scenario. His fate is succinctly suggested in the question, interrupted by echoes, he asks as he is dying: "Is there no . . . ? . . . No one here?" (II 595–96). Two successive echoes answer with the word "here" (aquí). The repetition of "here" underscores the fundamental paradox of this play. The Youth is no longer present but neither will he definitively disappear. He will occupy a different space or plane in an existential and theatrical equation in which "here" is a constant variable. The Youth's resistance to the directorial imperative of desire fails to stabilize an inexorable movement that, ironically, not even his death can halt.

In *As Soon As Five Years Pass*, Lorca intertwines empirical time with the dream state to create a hybrid scenario analogous to the relationship that exists between a photograph and the physical referent from which it receives its form. By locating the center of his representation offstage, Lorca is able not only to consolidate the poetic and directorial functions but also to displace the audience, to effectively suspend "stageability" as a criterion for theater.[12] If so inclined, an audience may choose to follow the "backward" trajectory of this representation. The play will have meaning, however, only if the audience is willing to adjust its epistemological criteria to a dramatic content that, ironically, portrays the impossibility of such a task for the Youth. The more one is able to comprehend the play's unorthodox viewing conventions, therefore, the more one understands that the representation is not a stage-centered spectacle that makes its visual-verbal reality available for an audience. The Harlequin hints at this when he responds to the Youth's desire to return home in act III, telling him that he is actually returning to a "circus," a stage "filled with spectators definitively silent" (II 571). This also implicitly asserts the requirements for the play's becoming a stage representation. The audience, in complete passivity, must be willing to house this dream in its imagination as it must also acknowledge, for the first time, a stage authority other than itself: an invisible presence under whose auspices the Youth's ruin has been authorized.

The Public

The Public is also about the ruinous contradictions of desire revealed in yet another dream scenario that exposes the theatrical and existential shortcomings of the Director, discredited as a consequence of his decision to use an adolescent boy in the role of Juliet in his production of Shakespeare's *Romeo and Juliet*. Although there are significant similarities between the two plays, the temporal context of *The Public* is much more ambiguous, indeed, chaotic in comparison to that of *As Soon As Five Years Pass*. The viewer cannot be certain if the action is consequent to the failure of the Director's production or if the initial tableaus actually precede the act of theater that brings him to ruin. It is even uncertain if the Director's production has been staged or if it exists simply as a vivid premonition in the dream. Whatever the true circumstances, he is violently dispossessed of his authority over a play that outrages its contemporary audience through exact faithfulness to Elizabethan conventions. The Director's production is further displaced by an extradramatic scrutiny of the causes, private and public, for its failure, which provides the basis for the play.

When at the outset the Director declares that "I have lost my entire fortune" (II 599), he is referring to the bankruptcy of his imagination that has nothing tangible to offer a private audience, the White Horses, potential sources for the imaginative energy necessary to stage successful theater.[13] Since the Director is without "financing," the horses abandon him to their successors, the Three Men, a second audience whose physical resemblance to the Director suggests that, as in *As Soon As Five Years Pass*, the Director is only the nominal protagonist, the public-professional aspect of a more complex and contradictory personality whose dream brings together this group of players. As the Director confronts his loss of authority in what appears to be a conventional "theater in the open air," he becomes the unwitting herald of an underground playhouse designated as the "theater beneath the sand."[14] Here he eventually discovers that his real motivation for the production has been to show "the profile of a hidden force when the audience has no further recourse except to pay full attention, filled with spirit and overpowered by the action" (II 665). The stage is not an autonomous finality but an open-ended medium, or tunnel, for the fuller materialization of this hidden force in public contexts: "I made the tunnel in order to take possession of the masks" (II 665). Stage characters must be instilled with the consciousness that they are not self-referential ends in themselves but rather the visible effects of an offstage authority that avails itself of the stage in order to extend, like a tunnel, into the imaginations of the theater audience.[15]

Also more pronounced than in *As Soon As Five Years Pass* is the disfunction of conventional visual-verbal signification that further in-

tensifies the phenomenon of indexicality in *The Public*. As empha-
sized by the use of a folding screen to effect character transformations
that are conspicuously incomplete, the full visual representation of a
character or character aspect is not revealed in one autonomous, self-
referring space but by means of a series of incomplete hybrid images
that extend across multiple planes. As the Director is forced to con-
front troubling aspects of his personal life instrumental in his casting
decisions, the play uncovers the fragments of a personal and profes-
sional reality revealed along a directional axis that exposes again the
error of wearing an unchanging public mask in this medium beyond
empirical consciousness.[16]

The Director's casting for *Romeo and Juliet*, a literal imitation of a
practice of convention in Shakespeare's time, becomes an intolerable
social/sexual transgression because the audience brings its own more
authoritative Shakespeare scenario to the theater. The "open air" and
underground theaters are similar in that both audiences displace the
Director as stage authority. Indeed, *The Public* becomes a confluence
of competing performance texts: the Director's "exact" imitation of
Shakespeare; the "open air" audience's version of Shakespeare; the pri-
vate audience, in the theater beneath the sand, that reveals the work-
ings of the hidden force at the further expense of the Director's author-
ity; and, finally, the Director's personal drama, as inseparable from
these audiences as are the competing versions of *Romeo and Juliet*.[17]
These simultaneously projected scenarios, which do not follow a
cause-and-effect progression, correlate well with the Harlequin's de-
scription in *As Soon As Five Years Pass* of one of the possible modes of
the dream state in which time is completely supplanted by effectively
unmediated images ("The dream goes on above time / floating like a
weathervane"). The Director fails to establish himself in either the
medium dominated by convention or the underground theater gov-
erned by an "abominable" force.

The final gasp of the Director's imagination witnesses the horses'
invention of a neologism—*blenamiboá*, a reversal of the syllables of
abominable—which succinctly characterizes the content of the play.[18]
Theater is constituted in *The Public* as a reverse direction, movement
through the unmediated indexical domain of the theater beneath the
sand. An open-ended tunnel rather than an enclosed space, the stage
functions as a medium through which antagonistic offstage forces in-

tervene to discredit the authority of those who continue to cling to the illusion of stage autonomy. The Director becomes the physical pretext upon which competing realities—expressed here as competing audiences—sustain themselves. *The Public* is, ironically, the truest name for Shakespeare's *Romeo and Juliet*. The only version of this play that the Director can legitimately bring to the stage is a performance text reformulated in the imaginations of generations of audiences. The Director was not the exclusive stage authority for this production. As a consequence, the public audience engenders a private audience of unrelenting critics, in the theater beneath the sand, to expose his failure to assert his authority.

The Director's reply to the First Man's assertion that "Romeo can be a grain of salt and Juliet can be a map" is that while private interpretations of these characters are possible, "they will never stop being Romeo and Juliet" (II 602). They are an inseparable part of the public imagination. As a consequence, his own attempt to reinterpret these characters, which features Juliet's role played by "a boy of fifteen" (II 657), becomes immediately transparent. As the Fourth Student later explains: "This is why the revolution has broken out. The stage director opened the trap doors and the people could see how the venom of the false veins had caused the true death of many children. It is not the disguised forms that bring forth life, but rather the barometric hair that lies behind" (II 653). Rather than becoming an innovative force, the Director succeeds only in exposing his own sexual ambivalence, which he is forced to confront, strongly resisting, in the theater beneath the sand. A deeper truth awaits him here, "a finale occasioned by fear" (II 605), the destructive consequences of an abiding fear of the audience and the truth of himself.

In the underground as in the "open air," an audience challenges the Director's authority to dominate the scene. Indeed, in the second tableau, subtitled "Roman Ruin" (*Ruina romana*), the Director is compelled to become an actor in a representation that further exposes his shortcomings. Two characters named Bells (Cascabeles) and Vine Shoots (Pámpanos), aspects or more honest visual projections, respectively, of the Director and the First Man (Martínez Nadal *Público* 48), emerge from the folding screen in order to reveal deeper truths about their counterparts. Their dialog, a series of hypothetical propositions followed by a logical response, underscores both the pretextual nature of their discourse and the incapacity of their utterances to stabilize their relationship, or even to establish their prominence, in a scene identified as a ruin. One of the more telling examples is the following:

Bells: And if I were to transform into excrement?
Vine Shoots: I would transform into a fly. (II 611)

Here a squalid medium determines the nature of the creature appropriate to such a scenario, which evinces both the mutual dependence and the self-destructive animosity of the parties as the consequence of an unwanted pairing. The culminating invocation is of "a knife sharpened during four long springs" (II 615), evocative of the latent violence inherent in the impasse of finding oneself matched in a relationship against one's will.

Indeed, the ruins become a visual correlative for ambivalence toward the other, as is further underscored by the entrance of the Emperor to proclaim the authority of the "one": "One is one and always one. I have slit the throats of more than forty boys that refused to say it" (II 618).[19] The Emperor, who champions resistance to the physical expression of homoeroticism, like the ruins over which he presides, cannot impose his authority over the scene. "Oneness" is an untenable position, the consequence of a refusal to acknowledge the truth about oneself and the nature of desire. As the scene concludes, the Emperor is embraced by Vine Shoots, which occasions the commentary at the beginning of the third tableau. The Third Man declares: "Those two must have died. I have never witnessed a bloodier feast" (II 621). Others offer different and contradictory opinions:

First Man: Two lions. Two demigods.
Second Man: Two demigods, if they did not have an anus. (II 621)

While there is the recognition of the validity, and even the potential superiority, of homosexual love, there is the equal appreciation that the inescapable necessity to express this love by physical means—that is, by means of two rather than one—negates its positive potential: "[t]he anus is the punishment of man. The anus is the failure of man, it is his shame and his death. The two had an anus and neither of them could fight with the pure beauty of the marble that was shining and conserving intimate desires defended by a perfect surface" (II 622).

The Emperor is ultimately the most prominent embodiment of the ambivalence that has authorized the ruin over which he presides. The creative search for the "one" inevitably summons an "other" and thus inexorable movement toward ruin: "The Emperor that drinks our blood is in the ruin" (II 623). The First Man, the character most sympathetic to homosexual love, wants to murder the Emperor and bring back his head to the Director. The Director agrees that this would make an excellent present, not for him but for Helen (Elena), the muse who has inspired his earlier theater. Like so many others, this exchange simply rephrases the conditions that have led to the Director's theatrical and existential crisis. Ambivalence to the authority of the hidden force has brought him to ruin. When the First Man reminds him that "the head of the Emperor burns the bodies of all women" (II 625), that his ideal is universally impractical, the Director abandons Helen as well—"No, do not call her. I will transform into what you desire" (II 627)—thereby reenacting the very abdication of authority that has brought him to the theater beneath the sand.

As an altercation between the Second Man and Third Man causes them to depart the scene, a more profound dimension of the theater beneath the sand reveals itself in Juliet, who arises from her coffin to complain: "I do not care for discussions about theater. What I want to do is love" (II 628). Righteously indignant at developments undertaken in her name, she lashes out at "four boys who have wanted to give me a clay phallus and were intent on painting an ink moustache on me" (II 632), a reference to the Men and the Director who have appropriated her form while concealing the passion that motivates it. This Juliet is not the character from Shakespeare's original or the Juliet of the Director's version. Shakespeare's Juliet has been appropriated by contemporary theater audiences who have bound and gagged her and have forced her to sit with the audience. The Director's Juliet is equally distasteful to her, however, for that Juliet, ironically, is simply another means to disguise her true potential.

Tied neither to any public audience nor to the Director, she is searching for an appropriate medium to invigorate with the form of love she has to offer. Her principal suitors here are the horses who had earlier abandoned the Director. They now proclaim "the true theater . . . the theater beneath the sand" (II 636) at the core of which is Juliet's form, the first visual expression of such a potentially rejuvenating force. Juliet's energizing presence allows the First Man to affirm that

"I have no mask" (II 637) while it also elicits the Director's continuing resistance and the opposite avowal that "there is nothing but mask" (II 638). Juliet proclaims that she cannot be domesticated, diverted, or used for a lesser purpose: "I am not a slave so that they can thrust burins of amber into my breasts, nor an oracle for those who tremble with love as they exit the city. My whole dream has been with the smell of the fig tree and the waistline of the one who cuts the ears of wheat. Nobody through me! I through you!" (II 636). From the depths of the theater beneath the sand, therefore, Juliet heralds the advent of an inspirational force more authoritative than the conventional imagination embodied in the horses.

Similar to the Youth's situation in *As Soon As Five Years Pass*, the Director's imaginative "bankruptcy" is a direct consequence of an unrecognized resistance to the hidden force. Although a much more palatable expression of the "abominable" forces impinging upon him, Juliet's demand for greater authority only inspires further conflict between the Director and the First Man. When the Director rebukes the First Man for embracing him in the company of others, the First Man's response is to proclaim his love "in front of the others because I abhor the mask and because I have succeeded in taking it from you" (II 639) and thus to press the Director to confront his insincerity with himself. Juliet's hopeful emergence from her coffin, however, is shortlived. As she returns to await a more propitious moment, three new character-masks appear to echo in parodic fashion the First Man's mourning of another lost opportunity.

By the fifth tableau, the contradictions of the Director's resistance to the truth become manifest as the scene returns, not to the coffin from which Juliet arose, but to the sepulchre at the site of the Director's ill-fated production. Interspliced with critical commentary from the Students is the slow, and sometimes comically ironic, agony of the Red Nude, the First Man in perhaps his truest aspect, now in the role of martyr for the sake of the Director's production. The Students characterize the Director's production as revolutionary ("he swept away the head of the professor of rhetoric" [II 650]), a break with the old rules of stage-centered playmaking. The Director's casting decision attempted to transform the script into something quite different by means of a manipulation of the scenario. It effected, however, an equally "revolutionary" intervention to restore the primacy of the poet—in this particular case, the "Bard"—tarnished by the Director. The angry mob from the "theater in the open air" finds the Director in Juliet's coffin, which, in its counterpart in the "theater beneath the sand," is where the Director failed to embrace Juliet's promise of a revitalized inspiration. As the Students continue to debate whether or not Romeo and Juliet need to be "necessarily a man and a woman for the sepulchre scene to be represented in a living and heartbreaking manner" (II 653), the scene switches abruptly to the Red Nude who is now finally acknowledged as an essential aspect of the Director's production. The Red Nude's sacrifice, clearly a parody of Christ's crucifixion, represents the literal, physical costs of the failed production. Under the nominal authority of someone less convinced than the First Man/Red Nude of the validity of this undertaking, the courage to bring such a production before an audience demands physical sacrifice as much as the expenditure of imaginative "capital." Although the Students strongly insist that "a spectator should never form part of the drama" (II 657), the audience's violent interruption of the representation becomes a final visual confirmation that stage authority resides elsewhere.

With the death of the First Man/Red Nude, the final tableau turns to a dialog between the Director and a new character, the Magician (Prestidigitador), who offers yet another perspective on the demise of the Director's production. In his discussions with the First Man, the Director had tacitly advocated a position recognizing theater as a trade-off between the naked truth—an impossible set of truths (veras)—and burlas, lesser or disguised truths that are nevertheless theatrically viable. The Director suggests to the Magician that his intention, via Shakespeare, was to make a statement about the universality of love no matter what the physical constitution of the partners,

> in order to express what happens every day in all the large cities and in the country by means of an example that, admitted by everybody in spite of its originality, occurred only once. I could have chosen *Oedipus* or *Othello*. On the other hand, if I had raised the curtain with the original truth, the seats of the theater would have been drenched in blood from the first scenes. (II 664)

Since the Director admits that his production was a compromise from the outset, the Magician criticizes him for not having chosen a more

appropriate play, such as *A Midsummer Night's Dream*, to introduce
the idea that "love is pure chance" (II 664), especially given the fact
that Juliet's counterpart in that play, Titania, falls in love with a don-
key. This would likely have spared the Director the violence that
brought him to the theater beneath the sand.

Now assuming a posture reminiscent of the First Man, the Director
vigorously defends the project and the inherent worth of the theater
beneath the sand, the most significant aspect of which has been the
opening of the tunnel between public and private domains: "My
friends and I opened the tunnel beneath the sand without the people in
the city's noticing it. . . . I made the tunnel in order to take control of
the masks and, by means of them, to reveal the profile of a hidden
force" (II 665). The tunnel is animated by desire, now understood as a
transcendent force, the creative-destructive potential of which the Di-
rector is now able to acknowledge:

> If Romeo and Juliet agonize and die in order to awaken smiling when
> the curtain falls, my characters, on the other hand, burn the curtain
> and die for real in the presence of the spectators. The horses, the sea,
> the army of grasses have prevented it. But some day, when all the thea-
> ters are burned, there will be found in the sofas, behind the mirrors
> and inside the goblets of gold cardboard, the reunion of our dead shut
> up there by the public. (II 666)

Indeed, the only character to survive this spectacle is the Magician,
an apparent master of disguise and stage effects. Nevertheless, there
emerges a much deeper appreciation of the relationships involved in
the act of theater. Lorca's challenge in the aftermath of this explora-
tion of the fuller geography of theater is to marshall these misspent
forces—the First Man's commitment to the authority of the script of
desire, the Director's will to represent such a commitment on stage,
the Magician's advocacy of a subversive expediency in the furtherance
of these goals[20]—in an attempt to achieve greater concert with the in-
exorable presence and direction provided by the hidden force.

Lorca's Experimental Plays in
Relation to Pirandellian Metadrama

There are numerous, especially formal, similarities between Lorca's
experimental plays and Pirandello's equally innovative "theater about

theater," the trilogy comprising *Six Characters in Search of an Author* (1921), *Each in His Own Way* (1924), and *Tonight We Improvise* (1929). Although the two dramatists corresponded, knew and admired each other's work, and had actually begun to collaborate (as mentioned above, Pirandello had made plans, although these were ultimately not realized, to produce *Yerma* in Italy in 1936, in cooperation with Margarita Xirgu's theater company), their dramatic visions nevertheless move in somewhat different directions. Ironically, Lorca's practical dilemma with *The Public* throughout the 1930s, the imposing problem of its stageability before a Spanish audience—the fear that lack of audience tolerance had relegated it, for at least the foreseeable future, to the status of a "poem to hiss at" (III 557)—paralleled trouble confronting Pirandello, who was forced to premiere *Six Characters* outside Italy, in Paris, precisely because Italian audiences were at that moment not yet able to tolerate its innovations.

As is the case with Lorca's early theater centered in what are generally considered the "lesser" theater genres, Pirandello's ideas about drama, aesthetics, and performance principles originate in a theory about humor, that is, the comic as opposed to the tragic, developed systematically in *L'umorismo* (1908). The underlying premise of *umorismo* is that beneath the surface appearance of a character or dramatic situation, to which an audience reacts intellectually, there is a deeper aspect, an emotional level, which transforms the initially comic impulse into a more profound experience. Integrally related to this concept is the idea of masking. All characters comprise surface appearance, their masks, and deeper content, which the act of theater undertakes to reveal to the spectator. Clearly, there is a strong overlap between the two playwrights in these respects. *As Soon As Five Years Pass* represents essentially a comic plot with a deeper aspect that reveals a greater seriousness. The figure of the Youth is but the most visible manifestation, effectively a mask, for the deeper dimension of a fuller personality whose multiple aspects are exposed over the course of the representation. Likewise, in *The Public* the Director is only the most prominent or stable of the many aspects-masks that constitute his full, or fuller, personality, a combination of both farcical/humorous and more serious/tragic aspects. The great difference between the two is that the "deeper dimension" of the Lorcan character is invariably expressed as another surface, another mask, which problemizes the question of the search for identity so prominent in Pirandello.

Lorca and Pirandello both use the idea and experience of theater as the means to represent a position regarding life and reality, and both prominently feature the figure of the stage director (or equivalent) who, within the action of *The Public* and across the three works by Pirandello, evinces a significant evolution with regard to his function. From greater centrality, authority, and unwillingness to participate with the characters that occupy the space of the stage, the Director (or his equivalent; in *Tonight We Improvise* that role is occupied by Dr. Hinkfuss) is displaced or replaced. Dr. Hinkfuss is thrown out by the characters who are then able to improvise. The Director of *The Public* mortally succumbs, leaving the Magician in his place at the conclusion. These parallel developments within and across works demonstrate as well that both dramatists have used playmaking not only as a representational vehicle but, indeed, as the ground for the material exposition of their thought.

The divergence between the two lies in the direction of their vision. With Pirandello the emphasis is upon evolution and an ultimate reduction in the tensions among the aspects of the theater/life equation, often characterized as the conflict between flux and form. As Roger W. Oliver suggests:

> *Tonight We Improvise* is the logical conclusion of the thematic and dramaturgic explorations that begin in *Six Characters*. Although *Each in His Own Way* and *Tonight We Improvise* both use the flux-and-form image more self-consciously than *Six Characters*, they ultimately affirm . . . synthesis . . . rather than the opposition of life with fictions seeking to delimit and stagnate it. . . . As *Tonight We Improvise* illustrates, even late in his career Pirandello created opposition and conflict in order to suggest the need for moderation rather than extremism. (122)

With *The Public*, however, the movement is not toward synthesis but rather toward a strategic reordering of tensions that remain undiminished. Just as the Youth's death in *As Soon As Five Years Pass* does not signal his definitive disappearance from an ongoing metadramatic scenario, so too the Director's death does not signify the complete overthrowing of his agenda, only that a perhaps foolhardy theater project must await a more propitious moment. Like Juliet before him, the Director himself returns to his own version of the tomb to await his resurrection and that of his theater, a moment of synthesis that must await until *Play Without A Title*. The figure for the moment dominating the scene is the Magician, much more adept than the Director at the types of disguises and masks necessary to keep the audience at a viable distance so that theater, if not at the present level of intensity, can indeed continue in some form. It was with regard to this aspect of the directorial function—the power to create a scenario "full of spirit and dominated by the action" that would leave the audience no choice except to be attentive to the hidden force—that the Director failed. His scenario was, in effect, too transparent, revealed too much and in the process ruined the illusion for everyone. Stageability and the commercial viability of future plays require the theater equation to acknowledge and to address the transparency that has resulted in destructive consequences. The figure of the Magician thus embodies the realization that the first goal of the directorial function must be to ensure the viability of the representation. Implied in the Director's experience, therefore, is the need to affirm greater visual density, a scenario that will facilitate the implicit presence in the scene of a hidden force whose fundamental essence remains unstageable. This, in effect, becomes the strategy of the commercial theater for the remainder of Lorca's career, to devise scenarios with sufficient visual denseness for the Director's agenda, through the auspices and manipulation of the Magician, to continue.

Little Puppet Stage and Two Prologs

In the aftermath of the experimental plays and also as a consequence of his practical experience as principal stage director of the La Barraca theater group, there is growing evidence of a different attitude toward commercial theater, in Lorca's appended prolog to the earlier *Tragicomedy of Don Cristobal and Miss Rosita* and in the related puppet play *Don Cristobal's Little Puppet Stage* (both around 1932), as well as in the prolog to the 1933 version of *The Shoemaker's Prodigious Wife*.[21] In the first of these, the irreverent mouthpiece, the Mosquito, begins with an acknowledgment of an infelicitous and frustrated theater past: "I and my company come from the theater of the bourgeoisie, from the theater of the counts and the marquises, a theater of gold and crystals, where the men fall asleep and the ladies . . . also fall asleep. My company and I were confined. You cannot imagine the pain we had" (II 105–6). In the context of the earlier theater, the Mosquito's censure, which appears to attack traditional middle-class forms of theater, is also a commentary on Lorca's sincere yet ineffective attempts to bring distinctiveness and originality to a confining theater environment.

Echoing the Director's even more disastrous failure in *The Public* in precisely a "theater of the bourgeoisie," Mosquito, one of the most insignificant creatures in nature, commands little actual authority. His observation about theatrical characters that reside "where the men fall asleep and the ladies . . . also fall asleep" sheds light on the reasons for this lack of authority. As much in allusion to an uninteresting theatrical content, Mosquito may also be referring to the consequences of the distancing of the theater audience so prominent in the structure of the earlier theater, a further acknowledgment of the difficulty in keeping "asleep" a more truthful theater content disguised and repressed in the earlier work.

Mosquito's most serious complaint, however, is about the collaborative nature of theater, which leads him to a further insight: "I opened my eye all that I could—the finger of the wind wanted to close it—and beneath the star, a wide river was smiling furrowed by slow ships. Then I warned my friends, and we fled through these fields in search of simple folk, to show them the things, the small things and the even smaller things of the world" (II 106). The reference to "the simple folk" could mean a nonbourgeois audience better able to experience and appreciate a spectacle in the open-air context of puppet theater. Yet these words equally refer to the company of puppets in the guise of more humble folk through whom the understandings of the "small world," the poet's private imaginative domain, are to be revealed. This would suggest that, more than playing to a new audience, the goal is to portray the current dynamic of forces with simpler and more straightforward masks. The pointed reference by Mosquito to the opening of his only eye suggests that there is a greater consciousness of the need to accommodate more acceptable and stable stage characters drawn from "simple folk" and "real life." This is precisely the direction Lorca takes in the rural plays of the mid-thirties.

As well as returning to the stage Cristobal and Miss Rosita, principals in the *Tragicomedy*, *Don Cristobal's Little Puppet Theater* also continues, in a more genteel fashion, the exchanges in *The Public* between the First Man, strongly identified with the poetic function, and the Director by means of extradramatic interruptions here by the Poet and the Director.[22] At the heart of their polemic is who ultimately possesses stage authority. The Director considers that paying the Poet for the script is all the authorization he needs to stage the play exactly as he pleases, the very attitude that Lorca himself confronted with the contemporary Madrid stage, dominated as it was by strong actors and impresarios and severely lacking in qualified stage directors. A problem immediately arises over the character of Don Cristobal, whom the Director considers to be "bad" yet of whom the Poet believes "in his heart he is good and perhaps he could be" (II 676). The Director's response is a familiar one. He demands the Poet's immediate silence: "Fool. If you do not shut up, I'll come up and split that cornbread face that you have" (II 676). This contrasts sharply with the Poet's demand in the prolog for the silent attention of the theater audience: "I want a silence so profound that we hear the gurgling of the fountains" (II 675). The Poet is reconfirming positions offered earlier that understand stage authority to derive primarily from the script and that consider the audience's distance from the stage essential ("The audience must fall asleep in the word and must not see beyond the column of bleating sheep" [II 653]). This Director, like his counterpart in *The Public*, is slow to comprehend that since the audience is the least controllable aspect of the director's responsibility, the Poet's advocacy of the audience's silence and distance is actually complementary to the director function.

The interruption of the representation, the cause of the Director's downfall in *The Public*, becomes the catalyst for an entirely different outcome here: the occasion to introduce to the stage a new language, coarse but invigorating, that will move theater toward closer contact with the spontaneity and vitality associated with popular traditions. The image-masks that dominated *The Public* are replaced with a swarm of discourse. The Poet's interruptions also draw attention to the Director's rather timid staging decisions, which are depriving his script of greater authority. Lorca is thus giving physical form to yet another aspect of an ongoing internal debate about the direction of his theater. If *The Public* examines the limitations of visual dominance as a vehicle for instituting an authoritative theater agenda, *Don Cristobal's Little Puppet Stage* responds to the poet's fundamental demand to be heard. The most prominent listener must be the stage director lest he find himself overwhelmed, as in *The Public*, by his audience. The Poet's demand to be listened to is a response to the implicit call in *The Public* for more original theater scripts, scripts that will be heeded because they are able to resist imaginative appropriation and circumscription by theater audiences. In the aftermath of the destruction of the characters embodying the functions of poet and director in *The Public*, Lorca has at last begun seriously to confront a long-standing internal dispute. Although it is the Director who concludes the farce and seems to have the last word, it is evident that the Director's words are now actually those of the Poet.[23]

The Poet's input throughout has been to call for a new and reinvigorating language in order for the values of "poetry"—scriptmaking— to shape and direct theater. The character who speaks at the conclusion is truly a composite figure, a Director who has assimilated the aims and purposes of the Poet. The Director celebrates the power of the coarse language of the common people, "crude words and expressions" (II 697), and their potential to infuse new life into a languishing theater scene: "Let us fill the theater with fresh ears of grain, beneath which will go the crude words that struggle on the stage with the tedium and vulgarity to which we have condemned it" (II 697). Coarse language (*palabrotas*) becomes a metaphor for the type of revitalized scriptwriting and scenemaking, heralded but unfulfilled in *The Public*, that now seems a more realizable possibility. The Director's final gesture is to link the Spanish Cristobal to a European puppet tradition, which further suggests that the revitalization of the Spanish stage cannot proceed in isolation from the rest of Europe. In the aftermath of his anguished experiments, Lorca takes an important step toward assuming fuller authority over his own mode of theater. Poet and Director, script and scenario, can work, if not in harmony, at least in mutual company and purpose to draw upon extradramatic forces that reside both in the underground and in the "open air."

The final step in the evolution toward a mature theater formula is the incorporation of insights from the experimental plays into a fully commercial production, which Lorca acknowledges in the revised prolog to the 1933 version of *The Shoemaker's Prodigious Wife*. A noticeable departure from the 1930 prolog is that the *autor* explicitly comments on a hidden aspect of the play, "where the creatures of tragedy wander" (II 376), a candid admission that his farce masks a different set of circumstances disguised by clothing "the dramatic example in the living rhythm of a common shoemaker's shop" (II 376). Equally significant, the activity of the characters is called "pantomime" (II 376), which suggests that they are visual stand-ins, masks or mediums for a more authoritative force in which their utterances originate. This, in turn, reveals a new understanding of the nature of stage activity, which, as the *autor* underscores to the impatient Shoemaker's Wife, extends fully into the theater audience: "your costume and your struggle will be the costume and struggle of each spectator seated in his or her seat, box seat, or general admission seat, where you flutter, large or small, with the same disillusioned rhythm" (II 376–77).

The phenomenon of theater is thus characterized in terms quite similar to those experienced by the Director in *The Public*. The audience is called upon to struggle with the characters but also as a character because theater is now fully understood to be a struggle for authority. The stage no longer functions as the unchanging, autonomous center of a representation upon which an audience is invited to project its imagination. In an exact reversal of the Director's fate in *The Public*, theater becomes the occasion to express the authority of the hidden force at the expense of the audience. While theater may begin on the public stage, its ultimate destination is a private scenario in the imagination of each member of the audience. Theater has thus fully become a struggle to expand the stage into the tunnel proclaimed by the Director in *The Public*. Near the conclusion, an apologetic *autor* asks forgiveness of the Muses "for having compromised myself in this prison of the little shoemaker's wife, for having attempted to entertain a group of people" (II 376), and he promises, in language evocative of the conclusion to *The Public*, "later, to open the trapdoors of the stage so that there will once again appear the false goblets, the poison, the libraries, the phantoms, and the make-believe moon of the true theater" (II 376). Indeed, rather than retreating from the insights of his experimental plays, Lorca's more mature theater, beginning with *Blood Wedding*, rededicates itself to confirming their authority.

5

BLOOD WEDDING

Oꜰ ᴛʜᴇ ꜱɪɢɴɪꜰɪᴄᴀɴᴛ works of twentieth-century Spanish theater, perhaps none has generated so many disparate readings as has *Blood Wedding* (*Bodas de sangre*). Two incompatible spectrums of critical opinion have emerged, one emphasizing the play's social-existential realism and another stressing the interplay of mythic-archetypal forces. For example, Reed Anderson considers that Lorca's intent is to expose the flawed principles of Spanish society, to demonstrate "the effect they have on the individual's humanity, on his actions and emotions" (*Bodas* 186),[1] a view that contrasts sharply with Louise Hutman's idea of the play as "a dual movement toward the core of each individual's being where he performs an absolute function and enacts an archetypal role" (330).[2] These antithetical positions suggest that Lorca actually wrote two plays: one social and didactic, the other descriptive of a repeated private spectacle. The weakness of these and similar arguments arises from formalist assumptions that *Blood Wedding* represents a self-referential dramatic space and from a consequent indifference to representational issues that tie it to his experimental theater and the wider agenda of Modernism.[3] Indeed, Lorca's greatest commercial triumph, conferring in large measure the type of stage authority to which he aspired, is more vitally connected to an alternative theatrical agenda than to the rural society in which it is nominally set.

In a 1933 interview during the run of *Blood Wedding* in Buenos Aires after initial success in Madrid, Lorca mentions, unnecessarily, that he has brought with him the manuscripts of the experimental plays, which at this moment he declares to be unstageable. *The Public* "is not a work to be staged; it is, as I have defined it, 'a poem to hiss at' " (III 557).[4] As late as the spring of 1936, however, Lorca continues to express a strong public loyalty to these largely unknown scripts: "In these impossible plays lies my true purpose" (III 674). His declared intention to bring *The Public* to the stage and his efforts, during the spring of 1936, to produce *As Soon As Five Years Pass* with the Club Anfistora (discontinued as a consequence of political instability preceding the Spanish Civil War)[5] suggest persuasively that these works remained prominent in his dramatic thinking until his death. Indeed, *Blood Wedding* offers the first vivid reflection of how the realignment of the theater functions in the experimental plays inspires Lorca's commercial theater.

In *The Public* the repudiation of mimesis is so thorough that the stage no longer serves as a stable repository for theater signs. Rather than representing fully drawn, that is, three-dimensional, temporally mediated scenes, the tableaus effectively function as translucent viewing screens for a projection that has its point of origin corresponding to backstage—to a point exactly opposite that of the theater audience. The onstage use of the folding screen, whereby characters emerge physically transformed as they pass from one side to the other, is also illustrative of the means by which images are produced in the theater beneath the sand. The requirement for spectator participation in this unconventional mode of theater, however, is unconditional acceptance of these alternative theater premises. The theater audience does not see in the usual sense but rather receives vision, almost as a by-product of a primary activity that does not include the audience. The Director's proclamations—"It is necessary to destroy the theater or to live in the theater! It's not enough to hiss from your window!"[6] (II 666) and "breaking all the doors is the only way that drama has to justify itself, seeing, through its own eyes" (II 668)—represent the ultimate generic transgression.

Rather than to offer itself for consideration by an audience, the immediate objective of the experimental theater becomes to see for itself. In *The Public*, the visible stage exists as an aspect of a more profound medium, the tunnel, that projects images to the spectator's imagination where they demand to be accommodated. At this point, the spectator is left very little choice: either to accept the representation, completely and passively, or to reject it. Resistance to such an imposing requirement, therefore, must invariably take the form of a disruption of the representation, a refusal, at some level, to continue viewing, which is perhaps why Lorca calls *The Public* an "unstageable" play. The spectator's resistance or acquiescence, therefore, lies at the heart of Lorca's fresh understanding of the theater functions.[7] In formal terms, the private projections of the hidden force, effectively two-dimensional or plane projections, clash violently with the spectator's requirement to render vision conventionally, in empirical, three-dimensional terms.

In *As Soon As Five Years Pass* the world of the Youth is also represented in relation to mutually exclusive domains: the Youth's volatile, uninviting life as part of the three-dimensional world of conventional space-time, to which he strongly resists accommodating himself, and the more constant two-dimensional, inner medium "without distance beneath your face" (II 505), which the representation makes available to the audience under terms less overtly threatening, if ultimately no different, than in *The Public.*[8] In terms of conventional mimesis, the Youth's story is equally "unstageable." Its greater visual availability than *The Public*, however, is the consequence of an "arranged marriage," the Youth's dream to the spectator's sense of conventional space-time ("space and time intertwined" [II 561]), which allows the Youth's private narrative to become visually available to an audience, provided, again, that the audience fully and passively accepts the conditions of this availability. *The Public* leaves its audience uncomfortable not only because it features discussions about homosexuality but because it makes no effort to initiate the audience to its unorthodox viewing assumptions. As the Harlequin intimates, *As Soon As Five Years Pass* could also have been represented from a much different point of view. Also directly inspired in the vision of an extended and changeable stage, at opposite ends of which are the hidden force and the audience's imagination, *Blood Wedding* represents one such alternate perspective.

The experimental plays emphasize that theater has become an ongoing search for the creative means to represent an understanding, a point of view, antagonistic to the values of conventional depiction represented in the audience. Rather than a turn toward more naturalistic representation, as a number of critics have suggested, *Blood Wedding* marks instead a moment of synthesis, the onstage wedding of Lorca's meditations about the authority of theater in relation to the audience. As in the experimental plays, of paramount importance in *Blood Wedding* are the conditions under which the play is made available to its audience. The act of seeing in *Blood Wedding* is intimately tied to the discovery in the experimental plays that the theater functions, if not actually "wedded," are nevertheless at the service of a more authoritative theater force, a unseen protagonist whose fullness the act of theater—that is, the collaborative efforts of script (the poet) and scene (the director)—can only approximate. The stage has become the vehicle for the fuller revelation of an agent whose authority extends beyond the space of the physical stage into the imaginations of the audience.

As *Blood Wedding* begins, however, the viewer's share of the representation can only be described as inordinate. The most striking feature of act I is the virtual absence of dramatic action, which in the first tableau consists in the Bridegroom's telling his mother goodbye as he departs for the day's work. In order to leave the house, the Bridegroom must eventually tell his mother to shut up and to shut off the bitter and obsessive vision of the bloodstained context of past losses. Offhand remarks made during the Mother's subsequent conversation with the Neighbor about the Bridegroom's intention to wed the Bride further illumine the dread which accompanies the prospect of such a union. The Bride was previously involved with Leonardo whose clan killed the Bridegroom's father and older brother. Both women self-consciously acknowledge that the authority of this unrelenting discourse on blood threatens to overtake the present. They decide that the only remedy is simply to repress it: "It falls to you and to me to keep quiet" (II 712). Indeed, speaking their minds freely only leads them backward, into the bloody past. Likewise in the second tableau, the young girl's gossip about the Bride's wedding present of silk stockings from the Bridegroom evokes the lingering past in Leonardo's imagination, which eventually disrupts the fragile veneer of tranquility imposed upon the scene by the earlier lullaby. Itself a thinly veiled poetic evocation of ambivalence in the face of desire, the *nana* becomes a presentiment of tragedy that the child is told he can avoid, again, only by repressing himself, shutting his *ventana* or window (see note 6), the medium through which he perceives the world, "with a branch of dreams and a dream of branches" (II 715)—that is, by means of a double dream to deny one reality as he imagines another.

If the idea of the wedding begins to distance the principals from the onstage present and to return them to the past, it works a similar effect on the spectator, in the opposite direction. From the outset the spectator occupies a privileged position in relation to the quite trivial and only minimally dramatic visual representations—saying goodbye to mother, talking to neighbors, singing a lullaby—occurring on stage. Even without knowledge of the title, which projects a bloody denouement before the fact,[9] the spectator is much better informed than even the well-connected gossipers for whom the past constantly threatens to superimpose itself upon the present. By the time the Bridegroom and the Mother arrive at the Bride's cave to discuss the marriage proposal with her father, there is literally nothing to say. Everyone, including the viewer, already knows why they are there. Indeed, the scene proceeds as if the conversation had already taken place, and the discussion, as in the earlier tableaus, is again confined largely to trivialities.

The presentiment of tragedy that the Mother has suppressed for the moment, however, remains with the spectator, who literally cannot help but sense a growing danger to the proposed union by virtue of his or her vantage point of near omniscience in act I. The fact that the stage performance consists largely of insubstantial conversations serves to undermine it as the true center of the representation, just as the Bridegroom's ignorance of vital information progressively invalidates his initial claim to an authoritative status. Indeed, the stage representation has been a pretext for the naming of a more powerful principal mover, Leonardo. As the Mother and the Bride's father are saying their goodbyes offstage, the spectator witnesses, from a different vantage point in the Bride's bedroom, her confession that Leonardo has been visiting her at night. The Maid is not satisfied with simply suspecting the truth—or even knowing it secretly—but interrogates the Bride relentlessly until she names Leonardo. As melodramatic as this scene may be, it makes unmistakable that Leonardo and not the Bridegroom is now the play's substantive protagonist. The Bride makes her confession only after the Maid forces her to look out of the window to the point from which Leonardo has presumably been watching all along. His visual penetration into the Bride's room further underscores his claim as the literal, as well as the imaginative, framer of events. An outsider has destroyed the Bridegroom's dream even before his proposal of marriage.

The juxtaposition of the nonevents of the tableaus in the spectator's imagination clearly signals a movement toward violence and bloodshed. As the parents set a time and place for the union, the Bridegroom is for practical purposes already cuckolded. Living for the moment when he will become the head of a new household, the Bridegroom seems especially ineffectual at this point because of his inability to see where events are leading. Disdainful of his mother's earlier obsessive representations and unaware of Leonardo's active pretensions to the Bride, the Bridegroom with his comparative lack of information is situated at the focal point of competing discourses: the apparently unremarkable stage events and the blood vision of the Mother, publicly dormant yet fully alive in the imagination of the spectator. It is the spectators who confirm this hidden scenario by representing to themselves in advance a drama different from the one being enacted before their eyes. The audience places the Bridegroom in a new frame from which he cannot extricate himself. His desire to make his own home by marrying and even his claim to the name Bridegroom are thus severely eroded by an irrepressible preexisting discourse that underpins the present and divests it of autonomy and authority.

The explicitness of the delineation of this triangle of desire further emphasizes its growing transparency in relation to another triangular relationship: the spectators' imaginative juxtapositioning of the stage signs that has allowed them to reach the same conclusion long before the fact. The specific mode of unfolding of this representation in act I has effectively transformed the play into a mental construct of the audience, for whom there is no mystery as to the true nature of the relationships in the play. In suggesting the preeminence of a viewer-centered "triangle of representation" over the onstage love triangle, I am invoking the dynamics of conventional one-point perspective, the fundamental representational paradigm of Western art from the Renaissance until Modernism. Succinctly stated long ago by Leon Battista Alberti, the principal tenet of this system is quite simple: a represented object "can never appear truthful when there is not a definite distance for seeing it" (57). The relationship formed between viewer and object is "triangular," extending to the picture plane which renders the illusion of depth as the representation extends "backward" to the vanishing point, beyond which it cannot be seen. Although the passing of time has made this mode of vision seem nothing less than a fact of nature, it is precisely during the early decades of this century when this system is rejected by artists in favor of more complex, less "natural," means of representation and viewing. Of seminal importance for the interpretation of *Blood Wedding* is that during Modernism this perspectival "triangle" is no longer understood as fixed but rather as capable of representing from a variety of locations within the same work of art. A quite similar phenomenon occurs, although more subtlely, from the beginning of the play by virtue of the viewer's privileged position in relation to the onstage principals. The Bride's naming of Leonardo as her lover is merely a reconfirmation of what the viewer has already represented to himself or herself: Leonardo is the true protagonist, the prime mover of present and forthcoming events. His emergence, however, also confirms the preeminence of the viewer in whose field of vision the trivial stage happenings have acquired greater significance. Supplementing the onstage scene, the audience has effectively fashioned an alternative imaginative space in which to center the representation.

In the Buenos Aires interview Lorca states that in *The Public* his intent is to have "file by in the scene the private dramas that each one of the spectators is thinking, as he or she is watching, often without noticing, the performance" (III 557). This is also what happens in *Blood Wedding,* the only difference being that the spectator has a much greater consciousness of the phenomenon as it is happening. In both cases, representation before an audience exposes a hidden agenda which undermines the autonomy of the actual stage representation because the relationships between the viewing subject and the dramatic object have largely been reversed. With the much more difficult to stage *The Public,* Lorca maintains that "the spectators would arise indignant and prevent the performance from continuing" (III 557). In *Blood Wedding,* the audience also effectively interrupts the stage representation in act I by means of its imaginative transformation and juxtaposition of disparate and apparently insignificant moments. Throughout the first act only the spectator knows the fuller story, the outcome of which the audience actually hastens by supplying the imaginative context within which such an all-too-familiar narrative proceeds. All that seemingly remains is to witness the bloody climax, already suggested in the title, to which events seem to be inexorably moving.

If in act I the representation acquires fullness by means of the constituting imagination of the spectator, a severe reversal occurs in act II. Left standing for the entire day in essentially the same space of act I where Leonardo stood earlier and observed the Bride outside her

cave,[10] viewers learn that their status as seers and projectors of a sce-
nario has also radically diminished as the wedding party gathers at the
cave, travels the ten leagues to the church for the wedding ceremony,
and then travels the same distance back for the reception.[11] Contrary
to the viewer's logical expectations and projections, the wedding takes
place without bloodshed, and without the viewer. As in act I, the two
tableaus of act II signify primarily by their relation to an offstage
event, which in this instance the spectator can only imagine after the
fact. Like an uninvited guest excluded from the community of wit-
nesses to the wedding, the viewer has had an earlier privileged vantage
point superseded by the one event that was necessary to that vision
and which has now unfolded in his or her absence. As Leonardo is
eclipsed as protagonist by the wedding—that is, the *boda*, always re-
ferred to in the script in the singular—the spectator can only project
backwards to imagine its uneventfulness. The feverish criss-crossing
of the stage by the guests throughout the second tableau parallels
the back-and-forth trajectory of the principals away from and back to
the same space. As the sun changes spatial-temporal positions over the
course of the act and the lovers decide in secrecy to switch allegiances,
the viewing assumptions of act I also shift.

Although it is rarely invoked in discussions of drama, the notion
of multiperspectivalism is clearly central to all Modernist schools
(Uspensky 130–72). This is especially true in Cubism where there is a
constant oscillation and tension between the three-dimensional world
of the viewer and the multiple light sources and two-dimensional
planes within the canvas that dramatizes the act of perception as it
also forces the viewer to shift to many different viewing points in
order to reconstitute the image-object in his or her imagination
(Mukarovsky 129–49). A similar notion of perspective is at work in
Blood Wedding: the spatial perspective shifts as the drama temporally
unfolds. The wedding that never manifests itself on stage, but never-
theless dominates the stage discourse that in turn delimits it, now un-
derscores to viewers their distance from a new representational center.
No longer the formulator and projector of a scenario, the spectator wit-
nesses the events of act II at a rather self-conscious distance from de-
velopments that have likely defied his or her expectations. As the
Bridegroom's desire to create a new space free of the Mother's obses-
sive blood discourse is superseded by Leonardo's irrepressible desire,

rendered ineffectual in turn by the wedding rite, so too the wedding reveals to the Mother, once it is learned that Leonardo and the Bride have fled, that it has been but a veil for the more intense scenario now unfolding in "the hour of blood" (II 772). As the Mother underscores in her exhortations to the pursuers—"Backwards! Backwards!" (II 772)—events have not been moving forward at all but rather backwards, away from the visual-verbal nonevents that constitute the stage representation. Seeing the dreaded scenario she has long carried with her now manifest itself publicly, the Mother confirms the presence of a new representation, the personification of forces and attitudes in a blood discourse that has remained suppressed until this point, its origin being indeed "backwards," in another space and time.

One of the central issues in *As Soon As Five Years Pass* was the idea of the interrelatedness of time and space, that space in any sense, whether a completely public space or the fundamentally private space of the individual psyche, is inextricably bound to the notion of time in some sense, if not conventional clock time then a more general time continuum in which consciousness and understanding develop. The reality of the Youth is determined to a large extent by the temporal epochs which both precede and follow him, as suggested by the Dead Child, who embodies a chronological time that has long since past but a psychic time that persists, ironically, as persistence and resistance to change and to the passing of one phase of life into another. This is exactly the same pattern that the Youth repeats as his drama is brought into clearer focus on the stage of the psyche. The intelligible context for the sequence of events that eventually require the Youth to cede his hegemony over the scene to a more mature aspect is not provided by the private space to which the Youth continues to cling but rather by the invasive presence of time. The inseparability of time and space in whatever medium in which they happen to coincide makes it possible to link what may initially seem to be unconnected images into an intelligible narrative. No space can effectively exist without the imposition, in some form, of an accompanying notion of time, even the private scenario of a dream or reverie.[12]

In *Blood Wedding*, however, which at a superficial level is easily understandable, the strong consciousness of the movement of time diminishes as the drama advances to the end of act II. As the Mother cries out "Backwards! Backwards!" (II 772), it has become evident to her that what has happened is not original or unique but rather a repetition of something that has persisted in the collective imagination. The spectator, however, has constructed an imaginative scenario premised on precisely the opposite agenda, to which temporal continuity—past and present are leading inexorably to a future—is absolutely necessary. Indeed, from the play's title and the explicitly delineated relationships made unmistakably clear to even the most inattentive theatergoer, everything points to a bloody denouement sited in the immediate future. The Mother, however, suggests that this future is not the legitimate center, that as the past reemerges, the notion of a linear progression of events through time is exposed as merely a phantom for a scenario in which "future" is actually "past." The Mother's mode of understanding, therefore, parodies the Old Man's constant admonition in *As Soon As Five Years Pass* to "remember toward tomorrow" in that remembering is fulfilled in a "future" in which the past has already established its authority.

It is, however, the audience's conventional notion of time, the assurance that events do move toward a future and, in this instance, that the audience plays an essential role in imaginatively shaping that movement, that accords this play representational power. At the outset, the theater audience strongly perceives that it is overseeing a predictable outcome. Indeed, this sense of temporal predictability actually diverts attention from striking incongruencies in the spatial aspects of the play. The audience has projected in its imagination a vast space for the unfolding of events in the first two acts. Broad distances lie between the lands of the principals, and the space represented onstage, the interiors and exteriors of the houses situated at opposite ends of this dissimilar geography, is only a minuscule part of the spatial territory upon which the rationale, primarily economic, for the wedding is premised.

Of the play's many departures from realistic detail, perhaps none is more striking than the shift from the Bride's semiarid "dry lands" or *secanos*—so desolate that the Bride's father remarks that "it has been necessary to punish them and even to cry over them so that they would give us something of profit" (II 725) and so apparently isolated that to travel to the Bride's cave requires "four hours on the road and [through it all] not a single house or tree [to be seen]" (II 724)—and the "giant humid trunks" (II 772) that comprise the scene at the beginning of act III, the forest to which the lovers flee. Although it is perhaps conceivable that a semitropical forest could lie in close proximity to what amounts to a desert, the scene represented in act III in many respects recreates the forest with "giant trunks" (II 560) that begins the significant metadramatic scene in act III of *As Soon As Five Years Pass*, in which a wood serves as the frame for the open-air theater from which the Harlequin pronounces upon the various relationships between time and dream. The forest suggests the confusion and unintelligibility of the dreamscape without the mediating presence of time. In *Blood Wedding* the forest fulfills the same function, to indicate, via the Mother, the supersession of the time-space, which had earlier been the almost exclusive province of the spectator, by a different scenario embodied in the wood to which the lovers now turn. The wood is suggestive of the deeper context to which the surface narrative is juxtaposed, the site where all the confluent narratives intersect, where the discourse on blood confronts the flesh-and-blood embodiments of its ongoing story line.

That the forest is evoked primarily by violin music strongly reinforces its metadramatic status.[13] As much as to a possible, if improbable, Andalusian landscape, this specific geography also vividly alludes to another powerful literary setting, the seventh circle of Dante's *Inferno:* the circle of the violent, which juxtaposes the burning sands of the sodomites, the violent against nature, and the doleful, bloody wood of the suicides, the violent against themselves, both of which are encircled by a river of blood, of varying depths, containing the souls of those who were violent to others.[14] In relation to *Blood Wedding*, this would include the Mother's husband and son as well as members of the Félix clan with whom they clashed. In a trajectory that parallels, in reverse, the Dantesque topography, Leonardo and the Bride flee from the dry lands to the forest en route to the river where blood is spilled after the lovers are encircled by horsemen who, especially in the context of the huge gathering for the wedding, quite implausibly "approach from all roads at the same time" (II 773) in a tightening circle. If acts I and II achieve greater fullness as the imaginative reconstructions of the spectator, so too the initial tableau of act III reveals its hybrid status as a response to a different mode of representation that has wed the present to the past, the public dimension of a story to a more imposing private narrative.[15]

It is quite appropriate, therefore, that act III begins in darkness as the disembodied voices of the Woodsmen disclose their confusion and ignorance of developments. This is also the predicament of the spectator, literally and figuratively in the dark, forced to overhear a conversation by characters who are themselves eavesdroppers. Alienated by now even from his own desire, the Bridegroom accepts with fury a new role in the long-suppressed blood narrative now visibly embodied: "Do you see this arm? Well, it's not my arm. It's the arm of my brother and of my father and of my whole family that is dead. And it is so powerful that it can uproot this tree by the roots if it wants to" (II 780). Within this discourse of generations, the Bridegroom and Leonardo are but pretexts—or, in the rhetoric of *The Public,* costumes or *trajes*—visible representations that mark its present margins yet driven all the while, like the flow of blood from a wound, to surpass them. As the emblem and icon of a peculiar way of viewing the world, blood achieves a perversely transcendent status that fully encompasses all aspects of life. The shedding of blood, therefore, is also a further act of transference to the collective memory which in turn enhances its effectiveness as a discourse.

The public manifestation in act III of the Mother's worst fears confirms the general acquiescence in a common vision-ideology—including by the Bride, who remains ambivalent to Leonardo even during their escape—unified under the concept "blood," its realm encompassing consciousness itself. The conflation of the blood discourse and the imagination-consciousness of the characters is further underscored in the appearance of the light of the Moon. By the present moment, literally everything has gone inward and backwards as vision and viewing now depend upon a source of illumination completely internal to the representation. The fact that the Moon is physically represented as emerging from the space of the representation—ascending from within, not descending from without—to disclose the lovers to their pursuers strongly suggests that the spectator's recovery of vision in act III is by no means a complete one. The viewer now observes only indirectly and at a significant distance. Illuminating what the characters themselves now understand as a self-conscious recreation of a repeated spectacle, the Moon also shifts the point, much further inward, from which these unfolding events may be viewed in true perspective. The spectator thus observes the action as if he or she were facing a translucent projection screen, much in the manner of *The Public.*

Contravening conventional empirical models, the vantage point of direct vision recedes over the course of this act to a vanishing point that can only be described as lying behind the stage. The Moon's brightness hastens the movement of the characters offstage while denying the spectator a direct view of what seems to be the new climactic moment: a second "wedding," Leonardo's and the Bridegroom's, in a new triangle of desire that exchanges the Bride for death, the Beggar Woman. As the Beggar Woman occupies center stage to spread her cape like a bird of prey, yet also like a small curtain, only Leonardo's and the Bridegroom's cries of death are heard, from offstage. More than as death, the Beggar Woman is a physical barrier to vision and thus a reminder to the audience of its blindness and distance from events literally disembodied from the moment of their representation. As the physical presence of the blood of these men is deferred from view, so too is the meaning of what has occurred, which can only be ascertained from a vantage point unavailable to the audience. The happenings at the end of the sixth tableau, therefore, do not signal a climax but rather the frustration of a climax or conclusion to a coherent story line.

Failing to consider that the tableaus offer different spaces from which to view the representation as it temporally unfolds, critical readings of the play invariably stop at this point. Although the final tableau has been consistently viewed as an excessively long and even unnecessary anticlimax (Edwards 165), it actually intensifies the undermining of conventional three-dimensional representation at work throughout the play. The physical setting itself suggests such a possibility. Although the setting is a "white room," it also possesses the "monumental sense of a church" (II 788), which suggests that it may be a church—perhaps the same church where the wedding took place in act II—or funeral chapel. The very peculiar ladders on both sides of the room that extend beyond the visible stage, however, suggest a less familiar scene. As the stage directions indicate, the whiteness of this room "with arches and thick walls" is deliberate: "There will not be a gray, nor a shadow, nor even what is necessary for perspective" (II 788). The deliberate undermining of perspective on the stage confirms physically what has been happening throughout the act: the audience is now watching the drama as if it were projected through a screen from a different set of eyes. By the time the bodies of Leonardo and the Bridegroom are returned to what may be the site of the original wedding ritual, roles and relationships have again changed. Declining to take a physical revenge upon the Bride, the Mother looks instead further inward, to confront the very structure of the discourse that has authorized this violence.

Of the many verbal and visual puns that pervade the drama, none is more suggestive than the Mother's apparently absurd detail in the midst of her passionate final lament, where she takes time to mention that the approximate hour of death of the two men was "between two and three" (II 798). These exact words are also immediately echoed by the Bride. Besides a strictly temporal reference, however, the Mother's and Bride's declarations may also be understood to allude to the problematical representational space in which these deaths and indeed all the action have emerged. Support for this interpretation is offered in the text itself since in both instances the temporal reference is clearly appended to phrases that would normally constitute the verse, forming something of a forced hemistich that inordinately extends the length of these verses to sixteen and eighteen syllables. The spatial extension of verses in the text, the only verses in the play that refer to clock time, underscores the other types of extension, and ostention, that have been visually expressed throughout the representation. Indeed, as the stage directions for this scene stress, the illusion of a stable, one-point perspective that faithfully mirrors empirical vision has disappeared. The three-dimensionality of the high realist stage and the spectator's initial illusion of an effectively omniscient perspective, extending across the vast spaces alluded to throughout the play, have collapsed. Since the tableau is set primarily in the noncolors black and white, the blood on the Bride's dress and the "red skein" that two young girls are winding into yarn become even more visually prominent. The girls' performed task, to make usable thread from a shapeless blood-red mass, constitutes a visual parallel to the Bride's and the Mother's commentary/interpretation about the shedding of blood. As this formless skein is transformed into an object of formal compactness (see also note 8), the representation itself is also acquiring its definitive form, abandoning the illusion of its unfolding in an immense space to achieve its truest form in a space that has effectively collapsed.

The progressive abrogation of perspective brings the viewer much closer to a more authoritative center where conventional laws of genre are rendered inoperative and where the words of the Director in *The Public*—"Breaking all the doors is the only way that drama has to justify itself, seeing, through its own eyes, that the law is a wall that is dissolved by the smallest drop of blood" (II 668)—now acquire transcendent meaning. *Blood Wedding*'s mission has been to establish the authority of a hidden force unassailable by the eyes, or imaginations, of the audience. As in the experimental plays, the visual and verbal signs of the representation again evince a strong indexical dimension[16] as they surpass self-referentiality in order to trace "the profile of a hidden force when the audience has no further recourse except to pay full attention, filled with spirit and overpowered by the action" (II 664). What has taken place, therefore, has ultimately been an extended act of pointing, backwards. The ultimate location of "backwards" (*atrás*), as the Mother suggests, is a space beyond the stage, beyond the domain of vision, "the site / where entangled trembles / the dark root of the scream" (II 799). At this moment, the knife, "a tiny knife / that hardly fits in your hand" (II 799), acquires its most authoritative form, not as an instrument of violence but as a stylus that has retraced the knife's path by means of the words of the script toward a space where the drama concludes only to affirm its origin. The ultimate effect is to transform the stage into a hybrid medium where the limits of vision become physically manifest at a point of convergence between the hidden force and the imagination of the audience, whose powers of vision, like those of the characters of *Blood Wedding*, it has both authorized and eclipsed. More than an exposé of barbaric societal codes, an identification with the tragic plight of his people, or a mythic-archetypal ritual, *Blood Wedding* is the commercial affirmation of Lorca's experimental agenda, a private vision that has authorized itself in the public act of theater.

6

YERMA AND *DOÑA ROSITA,*
THE SPINSTER

Successors to the popular triumph of *Blood Wedding, Yerma* and *Doña Rosita, the Spinster* (*Doña Rosita, la soltera*) solidify Lorca's growing stature as an invigorating force in Spanish theater. According to Fernández Cifuentes, by 1935 "García Lorca was beginning to impose the predominant theater formulas, while the Quinteros and even Benavente—still the most popular—were losing some of their authority or were being tacitly relegated to the passé" (144). In concert with interviews proclaiming a continuing loyalty to the experimental plays, Lorca's homage to Lola Membrives (1934) and "Theater Chat" (early 1935) also raise the issue of Spanish stage's lack of authority. Besides his criticism of blatant commercialism, the reiterated sentiment of these declarations is that "the public can be taught. . . . it can be taught, because I have seen them boo Debussy and Ravel, and then later I have witnessed the clamorous ovations of popular audiences to works that had previously been rejected. These authors were imposed by a high criterion of authority superior to that of the average audience, like Wedekind in Germany and Pirandello in Italy, like so many others" (III 460).

While the Spanish theater scene has strongly impressed upon Lorca that "an experimental theater . . . must necessarily be one exclusively of losses" (II 452), he is more optimistic about reversing the disequilibrium within commercial theater:

> Theater should be imposed on the public and not the public on the theater. For this reason, authors and actors must attire themselves, even at the cost of blood, with great authority, because the theater public is like the children in school: they adore the serious and austere teacher who demands from them and does them justice, and they fill with cruel needles the chairs where the timid and cringing teachers sit, the ones who neither teach nor allow others to be taught. (III 460)

Fully reflecting the realignment of the theater functions in the experimental plays, Lorca's commitment is to a "progressively better script and scenario" (III 461): challenging scripts accompanied by greater stagecraft and stage discipline in the form of "indispensable . . . authorized and documented stage directors who will transform the works that they interpret with their own identifiable style" (III 454).

Although these declarations strongly echo the Director's sentiments in *The Public* for a theater in which "the audience has no further recourse except to pay full attention," it must also be remembered that these words are directed to the practical-minded Magician. The imposition of a new dramatic agenda for the commercial stage requires that in *Yerma* the desire "to sublimely tame and to contradict and to attack [the audience]" (III 460) be tempered with pragmatism, the appreciation that the evocative and manipulable geography of a rural-pastoral setting offers an expedient means to accomplish such goals. In *Doña Rosita, the Spinster,* the physical removal of the stage set—which strongly recalls the Magician's avowal to the Director that "to remove [from the scene] is easy" (II 670)—communicates that play's most solemn message as Lorca continues to discipline audience imagination by an ingenious orchestration of temporal cycles inspired in the insights of *As Soon As Five Years Pass.* Together, these plays offer compelling testimony to the continuing legacy of the experimental plays and an idea of theater as a confrontation between private and public domains.

Yerma

If an all-too-familiar narrative dominates *Blood Wedding, Yerma* unfolds virtually without a story as a series of ever more obsessive meditations about Yerma's barrenness and, more generally, the possibilities of being fruitful and productive within the limitations of a given context. As suggestive as its title derived from *yermo* (wasteland), immediately establishing a sharp contrast between the lush physical scene and the protagonist's inner condition, is its rather ambiguous generic label, "tragic poem."[1] Lorca's statements about the play during its composition suggest that he draws upon two very different literary traditions—pastoral (which includes a rich Spanish tradition of rural-pastoral tragicomic plays) and tragedy—in order to create a unique form of tragedy that, drawing directly upon the insights of the experimental plays, departs significantly from classical models.

In a remarkable interview of early 1934, Lorca relates what he alleges to be an incident from his childhood that "revealed to me my first artistic experience" (III 600). While watching peasants till the soil with a new plow capable of penetrating the earth deeper than did traditional models, he saw the tiller become stuck on an object that proved to be a Roman mosaic (a literal "Roman ruin"), the inscription on which invoked for Lorca the names Daphnis and Chloe, principals in the classical pastoral narrative by Longus. This inspiring experience is further acknowledged as the foundation stone for an "agrarian complex," which Lorca credits with advancing his present theater:

> This, my first artistic astonishment, is tied to the earth. The names of Daphnis and Chloe have a taste of the earth and of love. My first emotions are linked to the earth and to the activity of the countryside. For this reason there is in my life an agrarian complex, which is what psychoanalysts would call it.
>
> Without this, my love of the earth, I could not have written *Blood Wedding*. And neither would I have begun my next work: *Yerma*. (III 600)

Insinuated in this rather contrived confession of an emotional attachment to the earth is the tunnel of *The Public*, which reveals the extensions of this complex "beneath the sand."

In a subsequent interview of early July, 1934, Lorca shifts the focus from pastoral to classical tragedy: "*Yerma* will be the tragedy of the sterile woman. The theme . . . is classic. But I want it to have a new intention and development. A tragedy with four principal characters and chorus, like tragedies must be. It is necessary to turn to tragedy. The tradition of our dramatic theater obliges us" (III 605). There is another calculated ambiguity here. Lorca is tacitly declaring that both the Spanish tradition of serious theater, which he does not identify with tragedy but refers to as "the tradition of our dramatic theater," and classical expressions of tragedy, which even at its most advanced moment never featured more than three principal actors, are insufficient models for what he hopes to express in a "tragedy with four principal characters." While there are a number of canonical Spanish plays that feature unhappy endings—some of the most famous of which are set in rural-pastoral locales—there are few, if any, that may rightly be considered tragedies in the pagan sense. Lorca is proposing a new form of tragedy that, nevertheless, must refer to classical models since high tragedy has never been part of the Spanish theater tradition.

Lorca uses the tragicomic tradition of pastoral and the Spanish *comedia* as a visual base upon which to construct a novel form of "four-actor" tragedy that emerges from the confrontation between Yerma's attempts to understand her dilemma and the vision-dominated values of her pastoral-agrarian society. As *Blood Wedding* has demonstrated, the realignment of the theater functions means that the scenario has become the primary vehicle to demonstrate the insufficiency of autonomous vision. In *Blood Wedding* the initial illusion of near-omniscient vision is followed by a severe undermining of conventional perspective as the play ultimately reveals that the true locus of vision actually resides in a point corresponding to backstage, exactly opposite the location of the audience. It is also at this point at which commercial stage authority is reborn as script and scenario ally themselves in the service of a theatrical agenda imposed upon the audience. In *Yerma*, Lorca's ongoing critique of the conventional generic boundaries of theater takes the form of a scrutiny of the very traditions that, arguably, have shaped the modern theater consciousness. Pastoral—typically a tragicomic genre, as are most of the serious classical Spanish plays—and classical tragedy thus become the vehicles for a further assault on theatrical complacency, the consequences of which are new insights into tragedy.

If classical tragedy typically depicts the excessive suffering that befalls noble if not preeminently virtuous individuals, many serious Golden Age plays instead feature *comedias* with unhappy endings, often called tragicomedies (*tragicomedias*),[2] which uphold the view of a providential universe and thus a system of just consequences for a character's actions, "poetic justice."[3] A number of the most outstanding classical tragicomedies—for example, Lope's *Fuenteovejuna*, *The Knight of Olmedo*, and *The Peasant in His Place* (*El villano en su rincón*) and Calderón's *The Mayor of Zalamea*—are set in rural-pastoral locales. In the *comedia*, peasants often meditate, like the melancholy shepherds of pastoral poetry, about the complexities of love. *Fuenteovejuna* features the incongruous scene of prosperous farmers and shepherds having extended philosophical discussions about Platonic theories of love. These plays, however, draw directly on a Renaissance pastoral legacy that includes Guevara's *Scorn for the Court and Praise for the Village* (*Menosprecio de corte y alabanza de aldea*), Garcilaso's *Eclogues*, and Montemayor's *Diana*. The pastoral setting offers a convenient pretext for the fuller development of intimate discourse that would likely be inappropriate, or even "unstageable," in an urban setting where complicating social, religious, and economic factors would inhibit these analyses and lamentations.

The Daphnis and Chloe fable that Lorca invokes in association with *Yerma*, among the last classical pastoral stories, offers, however, a delightful vision of love fulfilled. The shepherd Daphnis, so innocent that he possesses no instinct regarding sex, must be educated in the techniques of sexual practice by a go-between. Once his instruction is completed, he and Chloe eagerly consummate their desire for each other, the immediate outcome of which is their many children who thrive in a world of pastoral abundance. Since *Yerma* also focuses on the processes by which children are brought into the world, then, owing to what appears to be a lack of sexual instinct or inclination in both Yerma and her husband Juan, *Yerma* may be considered in parodic relation to the Daphnis and Chloe tale as well as to a wider tragicomic tradition of pastoral. A play that begins with a dream about Yerma's desire to have a child quickly metamorphoses into an obsession dominating script and scene as it involves all about her in making judgments about her plight. In keeping with pastoral conventions, a series of shepherds and peasants, primarily women but also men, offer further commentary as they assist Yerma in confronting a haunting "agrarian complex" of her own.[4]

As in the Daphnis and Chloe story, Lorca brings together a highly fertile and productive agrarian-pastoral scenario populated with characters whose vocation it is to emulate the reproductive example of the earth, which dominates their imaginations and values. The inhabitants of this area, most notably Juan, have succeeded in disciplining nature to a considerable degree. There is almost no hint of the problems faced by the historical Spanish peasantry from whom they are nominally drawn. Whatever their problems, they do not originate in a lack of material wealth or from an underproductive nature, often the catalyst for many an unhappy or tragic plot. Like their counterparts in pastoral, who in their court identities belong to a higher social class, Yerma and Juan do not evince a typically peasant outlook or mentality.

Indeed, it is only the rural location that makes them seem less than bourgeois. Juan's values are essentially capitalistic. As the years pass, his wealth grows considerably and he is able to pay in cash for the extensive property he continues to amass.[5] By the play's conclusion Juan can hardly be considered a peasant since he has progressed to the point where he needs to employ others to help him reap the abundant harvests which have allowed him to acquire extensive agricultural holdings. The genuinely pastoral components of this society, shepherds like Victor, steadily disappear as the landscape becomes transformed into a variation on the classical *locus amoenus*, reflective of Juan's growing stature in the community. Lorca, nevertheless, recreates the fundamental conditions of pastoral since Yerma's abundant free time—the consequence of her husband's success and her childless condition—allows her to dwell to excess upon love's infelicities.

Albeit quite different in form, Yerma's "love problem" coincides in substance with the dilemma of Longus's shepherds, the lack of sexual instinct. Like Daphnis, Yerma turns to the advice and services of third parties who assist her in articulating the problem and the available remedies. Much of *Yerma*, in fact, consists in what seems to be authoritative advice-giving and instruction, especially regarding the relationship between sexual instinct and barrenness. Early in the play, Juan takes the position that he does not care to have "children who waste" (II 805) since they represent an unwanted expense. His apparent lack of sympathy, however, has also been viewed as an awkward attempt to convey to Yerma his acceptance of a childless marriage, that he has other endeavors to which to dedicate himself (see González-del-Valle 144–46). Indeed, Juan later suggests to Yerma that they adopt a child, a notion she rejects (II 844). It is only after Yerma starts to wander from their cottage in search of answers to her obsession that Juan embraces the more stereotypical *comedia* posture of "defender of the family honor" by bringing in his spinster sisters to watch Yerma and keep her close to home.

Although Yerma is not content with a childless home, it was primarily for economic security, and not for love or children, that she acquiesced in the wishes of her family to marry ("My father gave him to me and I accepted him" [II 820]). An admitted earlier attraction to the shepherd Victor (II 818) further suggests that she may have forsaken a possibly more fulfilling life for one of greater comfort and economic security. Sexual activity for Yerma is not an instinctual response to desire. It is a convention endured in order to affirm a motherly role ("never to enjoy myself" [II 820]). Its all-important product ("the results" [II 857]) is considered separate and distinct from the activity, which possesses no inherent value.[6] This may well be why Yerma never seriously considers advice from the First Old Woman to have sex with another man in order to have a child. Since there is no intellectual-imaginative association between sexual desire and her desire for the child, Yerma clearly feels a much stronger compunction to conform to the conventions of her society than to listen to such advice. Yerma's desire to become a mother is, in fact, inseparable from her claiming the only social identity available to her. Having a child means achieving an identity and standing in her society, her only means not to feel "devalued to the utmost" (II 848).

Although besides the story of Daphnis and Chloe *Yerma* alludes to other renowned poems of the pastoral tradition—notably, Virgil's fourth eclogue addressed to a child at whose birth the Golden Age is to return—it ultimately departs from pastoral. Rather than as a backdrop for the shepherd's amorous lament, the *locus amoenus* becomes increasingly the visual confirmation of Juan's entrepreneurship and authority. As money becomes more important in this society, Juan's activity undermines the pastoral ideal of a simple life free of the marketplace. His success only magnifies Yerma's feelings of uselessness in the midst of the beauty that he alone is responsible for creating. Yerma's society, in fact, is governed by a strong belief in personal agency. Causes originate in people, who are responsible for their effects. As the women of this community reiterate, someone is to blame for Yerma's barrenness:

> First Washerwoman: He is to blame, him; when a father does not produce children he needs to take care of his wife.
> Fourth Washerwoman: She is to blame, the one who has a tongue like flint. (II 834)

Her strong commitment to her society's standards of personal merit or blame means that, ultimately, Yerma has little choice but to acquiesce in her failure to become a creative medium and thus to bear the responsibility for this loss and denial to the community. As suggested by the Second Girl, who has no desire at all for children and who does not feel diminished as a consequence (II 823), and María, whose long-ing for a child has endured much longer than Yerma's (II 867–68), the acceptance of childlessness is understood in Yerma's community as a type of choice. María's example also demonstrates that even in this restrictive society there are alternate states of mind by which despair and resignation to an unproductive existence may be postponed indefi-nitely. Yerma submits to Juan's demand near the end of the play to resign herself to barrenness, to end her obsessive wanderings and her conversations with others about a child that will never be hers.

By assenting to these demands Yerma also brings to an end all justi-fication for continued sexual relations. When immediately thereafter Juan becomes attracted to Yerma as never before, his invitation to en-gage in sexual activity betrays that he, along with the community, now perceives her as the sterile party. By acceding to her childless condi-tion, Yerma has actually increased the sense of blame and personal unworthiness that attaches to her name. In what becomes a final and cruel parody of the uninhibited and joyful sexuality of Daphnis and Chloe, whose lessons in love eventually brought them an abundance of children, Juan's calling upon Yerma now to embrace sex purely for its own sake is an invitation to continue to relive, in her imagination and through her body, the very scenario that Juan himself has demanded must end.

Only by ending Juan's life can Yerma enforce the demand that the discourse on the child forever cease. She will be able to sleep "without awakening myself in fear" (II 880) because his death also concludes the obsessive dream-complex about the child that, like a "phantom seated year after year over my heart" (II 858), had tormented her imagination. Rather than to clarify the dream, however, Yerma's violence summons yet another unsuspected meaning. During the course of the play, it is unclear if the shepherd in the dream—who stares intently at the sleep-ing Yerma as he walks on tiptoes holding the hand of a young child dressed in white—allegorizes her relationship with Juan (whose eyes in the play become progressively fixed on his wife's movements) or if he refers to the lost opportunity with Victor (or other more felicitous procreative partners), since the shepherd's eyes also seem to be implor-ing to Yerma, whose sense of duty does not allow her to respond. How-ever, since at specific moments Yerma wishes that she could engen-der children by herself (II 859), since she visualizes Juan as growing smaller and in reverse (II 804–5),[7] in effect becoming a child, and since during sexual activity she often sees herself as a child in Juan's eyes (II 820), the dream may in fact cast Yerma as the shepherd—a solitary yet impotent agent of procreation—as she herself suggests in the play's concluding words, "I myself have killed my child" (II 880). This apparent final acceptance suggests that, in keeping with "the tradition of our dramatic theater," Yerma is also invoking the authority of "poetic justice." Juan's death and the loss of all hope for the child mean that order, of a sort, has been restored and closure imposed.[8] If the play ends without Yerma's understanding why she has had to suffer, however, the discourse on the child is simply concluded, sadly, but not tragically, in deference to the tragicomic tradition.

Unaccompanied by an anagnorisis, or discovery, Yerma's peripateia, or reversal, is "just," especially in relation to the authority of the severe code by which these characters conduct themselves and judge each other. A number of characters less intimately involved in Yerma's immediate milieu, especially the First Old Woman, do not subscribe to this code. The First Old Woman, in fact, fully blames Juan for the absence of the child as she recommends to Yerma that she resolve her fertility problem by means of sexual relations with another man, her own son. In the process, she disparages the idea that a providential deity—and by implication an accompanying structure of "poetic justice"—is guiding the destiny of Yerma's community: "God, no. . . . When are you going to realize that he does not exist?" (II 821). Indeed, the First Old Woman is but the most obvious manifestation of an alternate value system that, as it refutes the premises of "poetic justice," critiques and supplements as well classical explanations for the causes of tragedy.

A tragic appreciation of *Yerma* begins in same the dream-complex that affirms Yerma's place in a pastoral tradition. The dream's full availability to the audience also makes it a type of prolog, a silent visual commentary entreating the spectator to confirm other dimensions to the play. If there is any initial confusion about the subject of the dream, it becomes unmistakably clear once the dialog begins that, in broad terms, the dream refers to Yerma's desire to have a child. In relation to the dream, Yerma's dilemma lies in discovering an agent-actor willing to assume the shepherd's role with sufficient authority in order to bring the phantom child into being. The eyes of the shepherd in the dream are replaced in waking reality by Juan's vigilance directed toward restricting Yerma's physical movement, itself a response to the growing power of the dream-complex to provoke her to stray from their home. Since the type of shepherd Juan has dedicated himself to becoming reflects his own goal of bringing together a grand pastoral scene, his watchfulness over Yerma is sporadic and rather ineffective. Juan's appreciation of his wife's situation, in fact, is clearly inferior to that of other characters in the play, de facto peasant "analysts," who offer opinions regarding Yerma's plight. Owing to its access to the dream and the numerous subsequent monologs that the dream-complex inspires, the audience is in a much better position to make judgments about Yerma's situation than even these authoritative-sounding peasants. Like the onstage characters who are most willing to assign blame to one or the other party for the absence of the child, it becomes almost impossible for the spectator not to use this information to make ultimate conclusions about Yerma's situation—that is, to impose an imaginative closure. The impetus for poetic justice in *Yerma*, for which poetic closure is both a precondition and a formal consequence, comes not only from Juan and the play's peasant milieu but as well from the spectator. By virtue of a privileged vantage point throughout the play, the audience's position is fully conflated with the repressive activity of vision taking place onstage and directed to bringing Yerma's search for answers to an end.

There are specific allusions to the fact that the real harm to Yerma's reputation as a consequence of her wanderings and public lamentations does not come from her immediate pastoral milieu but from distant, anonymous bodies of onlookers more willing to assign blame and to make damning accusations, referred to here again, as in earlier plays, as *las gentes:*

> First Washerwoman: But, have you seen her with another man?
> Fourth Washerwoman: Us no, but the other people [*las gentes*] yes.
> (II 833)

An associative chain thus extends from Juan and the immediate community to other less than sympathetic parties at the periphery, all of whom to various degrees are engaged in responding to Yerma's dream. The most authoritative of these *gentes* are the spectators in the audience. The diminishment of Yerma's resolve, bringing her late in the play to the conscious suppression of the dream-complex that in actual elapsed time endures for more than five years, is not simply the consequence of Juan but rather of the collective repressive force of a diverse and extensive community of onlookers effectively subsumed in the theater audience. As will become even more evident in *Doña Rosita, the Spinster*, the fact that an unusually lengthy amount of time passes between acts in *Yerma* means that the theater audience is forced to assimilate imaginatively quite disparate temporal moments, which requires an intellectual transposition of what is already a storyless play from the stage to the spectator's consciousness where, reassimilated, it acquires the characteristics of a more conventional representation. In a less threatening manner than in the experimental plays, Lorca is, nevertheless, forcing the spectator to accept the representation as a mental construct. As Yerma attempts to unfetter herself from the visual dominion of her husband in order to attempt to understand the forces working upon and through her, so too the spectator is required to reconvene the scene in imagination in order to be able to accept and understand the representation conventionally.

Yerma's feelings of uselessness amidst the visual beauty of the grand landscape that Juan's labor is creating underscore to her the worthlessness of vision since the only token of value, the child, remains a phantom. This raises another interpretive possibility for the dream: more significant than the shepherd's and child's visual appearance in the dream is their disappearance from the field of vision into a space beyond the limits of conventional perception. Perhaps the most profound meaning of the dream is a new orientation, in a direction that extends beyond a mode of understanding constituted by material-visual values. If the dream's center lies in a space outside the visual frame of reference, then there are indeed other possible actors besides Juan (or a sexual surrogate) and Yerma.

The high valuation of vision and material products—Juan's property and the child as a flesh-and-blood presence—frustrate Yerma's efforts to pursue her intuition of a space where she will encounter a more satisfying meaning to her dream. The domesticated beauty of Juan's property is unacceptable, as is the requirement to confine herself to the "four walls" (II 844) of the cottage. Staying within those walls is possible for Yerma only as a mother, which she intuits that she can become only through contact with a force residing beyond those visual-material limits. Indeed, her forays to a cemetery and to the hermitage are to sites beyond the repressive visual domain where Juan wants her to remain. The concept of "four walls," of course, also has strong currency in reference to the typical configuration of the realist-naturalist stage of the nineteenth and early twentieth centuries, typically an interior room of a house in which, from the fourth invisible wall, the spectator views the action.[9] Yerma's dissatisfaction with the four walls of her cottage thus reflects her growing dissatisfaction with conventional visuality since the requirement to produce a material-visual token, the child, marginalizes her and phantomizes her existence. As much as any specific personal agent, vision and materiality also thwart Yerma's attempts to achieve a satisfactory resolution and/or understanding of her plight.

If Juan and the immediate community are but the onstage expression of a wider repressive authority manifested through vision and seeing that ultimately centers in a third party or "third actor," the spectator, then Yerma's refusal to stay inside the "four walls" is also a positive response to her intuition of the presence of a "fourth actor," also beyond the physical scene, the antithesis of visual-material values. The "fourth actor" is a reorienting force, to which Yerma responds as if by hearing, that directs her to a much different scene. Given the values of her milieu, Yerma has little choice but to take forays away from those watchful eyes in order to search for answers. Her conformity to the will of an authority manifested visually and materially is thus undermined by her desire to listen to a different message. Yerma's first words to her husband in the play—"Juan, do you hear me? Juan" (II 804)—address, in fact, a deeper source of her suffering. No one, and especially not Juan, is capable of hearing the things that Yerma hears.[10] The incongruous juxtaposition of the visual-material values underlying Juan's pastoral *locus amoenus* and a private discourse that progressively captivates Yerma's imagination offers the raw materials for a "four-actor" tragedy. Yerma's dream can only be fulfilled in a location toward which the fourth actor directs her, beyond the visual authority of those who are watching her.

Indeed, the dimension of "voice," a private authority that suggests to Yerma that her fulfillment lies beyond what she can presently see, an alternative discourse in opposition to the visual-material values which she must constantly acknowledge, becomes as fully prominent as her guiding dream. Lorca also accentuates this at the outset, immediately following the dream, by means of a song, a lullaby sung by an offstage voice that does not belong to any specific character in the play. If the dreamscape may be interpreted to set the stage of Yerma's imagination, the lullaby serves, in turn, to comment upon a physical scene fully inadequate to such a vision. Indeed, the song heralds the aspirations of a married couple whose lives center in their young child, a couple that "as [our child] is sleeping we will build you / a little hut in the country / and in it we will all fit" (II 803). Rupert Allen, in fact, explains much of the underlying motivation for Yerma's behavior in the play as a function of the incompatibility of a couple that cannot hear or offer consolation to each other, expressed metaphorically in terms of voice and song, their inability to form a "singing" sensual union (146–53). Thus, according to Allen, part of Yerma's motivation to strangle her husband is also to destroy the sensual aspect of herself that she cannot accept. In other words, the "singing" that Yerma hears corresponds exclusively to the familial-maternal theme corresponding to the initial lullaby and to little else. Without the child, life within the "four walls" of the rustic hut is fully impossible.

In her private moments, Yerma consistently addresses her longing for the child in terms of a direction and a location, a point of reference that she intuits, or hears, lying beyond the present field of vision: "Where do you come from, love, my child?" (II 807). The intuition that the fulfillment of her dream exists beyond the visual-material scene once again evokes the phenomenon of indexicality so prominent in the experimental theater. The medium to which Yerma responds privately reveals itself through signs that are not ends in themselves yet the cumulative effects of which serve to redirect her imagination. The close identification here of agent ("love") and product ("my child") demonstrates that in her private meditations, Yerma's understanding of the procreative process is exactly the opposite of her publicly expressed position, where she draws a fundamental distinction between the sexual means of procreation and its product, or "results." Her later question, "What are you asking, child, from so far away?" (II 808), in reference to the dream (and to the lullaby) opens its interpretation further to suggest that the source of the insufficiency may lie in vision itself, that is, in the inability of the shepherd's eyes to sustain contact with Yerma. While this seems to give credence to the First Old

Woman's proposal that Yerma have a child in another locale, it more emphatically suggests that all conventional, visualizable agents of paternity are integral to the insufficiency dramatized in the dream and the lullaby, as Yerma herself relates to the Vieja: "What you offer me is a tiny glass of well water. Mine is a pain that is no longer a part of my flesh" (II 875). The fertility rituals at the hermitage, where Christian and pagan traditions intersect, only further underscore the insufficiency of these traditions to explain or satisfy her condition.

Barrenness is ultimately only a symptom of a deeper insufficiency in relation to the "fourth actor," an inspirational hidden force for which no suitable geography exists in which to realize its potential. The pagan-Christian backdrop of the final tableau—also evocative of the ancient communal competitions in which tragedy as an art form developed, in which author and actors wore animal costumes not unlike those of the Male (Macho) and Female (Hembra)—emphasizes that the predominant traditions of Spanish and western culture have been essential to the birth of the unique tragedy to which Yerma has given form. Their failure to fulfill her longing, intellectually and physically, brings Yerma to great suffering and a deep sense of loss but also to a deeper recognition and understanding. She is not a sterile desert but a "dry field where a thousand pairs of oxen plowing fit" (II 875), a vast dry field plowed in expectation of a future harvest, which suggests that her story remains as unfinished as it is unfulfilled. Yerma has not exercised the full range of options available to her. Her "pain that is no longer a part of my flesh" is a consequence of her recognition of the incapacity of these traditions and their discourses to do justice to her condition. Yerma's violence against her husband is thus not only an acknowledgment of her tragedy but also a redefinition of tragedy itself. As Juan admonishes Yerma for being unable to resist singing the wrong song, "this constant lament for dark things, beyond life, for things that are in the air" (II 877), he also, unwittingly, describes the real agent provoking her grief, an agent that expresses itself "by means of things that have not happened and which neither you nor I can direct" (II 877). Juan declares in the same breath that "what I care about is what I have between my hands. What I see through my eyes" (II 877); for him the choice is clear: simply abandon the thoughts that dwell in her imagination, the center of her humanity.

In the context of a new expression of tragedy, however, Juan's murder is not simply the response of an outraged spouse at the prospect of continued private indignities. It is nothing less than the confrontation of competing authorities, attitudes toward the world that in Juan's case represent themselves materially and visually and in Yerma's imaginatively and intellectually, in response to an alternative discourse expressed as "voice" and "song." The values of Yerma's community are expressed by means of visual-material products, in Juan's case is his property, which bears public witness to his prominence in his society. Yerma, who has no such token or icon, listens to the voice of a "fourth actor," a hidden force that inspires her to search for fulfillment by means of a different medium. Yerma ultimately discovers that her search for the child was instead the discovery of the conditions of her tragedy. Her suffering will be ongoing but for a purpose, so that she will comprehend the totality of the forces working and speaking through her.[11] The public declaration that Yerma makes to the audience that gathers after the murder affirms her acceptance of suffering but also her willingness to continue to search, no longer for the dream child but for the fullness of her tragic constitution.

Yerma finally understands that, however she may be publicly judged, there can be no closure to her situation. The child was but a symptom of a deeper cycle that her violence toward Juan has allowed her to acknowledge and to understand. In murdering her husband, Yerma destroys the only authorized material agent for bringing her a child under conditions that would be meaningful and, at the same time, destroys the toil of years that has reaped an abundance. As she strangles the life, and voice, from Juan, Yerma is figuratively blinding him as well, initiating a process by which his pastoral paradise will become transformed into a wasteland, the material-visual expression of the very force hostile to that vision and, indeed, to all visual mediums. Yerma's contact with the "fourth actor" transforms her into the dominant force in her community. No one, no successor, will carry on Juan's work, ultimately a labor as self-consuming as Yerma's dream of the child.[12] As she warns away those who gather to survey the scene, Yerma seems to reaffirm the standard of personal agency that underlies the values of her community when she says, "I myself have killed my child" (II 880). In fact, this affirms precisely the opposite, her public acknowledgment of an association with a hidden force that has brought her to a much different understanding.[13] Although Yerma destroys the visual expression of her desire, it now assumes another form: "I am going to rest without awakening myself in fear, to see if the blood will proclaim to me another new blood" (II 880). As the onlookers attempt to comprehend what has happened, Yerma awaits further direction, the inspiration of "another new blood" and a new phase of her life that now begins.

Doña Rosita, the Spinster

In *Blood Wedding* as well as *Yerma*, the most important actor becomes a hidden force that intervenes through human mediums to destroy the cohesiveness of these rural communities. *Doña Rosita, the Spinster*, set in turn-of-the-century Granada, is generally considered to be a departure from these plays. In terms of the options of individuals in the face of public expectations of their maturity and social stability, however, the play exhibits remarkable affinities not only with *Yerma* but with a larger cycle of theater that actually begins with *As Soon As Five Years Pass* and *The Public*.[14] Although less immediately evident than in *Yerma*, where resistance to public authority emerges from a context of extended exemplary conformity to its standards, Rosita's story develops in a similar fashion. Yerma and Rosita must both confront the issue of their ability to satisfy social expectations. Like Yerma, Rosita possesses a strong awareness that the test for such expectations is public and visual: not the physical presence of a child but the destructive transformation of her person as a consequence of time's passage. Rosita minimizes those effects by progressively confining her activity to her own version of Yerma's "four walls," the very space Yerma associates with sterility. Only when she ventures into the public gaze does the passage of time become a reality for her as it forces her to confront the deterioration of her position: "in the street I notice how time passes and I do not want to lose my illusions. . . . I do not want to find out how time passes" (II 921).

Rosita's resistance to the outside world becomes apparent in the context of her decision to wait indefinitely to marry her cousin, who must return to America to look after the family business. After fifteen years, he offers to marry her by proxy only later to marry someone else, again for the sake of business interests. By the time this fact is publicly revealed some ten years later, Rosita is beyond a marriageable age. Although her aunt criticizes her for her shortsightedness—"you have stuck to your idea without seeing reality and without charity to your future" (II 962)—in reality the opposite is true. From the outset, Rosita is very much aware of her circumstance in relation to what awaits her. As it emerges over time, her apparent exemplary faithfulness to her fiancé actually develops into a strategy of resistance to the expectations of maturity. Rosita's introverted attraction to someone in her extended family is indicative of a deeper unwillingness to engage the world. Her twenty-five-year courtship at a distance provides her an acceptable excuse for the indefinite postponement of her entry into the next phase of life, which will require a more intense commitment to the values of her community. Rosita's amorous ideal, therefore, may actually run in a direction contrary to marriage and motherhood.

Rosita does not lament the fact that her long wait for her betrothed denies her the possibility of children. Quite the contrary, it affords her the opportunity to remain youthful for an extended period of time. Although she shares traits in common with other Lorca heroines, Rosita ultimately resembles most the Youth of *As Soon As Five Years Pass*, whose ambivalence toward the socially appointed role of marriage elicited postponement strategies that prolonged the time of youth for so long that he had to be violently removed from "center stage" of the dream over which he nominally presided. Although it does not take place in a dream, Rosita's story is quite similar to the Youth's in many important respects. Just as the Old Man in *As Soon As Five Years Pass* suggests that the Bride's age, instead of years, could just as well be fifteen "snows," "airs," or "sunsets," so too time's impact in this play lies in the perception of change rather than the empirical fact of its passage. The play's truly destructive aspect is the acknowledgment of time's presence in the imagination, which again recalls the Harlequin's discourse on the arbitrary affiliations of time and space in *As Soon As Five Years Pass*. An unconventional idea of love offers Rosita an opportunity similar to that of the Youth to remain loyal to her youthful self, to prolong the time of youth, and to allow an image of herself to remain authorized well past the appropriate time for its discontinuation.

It is only after Rosita's aunt is informed, by means of a letter, of the cousin's marriage that Rosita admits that she has no further options and that she must now accept a different, and inferior, role. Although she knew the truth long before her aunt discovered it, she persisted in the earlier arrangement, for as long as Rosita was perceived to be a *novia*, she could remain young. After it becomes impossible to continue to deny reality, she is forced to acknowledge the ravages of time's passage all at once. Like the Youth's unconventional relationship to time in *As Soon As Five Years Pass*, Rosita's life has also been governed by a private discourse, as suggested by the play's subtitle, a "language of the flowers" allowing her to postpone the advent of an unwanted moment that, ironically, enacts its effects much faster upon Rosita than even upon the *rosa mutabile* with its rapid fading from rose to white, to which Rosita's life is compared throughout the play.

After workers remove all of the furniture from the house—their move the consequence of the uncle's poor financial management—Rosita, now dressed completely in white, enters the empty and darkened space for a final time. The inescapable reality of her new identity is underscored by the stage itself, which now evokes a black-and-white photograph. No longer able to protect her, the house—where Rosita developed and maintained a privileged image of herself—now actually assists in her exposure. The outside world succeeds in penetrating Rosita's private domain, transforming her from *novia* to matron and forcing her to acknowledge for the first time that her imagination and reality are the same. Bereft of her convincing public mask of a quarter-century, she finds time's destructive consequences converging upon her person and image in a single moment. This almost instantaneous, "photographic" transformation reaffirms that time and change are inseparable from the authority of the public consciousness. Since photographic images are considered to exist in a point-to-point, indexical relationship with their referent, the referent for Rosita's new identity-image can only be the mental image that the public has formed of her. A collective act of consciousness destroys Rosita's mask and forces her to acknowledge the new phase of her life that now begins. In contrast to the lifeless official portraits of Ayola, the official photographer of the Spanish royal family whose vivacious daughters visit Rosita in act II, the final image of Rosita is indeed powerful and alive. As in her earlier life, her new circumstances offer her new if limited choices, new possibilities for the imagination. Rosita can become bitter and hateful of everything, like her aunt's spinster sister, or she can continue to affirm the different course that has guided her to this point. Her declaration that "my eyes will always be young" even though "I know that my back will continuing curving more and more each day" (II 963) suggests that Rosita remains acutely conscious that the struggle between the public and private dimensions of her life remains ongoing, even in the aftermath of a public humiliation.

Rosita's public diminishment is accompanied by the loss of her house. Given the play's unusually extended temporal context, the relationships established in the act of theater effectively require that the house's space converge in the spectator's imagination for there to be any sense of continuity between acts separated by vast periods of time (respectively, fifteen and ten years). Rosita's story becomes recognizable as a conventional drama, therefore, largely because of the spectator's willingness to "house" in imagination a dramatic context that extends over a quarter-century.[15] To accept the representation as a drama requires that the spectator subjectivize the house and, in effect, refashion its reality as part of a mental picture, the truest form that reality assumes in the play. This, of course, duplicates what Rosita herself does in making the house a haven for her imagination against public intrusions. The house has been the privileged site of an unconventional understanding of reality, the dissolution of which is heralded by the play's final colorless image. Rosita's forced return to conventionality, a lesser form of reality, signals as well a devaluation of the house, which now fulfills a much different function. Bereft of the objects that have given it form, the house is ultimately transformed into a photographic medium, an exposure chamber that fully confirms Rosita's unmasking.

Ironically, Rosita's public exposure comes at the expense of the theater audience in whose imaginations her story has acquired representable form. Rosita's diminishment is accompanied by the closing of the house, which loses its significance as the center of an ongoing story as its occupants vacate the premises. With the intervention of the offstage public to which Rosita is accountable, the theater audience, on whose imaginative acquiescence the illusion of theater depends, loses authority as it is forced to confront its own displacement from the story that it has "housed." The theater audience's authority has depended on another offstage force that, like Rosita's society, has manifested its effects from the opposite side of the stage. At the conclusion, therefore, Rosita becomes a living index of the effects of the public consciousness upon her person—which, ironically, also assigns to the theater audience the same restrictions and diminishments placed upon her. In a real sense, Lorca is again fulfilling on the commercial stage his intentions in the experimental plays to make the stage an extended medium for the participation of offstage forces. Just as the slightly ridiculous if sincerely frustrated teacher-playwright Martin persists in writing plays essentially for himself because "it is the only thing that pleases me" (II 954), so too Rosita's entire youth has been spent in enacting her own personal drama, to herself, for essentially the same reason. Her contradictory qualities of resistance within a context of apparent conformity also succinctly characterize the practice of Lorca's mature commercial theater, situated at the margins between the two dissimilar modes of theater proclaimed in *The Public*, one public, the other private. As in earlier plays, Lorca's task here has been to achieve a viable theatrical experience from "unacceptable" theatrical premises, specifically accomplished in this instance by providing "temporary housing," via the imagination of the theater audience, for an uncontainable hidden force.

7

THE HOUSE OF BERNARDA ALBA AND *PLAY WITHOUT A TITLE*

A DIVERSE AND provocative array of posthumously collected working ideas and partially completed scripts—which include *The Dreams of My Cousin Aurelia*, *The Destruction of Sodom*, and *The Black Ball* (*Epentic Drama*)—testify to the continuing intensity of Lorca's dramatic imagination at the untimely end of his life.[1] The most fully developed of these works in progress is *Play Without A Title*, drafted along with *The House of Bernarda Alba* during the first half of 1936 (Andrew A. Anderson "Strategy" 212). Characterizing commercial theater in *Play Without A Title* as an entertaining "game of words . . . a panorama where one sees a house where nothing happens" (II 1069), the principal character, the Autor, offers his audience instead a much different space, "a small corner of reality" (II 1069), a metatheatrical reality intended to reveal a more profound set of stage relationships. This is also a succinct description of the most significant dimension of *The House of Bernarda Alba* whose *advertencia*—both a warning and a declaration of intentions from behind the stage—alludes to the nature of the theatrical experience about to unfold: "The poet cautions that these three acts are intended as a photographic documentary" (II 973). Rather than the return to a more conventional theater that many critics have suggested it is, *The House of Bernarda Alba* in fact represents a continuation and intensification of Lorca's efforts to integrate the insights of the experimental plays into his commercial theater. Together, these plays offer as well the most profound expression of the extended dialectic on stage authority that has guided the steady evolution of his theater.

The House of Bernarda Alba

The specific words of the *advertencia* also invoke the dramatic structure of *Doña Rosita, the Spinster,* three effectively discrete acts separated by vast periods of time culminating in a climactic white-on-black photographic moment. The largely black-on-white images of *The House of Bernarda Alba* extend and strengthen the association with photography. Resolving to keep her own "small corner" and its occupants from public view for an extended period, Bernarda admonishes her daughters to conduct themselves as if the house's doors and windows were physically sealed with brick and mortar. The only authorized exception to this directive, the brief opening of the shutters of one window late at night, allows Angustias to converse with her fiancé, Pepe el Romano. Bernarda's imaginative and physical reordering of her house demonstrates striking—if not immediately apparent—affinities with the principal features of a camera. The mechanism of the camera obscura is a modern metaphor for the mechanisms of the human mind and cognition, given the capacity of photography to render, and to document, instantaneously upon a blank surface the received materials of sense perceptions. Similarly, the special configuration of the stage is a concrete, physical means for Lorca to allude to the truest agents of this representation—not the activity within the house itself but the intrusions upon this activity from two distinct points beyond its visible range, in the form of the disrupting effects of Pepe el Romano and the most authoritative witness to the trajectory implied by those effects, the spectator in the theater audience. The house's status as a completely enclosed space further makes problematic the conventional "four walls" relationship since, in effect, it leaves spectators little choice but to consider themselves physically present in the house. If the spectator's imagination is called upon in *Doña Rosita, the Spinster* to "house" disparate temporal moments, in *The House of Bernarda Alba* it acquires an additional and more intimate role as a revelatory medium that, in the manner of a photographic negative, cannot but document the relentless degradation of this privileged space by forces that never assume visual form.

Recent criticism, which has noted an intimate correspondence between Bernarda's house and the town,[2] has also begun to consider the spectator's role in relation to these inner and outer spaces. Nina M.

Scott suggests that "the viewer becomes as much a prisoner of the house as the five daughters" (298) while Morris equates the house with "the space that encloses the reader or spectator together with the characters on stage" ("Austere" 129). While there is merit in these views, it does not necessarily follow that the spectator's visual perspective parallels that of the daughters. Rather, the audience shares more in common with the servants, especially La Poncia—clearly a more perceptive observer than are Bernarda or the daughters—who more fully comprehends the danger threatening the house, which she characterizes as "something extremely large" (II 1031). If she ever did, Bernarda does not now consider the servants part of her extended family but simply paid help to whom she is not obliged to listen. Like La Poncia, the spectator quickly understands that Bernarda's unwillingness to acknowledge a hidden agenda within the house compromises her authority.

That the play has been frequently discussed as a return to greater realism is also a partial consequence of the *advertencia*'s explicit invocation of photography.[3] While recognizing that Bernarda's household is not at all typical of Spanish social reality and, if anything, is an extreme case, Andrew A. Anderson nevertheless classifies the play as a work of realism because it is "ordered upon a basis of contrasting blacks and whites, which is precisely what a photograph from the period would offer" ("Strategy" 221). This opinion, however, overlooks the significance of photography to Modernist aesthetics. The Surrealists were especially fascinated with photography because, as Krauss has demonstrated, they considered the photograph to transcend mimesis altogether, indeed, to be the visual equivalent of automatic writing. Photography is not iconic representation in the conventional sense but rather "an imprint or transfer off the real . . . a photochemically processed trace causally connected to that thing in the world to which it refers in a manner parallel to that of fingerprints or footprints. . . . The photograph is thus generically distinct from painting or sculpture or drawing. . . . [D]rawings and paintings are icons, while photographs are indexes" (26).

Photography is understood to establish an immediate, point-to-point relationship with a real object. Rather than as copying or reproducing an object, artists "from the period" typically considered the photograph to be the indexical trace of an actual presence. In this context, therefore, the *advertencia*'s declaration of a photographic intention is actually a subtle repudiation of mimesis: a warning to the spectator—not unlike the many warnings that Bernarda receives from others in the play—that a hidden force, unacknowledged, indeed, unacknowledgable in empirical understanding and representation, is also at work here.[4] It is through these other indexical manifestations on and off the stage that Lorca alludes throughout the play to a presence that surpasses and subsequently invalidates Bernarda's more limited mode of understanding.

Although the principals approach their new situation after the death of Bernarda's husband with an already well developed theatrical sense—that they are the objects of public scrutiny, actors in a never-ending spectacle—their most significant metatheatrical role is to embody the theater functions whose contentious realignment in the experimental plays has been instrumental in Lorca's subsequent commercial successes. The *advertencia* is also a subtle restatement of Lorca's mature formula for the act of theater, "three acts" that unite as a play only as a consequence of the essential participation of a three-actor "company" comprising the stage director, the poetic function, and the spectator. Bernarda approaches the task of consolidating her authority over her household as if she were a director in charge of a theatrical production.[5] Indeed, Bernarda's comment after the mourners leave could easily express a stage director's thoughts after a performance: "Go back to your houses to criticize everything that you have just seen!" (II 984). Her house becomes center stage for a peculiar yet exemplary representation, the content of which is authority itself. The viability of this production, however, is premised on a repudiation of conventional theater tenets. Bernarda not only directs but is the exclusive audience for an inverted production, the success of which demands that it remain publicly silent and visually unavailable to a disapproving outside audience in the town. Bernarda's situation thus strongly recalls the predicament of the Director of *The Public*, whose lack of moral-existential "capital" forces him to retreat to an equally isolated stage space.

Bernarda's decision to close off her house is motivated by essentially the same force. There is simply not enough money (or *finanza*) for her to continue to risk her moral standing by appearing in public before a town that she resentfully regards as a hostile audience. As the director of a scriptless private scenario, Bernarda understands her task in terms of visual dominance—"My vigilance can do everything" (II 1051)—despite repeated warnings that her eyes are betraying her. Since the failure of the type of vigilance Bernarda undertakes is expressed in the town destructively in brutal public condemnations—leveled by Bernarda herself in her role as the town's condemnatory mouthpiece—any negative consequences for Bernarda ultimately portend a confrontation with herself, a self-condemnation authored in a loathsome public discourse organized and authorized around her person. Bernarda's will to create an absolutely private space, however, actually hastens the collapse of the distinction so important to her between inside and outside spaces.[6] Allowing the house to become exposed to criticism, therefore, means self-exposure, by her own public referent, under conditions fully analogous to photography, where unmediated images emerge instantaneously as if the space between medium and referent did not exist.

The inherent vulnerability of Bernarda's private medium is alluded to from the outset as the Servant complains about the physical effects of the mourning bells that have penetrated the house's thick walls: "I already have the tolling of those bells deep within my temples" (II 973). Their largely unmediated effects mark but the first instance of a subsequent pattern of involuntary or spontaneous intrusions into the space of the house communicated through indexes whose effects herald Bernarda's failure to maintain her enclosed space. With the exception of Angustias, the death of Bernarda's husband leaves everyone, and especially Bernarda, insecure and economically vulnerable.[7] The prospects of reduced economic circumstances may also offer an explanation for Bernarda's severe treatment of La Poncia, whose earlier more intimate role in the house is now abruptly curtailed: "You serve me and I pay you. Nothing more!" (II 991). Bernarda's disparagement of the poor ("the poor are like the animals; it seems as if they were made from other substances" [II 979]) is a further reflection of her insecurity in a space ordained as private but which she must continue to share with those whom she considers outsiders.[8] In a manner paralleling that of her mistress, La Poncia's response to Bernarda's rebuffs is to retreat into a more conventional servant's role and to refrain from offering further unsolicited advice. By the time events reach a critical point, La Poncia has become little more than a bystander.[9]

La Poncia's many unheeded admonitions are unmistakably communicated, however, to the spectator, who quickly becomes privy to a much different understanding. If La Poncia's warnings and the steadily more bitter and jealous exchanges among the daughters about Angustias's pending marriage are not enough, explicit declarations by the lucidly demented María Josefa summarize clearly what is happening to the house and to Bernarda's daughters: "Pepe el Romano is a giant. You all want him. But he will devour you because you are grains of wheat" (II 1058).[10] As in earlier plays, the audience occupies a privileged position in the house where very nearly everything points to the untenability of Bernarda's intentions. In a scene also filled with "pictures with inverisimilar landscapes of nymphs or legendary kings" (II 973), it becomes very nearly impossible for the spectator to fail to recognize the inappropriateness and insufficiency of Bernarda's response to such powerful developments.

The overabundant evidence of the deterioration of Bernarda's position makes it clear that a different point of view is progressively assuming control of the scene. Bernarda's ability to direct her household is steadily undermined by the discourse on Pepe el Romano that erupts from the very space designated to embody her authority. Bernarda's pretensions to control are thus discredited almost from the outset since the spectator clearly understands that something more powerful ("something extremely large") is making its uninvited presence felt in her private scene. The spectator emerges as an authoritative observer as a consequence of understanding Pepe el Romano, and not Bernarda, as the play's true protagonist. Although he is never visually present on stage, Pepe's prominence is communicated through his disruptive effects on the daughters, as the "author" of a "dialog" that spoils the house's silence. In relation to the theater functions, Pepe, in effect, usurps the poetic function and the script banished from Bernarda's scenario. From the outset, Pepe enjoys an unusually favorable position. His interest in marrying an unattractive, nearly forty-year-old spinster unsuitable for childbearing leaves little room to doubt Magdalena's contention that he comes to the house "for the money" (II 997), Angustias's considerable dowry. More than simply to grab the lion's share of assets that still accrue to the estate, Pepe eventually takes from Bernarda something that she values much more highly, her moral authority. The scandal provoked by Adela's suicide, however, also prevents Pepe from profiting from this lucrative arrangement. Instead of fathering the child that Angustias will be unable to bear, which as La Poncia envisions will leave him free to use the money as he pleases and also to marry Adela, Pepe instead becomes the agent of something far more destructive, a series of exchanges within the house that eventually discredits all involved. If Pepe does indeed come "for the money," he not only leaves penniless but comports himself, like Bernarda, in a remarkably inept fashion that fully undermines any such intention. By becoming enmeshed in the very sexual desire that enhances his authority in the house, Pepe also falls victim to something unforeseen that originally seemed to center in himself.[11]

Angustias's admission that when she attempts to focus on Pepe intently "his image is effaced right in front of me" (II 1047) suggests that a significant shortcoming of the house's occupants is their inadequacy as mediums. According to María Josefa, Pepe's effects have degraded and transformed them into "tongueless frogs" (II 1058), croaking mouthpieces of a force over which they have no control.[12] By the time Bernarda acknowledges late in act II that Martirio's stealing of Pepe's photograph signifies something more serious than a joke (*broma*),[13] it is clear that Pepe's most significant penetration of the house is as a "photographic" trace upon a sensitive yet fragile medium. Mocking the type of authority that Bernarda commands in the community, Pepe also manifests a dual presence, inside and outside the house. In distinct contrast to the unchanging silence that Bernarda covets, Pepe is progressively redefined and imaginatively aggrandized by the daughters, especially Adela.

Traditionally considered a freedom-loving rebel, Adela demonstrates essentially the same weakness of imagination as Bernarda in the face of the challenge of a force summoned in the name of Pepe. Adela progresses through what appears to be a steady intensification of her resistance to her mother in an apparently valiant quest for personal autonomy. In act III, she gives an explicit indication of what she has been imagining when she associates Pepe's sexual authority with the stallion in the adjoining stable, the creature whose sexual intentions are unmistakably communicated by the thunderous effects of his hooves against the walls of the house—that is, by indexical means.[14] Adela simultaneously reveals, however, that she also remains dominated by the idea of the house, that she does not possess the strength of imagination necessary to envision a fundamentally differ-ent mode of existence, even with Pepe. Discounting La Poncia's advice to bide her time, Adela declares instead late in act III her resolve to become Pepe's mistress: "I will put on the crown of thorns that be-longs to those who are the mistress of some married man" (II 1062). She is willing, therefore, to exchange one house where she is kept for another: "I will go along to a little house where he will see me when he wants, when he feels like it" (II 1062). Desire is not liberating for Adela but rather accords her a dubious authority, to declare that "in me no one except Pepe gives the orders" (II 1063). Whatever individual identity and dignity she commands as Bernarda's resistive daughter is exchanged for the power to lose herself in Pepe.

The play's climactic moment is ordered around another index, Ber-narda's shotgun blast intended for Pepe—a spectacularly ill-consid-ered act that instantly destroys the coveted public silence of the house—which instead triggers Adela's suicide.[15] So desperate to be seen that at one point she had even begged the chickens to notice her (II 995), Adela also takes the word of a jealous and untrustworthy sister of Pepe's death—that she will now be forever separated from Pepe's gaze—and rushes immediately to put an end to herself. Not high trag-edy but a deluded *broma* "brings down the house," a stage trick worthy of the Magician in *The Public* who so efficiently removed objects from the stage and whom Bernarda parodies at this moment as she waves her malsonorous "wand" at Pepe, only to make Adela disappear. Adela's suicide is also the consequence of her own narrow understanding of a scene in her imagination intended for only one person. In "death," Pepe attains his most destructive form. Bernarda's acquiescence in Martirio's "joke" authorizes one form of Pepe to suppress another. Pepe's absence destroys Adela, the human medium in which he at-tained his fullest presence, along with destroying the idea of the house that Bernarda envisioned. That deluded understanding, nevertheless, is the exclusive means by which the spectator has been able to obtain an enhanced perspective. The status and significance of the house resides in the fact that it is a closed space, and the spectator's perspective rises and falls along with the space of the house. At its most essential level, the play has thus been a temporal-spatial embellishment upon the words of the *advertencia,* which apprise the spectator of the poet's in-tention to bring to the stage a photographic documentary. Exactly in the manner of the *advertencia*'s relationship to the play—as an "outside text" not part of the representation—the real authority in Bernarda Alba's house is neither Bernarda nor Pepe but a hidden force that collapses mimetic space as it leaves its "photographic" trace on everyone in the house, including the spectator.

Clearly the best-informed and most competent medium in the house is the audience, whose near omniscience throughout the representation fully conflates its position with the house itself. Like La Poncia, who worries about how a scandal will affect her own standing in the community, the spectator depends for authoritative perspective on the house's continued stability as an enclosed and publicly silent space. The scandal that comes to the house, which forever destroys the silence that no amount of insistence by Bernarda will be able to reimpose,[16] means that the theater audience's own authoritativeness as a repository of privileged information is also decisively overturned. As the scandal in Bernarda's house becomes known, the importance of the house as the privileged container of the scene disappears along with the audience's role as its best-informed party. Bernarda's loss of standing, evidence of which is her vociferous attempt to reimpose her interpretation upon events, is paralleled in the audience's equal incapacity to stabilize the scenario over which it has visually presided. At the play's conclusion, that authority, which never centered in Bernarda but became closely identified with the spectator's powers of vision, fully belongs to "something extremely large" which succeeds in exposing Bernarda's private scene to the outside public.[17] As a second audience of townspeople emerges, the theater audience as well must confront the ruinous effects of a force that has diminished everyone. Upon the scandal's becoming public, the spectator's knowledge is no longer privileged or unique, and thus the audience is forced to become—like Bernarda herself, screaming in public—merely one of a growing crowd of critics and commentators.

As the townspeople, whose values and outlook are also intimately conflated with Bernarda's, begin to be made aware of the details of what has happened, they are also diminished. The scandal now makes it more difficult for the community to sustain the exemplary way of life epitomized in Bernarda. A second representation injurious as well to the *pueblo*, and the theme and content of which are also "the house of Bernarda Alba," thus begins in the imaginations of the townspeople.

The final moment, announcing the entrance upon the scene of the second audience, again recalls the conclusion of *The Public* in which the Director's last act before expiring is to welcome the entry of another audience to a scene of relentless destruction. As in *The Public*, the most significant dimension of this production has been the progressive revelation of the authority of a hidden force that has conflated and collapsed the space of the stage in a manner which also exposes the insufficiency of conventional mimeticism in relation to a superior indexical-"photographic" medium. What most critics consider to be Lorca's most realistic play demonstrates fundamental affinities with the avant-garde *The Public*, also a response to the need to "reveal the profile of a hidden force when the audience has no further recourse except to pay full attention, filled with spirit and overpowered by the action."

As for the Director in *The Public*, the struggle here has been to manage a force that, in the manner of Pepe el Romano's marriage arrangement, exacts impossible terms from all those called upon to house its debilitating effects. Amelia's complaint of "this criticism that does not allow us to live" (II 993), Martirio's cry that "I see that everything is a terrible repetition" (II 993), and Magdalena's lament that "not even our eyes belong to us" (II 1020) refer to their own predicaments but also to the accumulating effects of a tormenting force that disrupts their sense of belonging to a stable scene. Just as Bernarda fails to maintain the autonomy of her house "erected by my father so that not even the grasses would learn of my desolation" (II 1029), so too her dramatic father, who must likewise establish and affirm his own authority in a "house," has understood that, whatever else it may become, theater is also a continuing response to the recognition of its own inherent vulnerability.

As it manifests itself in this play, the most powerful demonstration of authority is to discredit a mimetic understanding of a play that seems to be Lorca's most realistic and socially sensitive undertaking. Paralleling that of his principal character, Lorca's social awareness expresses itself not in terms appropriate to social realism but in the particular, and peculiar, terms of what goes on in one specific house, a theater dedicated to obliging its audience to acknowledge the human price of exercising authority over a "small corner of reality." More than condemning the tyrannical will of Bernarda Alba, Lorca exposes the tormenting paradox of authority: it can only exist in the context of an audience. More than to direct the scene of her authority, Bernarda wishes to free herself altogether of the burden of having to satisfy the demands of her public. There is, however, no such space. In the public house of theater, an invisibly present agent becomes "something extremely large," not only in relation to onstage events that it ultimately dominates, but also in relation to the theater audience whose acquiescence in Bernarda's private *mise-en-scène* also exposes the spectator as the final unsuitable medium to contain a force that exceeds all attempts to understand it conventionally. Along with the house of Bernarda Alba, two audiences, in the town and the theater audience, are diminished as the hidden force, finally, exposes the limits of its own authority in relation to these spaces—acts of consciousness that are also acts of theater—which together produce a negative image. The "rapid curtain" with which the play concludes is thus both a final curtain and a final allusion to the shutter movement of a camera that has documented the trace of the presence of a hidden force upon fragile and insufficient imaginative mediums.

Lorca's Last Plays in Relation to Antonin Artaud's "Theater of Cruelty"

Before discussing *Play Without A Title* as a separate work of theater, it will be useful to examine it and *The House of Bernarda Alba* in relation to Antonin Artaud's theoretical pronouncements in *Theater and Its Double* as well as in *The Cenci*, both of which had begun to make their initial impact on the European stage at the very moment that Lorca was writing what proved to be his last works for the stage. Artaud considers French theater little more than spoken dialog that has not fully acknowledged the directorial function or the concept of the performance text ("if the term staging has assumed such disparaging meaning, this is the fault of our European concept of theatre, making speech predominate over other means of performance" [81]). It is notable that in comparison to a wealth of provocative statements about the necessity for the reform of the theater, Artaud's most significant theater production, *The Cenci* (1935), although indeed controversial because of scenes featuring violence and torture, nevertheless offers a stage spectacle that in many respects is rather conventional. The most important dimension of this play appears to be an attempt to give physical/visual form to Artaud's theoretical ideas about "cruelty" in *Theater and Its Double*, as embodied in the principals, Cenci and his family. What is significant about Cenci's cruelty is that it is exercised as a demonstration of his will and authority over his family and to enhance his political position by virtue of the impunity with which he is able to terrorize his immediate social milieu. In this sense, there are striking parallels between Cenci and Bernarda Alba, the "tyrant of all those who encircle her." The source of their authority lies not in their ability to achieve their ends without overt coercion but rather through a process of mental discipline.

Discipline, specifically "strictness, diligence, unrelenting decisiveness, irreversible and absolute determination" (77), the authority to bring greater discipline to both the theatrical production and the consciousness of the theater audience, lies at the heart of Artaud's conception of cruelty. "Cruelty," therefore, does not consist in overt acts of physical assault but rather in their intellectual equivalent, a relentless bombardment (Artaud's precise word) in which "violent physical images pulverize, mesmerize the audience's sensibilities, caught in the drama as if in a vortex of higher forces" (63). It is "cruel" in the special sense that the audience is afforded no opportunity for emotional retreat, is required to participate in productions in which the sense of distance has effectively disappeared. Cruelty, therefore, is primarily an intellectual process, an assault upon conventional consciousness "imprinted with terror and cruelty" (65) whereby both the theater production and the audience submit to the discipline of a higher authority. Indeed, an essential component of Artaud's plan for the reform of the theater is for the poetic and directorial functions of theater to merge— for one authority, a playwright who is also the producer of his scripts, to assume authority over the stage: "the old duality between author and producer will disappear . . . replaced by a kind of single Creator using and handling this language, responsible both for the play and the action" (72).

This is, of course, almost identical to Lorca's ideas from *The Public* and his numerous pronouncements on the need for greater stage discipline, all of which are refined and embodied in *Play Without A Title* in the figure of the Autor. The essential ingredient of Lorca's experimental theater is precisely the audience's acquiescence in what amounts to an assault upon its conventional consciousness, which—as Artaud himself in Paris was forced to understand with the commercial failure of *The Cenci*—Spanish audiences were not yet disciplined enough to accept. Lorca's response, unlike Artaud's rather resigned acceptance of his commercial failure, is to devise less demanding means by which to achieve fundamentally the same theatrical effect. Rather than to bombard the audience, Lorca overcomes dramatic distance by ceding effective omniscience to the audience, only to use that privileged vantage point to manipulate it in more subtle ways.

In *The House of Bernarda Alba*, while the audience is not bombarded with "cruelty," the sense of distance between Alba's house and the consciousness of the spectator is nevertheless almost completely erased. By more comfortable means, therefore, Lorca establishes a dramatic space that not only includes the spectators but ultimately demands that they become part of the physical space of the stage, that the spectators, in effect, "house" a production of which content is rather cruel if also, like that of *The Cenci*, seemingly "conventional" in many respects. Ultimately, Artaud's and Lorca's goals are similar in that both have come to understand theater in terms of performance and further, that the end of performance is discipline, of the stage itself and, through the stage, of the audience. Both advocate reform in national theater by means of an enhancement of the directorial function, and the goal of both is indeed a theatrical atmosphere in which the audience is emotionally and intellectually enthralled and overpowered by the action. It is significant that what proved to be Lorca's last autonomous piece of theater, *Play Without A Title*, concludes in a literal sense with an aerial bombardment of the stage, for the theater of both Artaud and Lorca, each in his own way, is dedicated to precisely such an idea, an unrelenting assault on the complacency of conventional consciousness on both sides of the stage.

Play Without A Title

If *The House of Bernarda Alba* examines the impasse of authority, *Play Without A Title* offers a more optimistic outlook and direction for what has become the dominant issue of Lorca's theater. The present play may also be understood as a condensation and refinement of the experimental plays, especially *The Public*. The principal character, the

Autor, is a much stronger successor to *The Public*'s Director, better able to defend himself against unwanted audience intrusions. In *The Public* Lorca is just beginning to confront the issue of stage authority, its relationship to his understanding of love and tragedy, and the direction in which such intuitions are taking him. By *Play Without A Title* he has largely concluded this exploration and, indeed, seems to be embarking on a new phase of his theater in which the earlier contradictions no longer present the same obstacles to authoritative representation. Far from abandoning his avant-garde agenda, Lorca is poised to affirm a more constructive relationship with the hidden force whose creative-destructive energy is portrayed metaphorically in more public terms, as a proletarian audience of workers—the very class of people which Bernarda Alba held herself above—a force with great destructive potential that threatens to assume control of the stage yet nevertheless drawing the Autor to its energy. What many have considered a prolog or initial scene to a larger work serves equally as the introduction to a new phase of Lorca's theater.

This fresh direction proceeds as the evolutionary consequence of a cycle that has now run its course, culminating in Bernarda Alba's private *mise-en-scène* that was itself also something of a parody of the mode of Lorca's very earliest theater, similarly poorly equipped to accommodate its public audience. Although most of the truly radical qualities of *The Public* are absent from *Play Without A Title*, the play nevertheless dedicates itself to revalidating the experimental cycle by making its message publicly accessible. The Magician's recommendations in *The Public* against *Romeo and Juliet* and in favor of *A Midsummer Night's Dream* as a more suitable medium to raise the issue of love's accidental nature, "an accident [that] does not depend on us in the least" (II 1081), are fully heeded in *Play Without A Title*. Although love's tragic potential remains unchanged as "a destructive truth [that] can lead to suicide" (II 1081), the Autor also realizes that "it is necessary not to think about oneself but rather to think about the others" (II 1081). Thus while recalling especially the Emperor's violent obsession in *The Public* with "oneself" (*uno*), the Autor is signaling here a revaluation of earlier priorities, that the new emphasis will be collective rather than the particular complaints of his predecessors. As the Autor makes clear: "I do not want to correct anybody. I only want people to tell the truth. And to be saying it in public" (II 1078). A truly authoritative theater must emerge from the underground to speak its truth in the "open air." Although the objective conditions remain unfavorable because the truth "is still poorly illuminated" (II 1078), the Autor nevertheless dedicates himself to that more universal version of the truth in the play.

It is in the audience to whom the stage discourse is directed, rather than in the dramatic content, that *Play Without A Title* differs from *The Public*. Indeed, both transpire in a metadramatic space in front of an inner audience that occupies the same space as does the central character. Although the characters—that is, the "people who impede the representation" (II 1093)—in *Play Without A Title* are of the same essence as the horses and men of *The Public*, they are located in a slightly different position, which corresponds to the seats in the theater rather than the space onstage, where the Autor is situated. If the Director of *The Public* was eventually overwhelmed by the presence of an onstage audience that disrupted his intention to represent the truth of love, the Autor in *Play Without A Title* commands a much greater authority from the outset to fulfill those elusive goals. It is precisely the space of the stage, which did not belong to the Director, that measures the Autor's authority.

The play begins in the manner of a prolog similar to others that have accompanied Lorca's productions, especially that to *The Shoemaker's Prodigious Wife*, in which the Wife interrupts the *autor* to demand that she be allowed to enter the scene and to begin the play. A similar situation obtains here as one of the spectators interrupts the Autor's harangue with a rhetorical question regarding how the salty smell of the ocean could be brought to the enclosed space of the theater. The fact is that although the Autor is occupying the role of one who is supposed to be introducing a play, he has no such play to introduce. The prolog is his play, or sermon, as he refers to it, its content solely the present state of the theater and the authority it commands. Although the Autor raises issues fundamentally no different than before, his attitude is much more confident than that of his predecessors. His purpose is not to convince his audience of anything but simply to present a new agenda for theater: "to move your hearts by showing the things that you do not want to see, shouting the simplest of truths that you do not want to hear" (II 1069). Accompanying his dissatisfaction with the artifice of drama and the difficulty of representing reality to an

audience—since "reality begins because the author does not want you
to feel that you are in the theater, but rather in the middle of the street"
(II 1070)—is his thought that "how beautiful it would be if suddenly
they would call to the spectator from the stage and make him speak"
(II 1070), which is what happens shortly thereafter.

Although the abrupt interruption of the Autor by the First Male
Spectator parallels the Director's unfortunate experience in *The Pub-
lic*, there is a significant difference in the point of origin of these re-
spective audiences. If in *The Public* the Director is interrupted by
nightmarish figures that incarnate aspects of his person, the spectators
in *Play Without A Title* are simply aspects of an ongoing discourse on
theater. Their questions, which accentuate the proper relations be-
tween spectators and the dramatic action, offer pretexts for further
comment on the even more important issues of the relationship be-
tween reality and dramatic illusion and the authority of the stage to
provide convincing models of reality. The characters who initiate the
dialog here are neither emanations from a dream nor do they belong
to any theater audience that may be watching them. They are instead
characters whom the Autor has summoned to question his authority.
Their outlooks and attitudes, however, closely resemble those of "real-
life" spectators which every dramatist must confront. Lorca thus re-
turns both to the primal scene of his theater, an enclosed space that
houses his dramatic ideas represented before an audience of one, and
to the setting of his most serious mistakes. Here, in another theater
not for spectators yet at which spectators are present in abundance and
on many levels, the Autor conducts what amounts to a master class on
the limits of theatrical authority.

The First Male Spectator claims the right to interrupt the Autor be-
cause "I've paid for my seat!" (II 1071), to which the Autor replies:
"Paying for your seat does not imply the right to interrupt the one who
is speaking, much less to judge the work" (II 1071). The Autor con-
cedes that the spectator can like a play or not like it, applaud it or reject
it, but never judge it, to which the First Male Spectator replies: "The
only law of the theater is the judgment of the spectator" (II 1071).[18]
These attitudes lie at the heart of the act of theater and reveal the two
classic perspectives at work in every theater production. The specta-
tor's very presence in the theater instantly confers the status of judge
and critic, along with the power to bestow success or failure upon the

production. In this regard, there can be little doubt that what the First Male Spectator says is true. Because it may be true does not mean that such a viewpoint must prevail. The Autor exemplifies an attitude toward theater that, if it were dominant, would assure the autonomy, and thus the authority, of every theater production. Every decision to bring a work of theater to the stage would be strictly an artistic one and not the consequence of "the economy of the theater" (II 1086).[19]

The Autor's reply to the First Male Spectator's persuasive argument is to remind him of his metadramatical status: "Here we are not in the theater" (II 1072). The First Male Spectator is part of a much more ambitious theater project than he could ever imagine because the Autor wants to "tear down the walls so that we can feel that we are crying or murdering or snoring with the shriveled up stomachs of those who are outside, those who do not even know that the theater exists" (II 1072).[20] The First Male Spectator, however, claims that he is too close to reality to give credence to such theoretical arguments, to which the Autor replies that there is no reality, that death awaits in the form of "four coffins" (II 1073) for all those listening to him at this moment, which may also be an allusion to the "four walls" configuration of the contemporary stage exercising a similar debilitating effect on Spanish theater. The First Male Spectator replies that if Spain were not a "country so wild about death" (II 1073), the Autor would have been booed off the stage long ago. He then strongly reiterates his demand for entertainment ("I thought I was in the theater" [II 1073]), to which the Autor replies with yet another negative affirmation: "We are not in the theater. Because they are coming to tear down the doors. And we will all save ourselves" (II 1073). Neither is part of reality or the theater because both are awaiting a higher purpose, the moment in which the distinction between the theatrical and the real is no longer a refuge for playwright, actor, or spectator. The Autor wants actors to be "men of flesh and women of flesh" (II 1073), to act as if there were no audience. Only when the theater acquires enough authority to communicate its message by means other than pandering or preaching will it begin to meet the fuller conditions of "reality."

As the Autor patiently and confidently awaits this moment he senses to be near, the First Female Spectator continues the dialog. She does not want to leave the theater because she is interested in the "plot" (*argumento* [II 1073]), here a double reference to the present discussion about theater and to the theatrical plot, which for the Autor means *vida* (II 1074), "real life." At this point the Autor alludes to an outlandish example of plot that he claims to have presented tearfully on this very stage before a few of his friends; he is sure that the First Male Spectator will not believe the plot. This is clearly an allusion to the experimental plays and a further reflection of the considerable personal suffering that their stories have occasioned. The plot deals with the starvation in a small room of a woman whose famished children play with her hands after her death as if they were "yellow breads" and then fall asleep on her breasts after eating the contents of a tin of shoe polish. As predicted, the First Male Spectator rejects the story as an exaggeration. The First Female Spectator is horrified, however, by the thought that the story might be true, which causes them to leave and to call for the Autor's arrest by higher authorities. This, in essence, recreates the attitudes that have made the experimental plays unstageable. Yet as the First Female Spectator's reaction suggests, the real reason for their unstageability may well be their "realism." Rather than being "original" stories, they may instead evince correspondences with the spectator's most intimate thoughts, as Lorca has suggested, "making file by in the scene the private dramas that each one of the spectators is thinking, as he or she is watching, often without noticing, the performance." The stage thus becomes an intolerable intrusion and "the spectators would arise indignant and prevent the performance from continuing" (III 557). Significantly, the representation does continue, as does the hope for bringing the experimental plays to the stage in the future.[21]

At this point the Youth enters, wearing a dress coat, which again recalls the costuming of *The Public* and *As Soon As Five Years Pass*. Entering the scene with a somewhat outmoded and unrealistic view of the theater, as if time had passed him by, the Youth shares some affinities with the Youth of *As Soon As Five Years Pass*, who resisted the inevitability of change and time's passing. His Servant, who also bears a resemblance to his counterpart in *As Soon As Five Years Pass*, continues the allusions to the experimental plays by recounting two stories that recall their dark humor. In the first, a group of drunks has a contest to see whom they can intoxicate more quickly, a young child or a giant turkey. The child gets drunk first and beats his head against the walls of the bar while the turkey, whose throat the drunks have slit with a jagged-edged blade, requires half an hour. The second deals with a drunkard who during Carnival makes a violin using a cat—which recalls the Dead Child's companion in *As Soon As Five Years Pass*—crucified to a washboard, which also evokes another crucifixion parody, the Red Nude's in *The Public*. The drunk plays by scratching the cat with burrs, causing it to howl loudly, which in turn inspires two women dressed "one as Pierrot and the other as Colombina" (II 1077) to dance. Although the Youth considers the Servant's stories inappropriate and barbaric, the Autor does not reject them because he understands them not as cruelties but as vehicles by which to "open the eyes of the spectators, even though they may not wish it" (II 1077), which was also certainly part of the motivation for the experimental plays.

The Servant's fear of walking into the darkness backstage elicits a call from the Autor to turn on the lights, which brings forth the unexpected presence of a new scenario, "an inverisimilar palace" (II 1080), that indicates that rehearsal for a play—Shakespeare's *A Midsummer Night's Dream*—has now begun. This abrupt transition strongly reinforces the idea of a multidimensional reality, a changeable scenario featuring a script, or *argumento*, that remains rather constant. The Autor's serious interpretation of this light-hearted play supports such a view. He declares it to have been seriously misunderstood, the basis for its "somber plot" (II 1080) being precisely the view of love it develops: "love, of whatever kind, is an accident and does not depend on us in the least" (II 1081). No one has the power to question the authority of love; one must either obey desire or be consumed by one's resistance to it. Lorca's theater has been grounded in this simple idea which has demanded extraordinary personal effort to acknowledge its fuller truth. The Autor's commentary on this play is, therefore, tantamount to a public confession of an eccentric sexuality. In contradistinction to the homosexual self-hatred expressed by the Men in *The Public*, which eventually consumed and destroyed the Director, the present play evinces a much greater acceptance of an unquestioned fact. What was previously "a terrible truth" is now a more universal form of understanding of love, in the form of "truths that build" (II 1081).

Upon acknowledging this major impediment to his dramatic authority, the Autor is confronted by the act of theater itself as he is now forced to become the director of the Shakespeare production. When the Prompter asks him how they should imitate the air that will be blowing in the woodland scenes, his flippant reply is, "However you want. Singing with your mouth closed" (II 1081). What this more importantly demonstrates is a resolve to settle the problems of staging through the spoken word. Rather than continuing to allude to an off-stage agenda, the Autor is anticipating the time when theater will speak freely in the open air. The Actress's claim to be uttering an "original" statement never before part of any work of theater merely draws attention to the fact that "originality" is as multidimensional as reality. The act of theater is but one step in a creative process that begins in a private space, the imagination of the dramatist, whose "original statements" are themselves adaptations of a preexisting plot.

Echoing sentiments that align her with the conventional stage, the Actress inspires the Autor's denunciation of the contemporary theater scene: "I am certainly going to leave you, your society, your inconstancy" (II 1083). Recalling the debate in *Don Cristobal's Little Puppet Stage*, the Actress's final gesture in order to be able to accompany the Autor to his new destination is her threat to use offensive language, which presumably would be enough to banish her from her present set of theatrical circumstances. All she succeeds in accomplishing, however, is to transform herself from Titania into Lady Macbeth, hardly a change for the better. As the scene is now interrupted by the sound of gunshots, the threat of violence causes the Actress to demand that the doors of the theater be closed, to which the Autor replies, "Let them be open! The theater is for everybody! This is the school of the people!" (II 1085). When the Actress worries over the possible destruction of the props and scenery, the Autor even more emphatically replies, "Destroy everything!" (II 1085). The false blood of the conventional stage, "the walls of lies" (II 1086), must not be allowed to become mixed with the "true blood" (II 1086) about to be shed in the name of a new theater.

His harshest remarks are reserved for when the Prompter reminds him of "the economy of the theater" (II 1086), the universal impediment to a more truthful stage. The Autor's condemnation of theater economics is also a rejection of a formula for playmaking that has compromised Lorca's stage throughout his career. Thus while the Autor well understands that "gunpowder kills poetry" (II 1087), he is also aware too that the new destructive force now making itself manifest, "the tongues that want to destroy what is already established" (II 1087), constitutes salvation. As the rebellion from "outside" mounts, the Autor casts aside his doubts and his former loyalties to proclaim that he no longer wishes to belong to a decadent theater elite: "I am not a gentleman and neither do I want to become one. I am one who is dying for God" (II 1090).

During the continuing pressure on the area of the stage from the invaders, the Autor leaves the scene momentarily by climbing a set of stairs, which places him at a different vantage point from others like the Second Male Spectator, who complains bitterly about "those people who impede the representation" (II 1093). These words, of course, are ironic since they are uttered by actors who are themselves embodiments of the agents that prevented the earlier versions of this play, one of what Lorca was at this time calling his "unstageable plays" (III 674), from achieving their full expression before an audience. As the Second Male Spectator and the Youth recall earlier times, the bombing increases, forcing them to flee. At this moment a new group of characters enters dressed as fairies and sylphs—recalling the "old sylph of the forest escaped from a book by the great Shakespeare" (II 6) that provided the inspiration for *The Butterfly's Spell*—as a dying worker shouts a *viva* for the revolution. As the Second Female Spectator laments for her children, the Actress now begins to criticize the falseness of her voice, which the Actress understands will move no one to pity. Finally, the Autor reappears on the scene to proclaim the triumph of the new revolution: "Tell the truth above the old scenarios. Drive nails into the old thieves of oil and bread. May the rain wet the looms and take the paint off the flies" (II 1095). As a voice shouts, "Fire," the Autor repeats the message of affirmation via destruction, following it offstage accompanied by the Actress, who calls out to him in a low and trembling voice.

The Autor's ultimate destination is once again to the starting point, to the offstage space that has consistently been associated with the hidden force and with the bringing into public view of a more authoritative stage agenda. The distinctive element in *Play Without A Title* is that "offstage" is also the place where the hidden force is now assigned a physical form, as an entirely different class of theatergoers, the workers, whose destructive mission is truly revolutionary.

Owing to other destructive events that cut short his life, Lorca's *Play Without A Title* becomes his final statement about the direction of his theater. Everything about it, however, suggests that he was

poised to embrace a new and more authoritative moment for his thea-
ter, won as a consequence of the ongoing dialectic between his private
agenda and his audience. The *Play Without A Title* is Lorca's acknow-
ledgment that his theater public has grown more diverse, that he does
not necessarily have to pander to a narrowly defined range of aesthetic
preference. Indeed, it is the growing authority of his theater that has
allowed Lorca to conceive of the Autor, for whom the prospect of the
destruction of everything traditional and conventional about the Span-
ish stage offers the most sincere expression of belief in the forces of
creation. The "workers," therefore, are ultimately the embodiments of
Lorca's desire to embrace a much wider audience. As the Autor exits
the stage, he affirms both the hope for a new direction but also his own
author's awareness that he has arrived at the threshold of a new rela-
tionship with a more diverse audience, the consequence of a vision of
the stage as the authoritative locus for "the definitive transfer; from
the mind to the scene" (III 629), where the authority of a private vision
is publicly confirmed. It is to this unending process that the Autor has
fully dedicated himself as he departs the stage in order to start anew.
This was also Lorca's position in an interview not long before his own
unfortunate disappearance from the scene: "I can't give an indication
of my preferences among works already staged. I'm in love with the
ones that I have yet to write" (III 629).

CONCLUSION

THE VIEWS OF García Lorca's theater that emerge and solidify shortly after his death have almost invariably stressed the thematic and/or social messages of his theater. This study has suggested instead that a full accounting of Lorca's theater must acknowledge as well the constructive pathway he was building toward the type of stage authority that he knew was necessary to bring his theater—and Spanish theater in general—into the European mainstream. Lorca could not and did not write his plays in isolation from the major developments of continental Modernism. Yet despite a wealth of interpretive commentary from other European literary-critical traditions, Lorca has only rarely been studied from this perspective by Hispanists. With few exceptions, noted in the introduction, Lorca's theater has been examined at the formal level from the high rationalist, empirico-mimetic premises that he found confining and detrimental to the evolution of his theater.

Indeed, the principal casualty of the Modernist rejection of empirico-mimeticism is the very idea of a fundamental interrelationship, or bond, between visual and verbal signs: that words and images can, and do, faithfully translate each other as they become the exclusive participants in the creation of an autonomous, auto-referential fictional world. At the formal and political extremes of Modernism, this is expressed in the attempt to hybridize the separate functions of words and images in the creation of a modern hieroglyphics that effectively fuses their separate functions. Rather than a mimetic re-presenting, the Modernist becomes more concerned with rendering actual presences, "primary apparitions" or traces of a more significant reality that assume various forms, from the exalted image and short poem of Imagists to the automatic writing of the Surrealists. While even the most extreme manifestations of Modernist art center themselves in a ground of "realism" upon which they invariably draw, it is equally true that the Modernist artist does not consider himself or herself bound by the conventional limits of mimesis. Indeed, the Modernist is invariably dedicated to a vision at odds with, and superior to, the ordinary "reality" that he or she is superseding. This not only produces a different mode of art but as well the necessity for a different set of explanations for the process of art.

High stage realism, like its counterpart in narrative, is premised on the complementarity and interchangeability of visual and verbal signs that in turn produce an autonomous, self-referential artistic space. Modernist art posits that spatial autonomy is always incomplete at best as the artist's designs for a better reality invariably clash with the structural and ideological premises of the mimetic paradigm. It is a mistake, therefore, to call Lorca a realist by qualifying that "realism" with some other term (for example, "poetic" or "magic" realism). At no time is Lorca a realist in the traditional sense, and this is especially true of his most mature plays, which witness a progressive enhancement of the more significant metadramatic dimension from which all his mature drama draws its strength and direction. Lorca's social message, if one can truly call it that, is inextricably bound to his vision of theater, which departs significantly from the mimetic tradition of straightforward social messages. This study has sought to account for the neglected dimensions of Lorca's art and thereby to develop a new reading of his theater premised on the most significant reality for Lorca as a dramatist, his authority in the face of a body of theatergoers ill-equipped to accept an innovative agenda for theater.

The intuition of the existence of an "outside" authority that progressively dominates and directs the activity of the stage—an authority Lorca refers to as the "hidden force"—is simply the conceptual/intellectual manifestation of the foundational tenet of Modernist aesthetics. As I have developed at greater length, others in Lorca's immediate poetic circle invoke similar agents/authorities in order to objectify their inspiration in an alternate medium which surpasses the discourse of empirico-mimeticism. In *Reality and Desire* Luis Cernuda proclaims the existence of a "daimonic power" that he senses has assumed authority over his life and art and is controlling his destiny. In *Concerning the Angels*, Rafael Alberti becomes aware of "angels," the persistent empty images of a now spent youth that expose the untenability of his present life. Vicente Aleixandre and Pedro Salinas allude to a transcendent "female" force that provides their art with the direction and sense of satisfaction that their lives in ordinary reality lack. Finally, in "Farther Away" (21) from *Canticle*, Jorge Guillén proclaims the presence of a "better" reality centered in a privileged plane of consciousness where the chaotic elements of ordinary reality are willfully reassimilated into a more significant understanding. In all these poets, mimetic understanding is invariably subverted in favor of a new configuration that supersedes the premises of the earlier paradigm. Whether this subversion proceeds by willful means or by an "automatic" process that the artist considers largely beyond his or her control, the guiding idea of this poetry is that ordinary reality and consciousness are insufficient to account for more significant emergent modes of understanding, the "better realities" that become perhaps the most universal characteristic of the new aesthetic that sweeps Europe during the 1920s and 1930s.

This new aesthetic orientation demands that the nineteenth-century idea of an autonomous and self-referential theater space become instead an arena for the emergence of the "better" reality, or as Lorca expresses it, the "hidden force" that progressively assumes command of the stage. Lorca is very much in line with his Modernist contemporaries throughout Europe as, especially during the thirties, he devises the aesthetic means to bring his intuitions to greater prominence onstage. The presence of the hidden force reorients the visual-verbal sign relationships obtaining in the conventional "four walls" configuration, transforming them instead into indexes that refer the activity on stage to the alternative reality/referent understood to animate it. Lorca needs to be understood as a full participant in the epistemological and ideological overturning that takes place during Modernism. His subversion expresses itself formally in the enhanced prominence of "unstageable" theater signs, indexes and indexical relationships that typically allude to spaces beyond the visible stage. This is most explicitly manifested in *The Public* in the existence of the underground "theater beneath the sand," a presently unstageable theater agenda of which the goal is nevertheless to establish itself authoritatively in a public forum.

Integral to Lorca's understanding of dramatic authority is a fundamentally metadramatic approach to theater that intensifies as he writes what most of his critics have considered to be his most realistic theater. Rather than returning to greater conventional realism, Lorca's most mature theater actually intensifies the subversion of mimetic reality. More important than any social message is his understanding of theater dynamics, which witnesses the creation of a more authoritative theatrical model. As the title of this study suggests, this is perhaps the most significant contribution of his theater, which progressively attempts to bring greater stage authority to a theater scene that had all but abdicated an artistic mission. Performance theory has afforded a working model by which to measure the extent to which Lorca's plays anticipate modern theoretical approaches to theater. To a significant extent, Lorca advocates a theater along the lines of director-centered performance models that assign greatest value to the performance text. Lorca's ideal form of theater, however, is perhaps less collaborative and more hierarchical, closely paralleling Artaud's idea of a Creator "responsible both for the play and the action" (72), the sublimely authoritative synthesis of the functions of the scriptwriter and stage director.

Lorca's response to his critical awareness of the necessity to challenge his audience's control of the stage is to realign the functions of the script and scene in favor of the emergence of a more authoritative agency embodying a model for theater that recognizes the inseparability of these functions. He acknowledges this explicitly in *Don Cristobal's Little Puppet Stage* as the tension between the Poet and the Director results in an unusual resolution: the emergence of a stage director who has fully assimilated the values and discourse of the scriptwriter. This also marks the moment of greater maturity in Lorca's theater as the insights from earlier plays are incorporated into a revised model of playmaking, its ultimate goal the recovery of the space of the stage from the audience. The theater of the 1930s demonstrates the full emergence of Lorca's alternative understanding of theater in an extended process that witnesses the overturning of the theater audience's previously authoritative position. The truest content of the more mature theater is authority itself, as a theatrical and metatheatrical phenomenon. Lorca aggrandizes the audience's powers of vision in these plays to the point of near omniscience, only to diminish that vision severely over the course of the representation in order to herald the presence of a different form of authority, "the profile of a hidden force," that brings into greater focus the offstage agenda announced in *The Public*. As fate would have it, the most fully developed moment of this evolutionary process occurs in Lorca's last autonomous piece of theater, *Play Without A Title*, in the Autor, a creative authority willing to make the sacrifices necessary for the institution of a truly invigorating theater.

The more optimistic and confident direction charted in the *Play Without A Title* as well as the impressive and provocative legacy of ideas for future plays leave little doubt that Lorca would have continued to contribute significantly to the development of Spanish theater had he survived the Spanish Civil War, whether in Spain or abroad. Had he realized his goal of bringing his experimental plays to the stage, the history of the criticism of his theater would certainly have been much different, as Andrew A. Anderson suggests: "Had his experimental plays in their final versions been widely known in the postwar period, it seems to me likely that the textbooks of twentieth-century European drama, concentrating as they do on Pirandello, Eliot, Brecht, and Beckett, would have been written differently, with Lorca on, at the least, an equal footing with these playwrights of international renown" ("Strategy" 223–24). The antithetical views of Lorca that emerge after his assassination, and that persist to this day, might well have been reconciled by the growing authority of Lorca's theater, which, especially in *Play Without A Title*, seems to be moving to surpass the private-public dialectic that dominates but also restrains his theater during the thirties.

Carlos Rojas's prize-winning novel *The Ingenious Gentleman and Poet Federico García Lorca Ascends to the Underworlds*, in fact, examines possible future destinies that Lorca's life and career might have expressed had he not been arrested in Granada at the Rosales house and thereafter assassinated. The novel begins in Lorca's afterlife, the setting for which is a vast theater with multiple stages situated at the different levels of an endless spiral. Here the poet relives scenes from his life and assassination as well as other possible destinies that might have been his. One of these alternative lives is simply to have remained forever waiting at the Rosales house for soldiers that never came to arrest him—a fate that would actually have satisfied the truest yearnings of Bernarda Alba, to remain forever hidden behind the walls of her house "so that not even the grasses would learn of my desolation" (II 1029). The other is to have escaped the war and to have emigrated to the United States in order to become a poet-professor in the manner of others of his early poetic circle who found a comfortable life outside Spain. Finally, Rojas's Lorca publicly scorns official adulation by refusing to accept the Nobel Prize for Literature. By this gesture Rojas's Lorca reaffirms the authority of his work as against the force of official public opinion; the gesture is also fully reflective of the spirit underlying the Autor's judgment in *Play Without A Title* that the public has no right to interfere, "much less judge the work" (II 1071).

Rojas has brilliantly understood the contradictions of Lorca's life in an historical and political context but also, and perhaps better than most literary critics, expressed the fundamental divergence between private and public existences with which Lorca struggled throughout his lifetime. Such possible afterlives are plausible because these alternative destinies are fully grounded in the dialectic that constitutes Lorca's art. As the Spanish Civil War erupts, Lorca's private civil war, most ironically, may well have been approaching something of a resolution, in the form of a greater self-acceptance. Projected works such as *The Destruction of Sodom* and *The Black Ball* suggest a mature willingness to continue, yet with much greater authority, the agenda begun earlier in *The Public*. That the Autor of *Play Without A Title* welcomes the destruction about to overtake the stage suggests that Lorca was ready to move forward to a new moment in his theater, a phase that would not only have witnessed the reconciliation between the "theater in the open air" and the "theater beneath the sand" but that would also have made these concepts publicly available. The authority that Lorca envisions is the freedom to speak truthfully to a wider audience. The revolution proclaimed in *Play Without A Title* simply acknowledges the next logical step in the evolution of a theater that may well have witnessed the full emergence of Lorca as an *autor*, a figure of unquestioned authority—as scriptwriter, stage director, and theatrical producer—fully empowered to revitalize the Spanish stage and thus to accommodate a more generous idea of theater and "the profile of a hidden force when the audience has no further recourse except to pay full attention, filled with spirit and overpowered by the action."

NOTES

Preface

1. What the *Obras* calls "Love Sonnets" are better known as the *Sonnets to Dark Love.* Christopher Maurer and others have considerably increased the volume and availability of Lorca's letters, which reveal the personality of the writer in a greater variety of moods and attitudes. Eutimio Martín has brought to light significant information regarding Lorca's juvenile production, especially his dialogs. Finally, Mario Hernández has assembled a rather comprehensive catalog of Lorca's drawings.

2. Ian Gibson's thorough account of Lorca's life (*Lorca*) is a significant improvement over earlier accounts and testimonies, notably those of Carlos Morla Lynch and Francisco García Lorca that purposely omit important information, especially regarding Lorca's homosexuality.

3. One of the first to advocate such a position is Arturo Barea who, in the aftermath of the Spanish Civil War, labels Lorca a "poet of the people." This view of Lorca as a social dramatist has been championed in recent years by Reed Anderson (*Lorca*) and Andrew A. Anderson ("Strategy"), both of whom view Lorca's avant-gardism at the service of a social message.

4. Among the first to see "Spanishness" as a central aspect of Lorca's work is Dámaso Alonso ("Expresión"), followed by a host of other critics, notable among whom is Cristoph Eich.

5. An earlier generation of mythic/archetypal readings of Lorca's poetry and theater generally inspired in Jungian psychology (Correa [*Mítica*], Allen, et al.) has been succeeded by Freudian and Lacanian readings (Feal Deibe [*Eros, Tragedia*], Ramond, et al.).

6. All quotations from Lorca's writings and public statements are taken from *Obras* with volume and page number given in the text, unless otherwise indicated. I have provided my own translations of all quotations in Spanish; the page references are to the original Spanish text.

7. Lorca himself has given ample testimony that he resented the label of a spontaneous talent. Well-known are his complaints to Jorge Guillén about the myth of his "gypsyness" in the aftermath of the publication of *Gypsy Ballads* (*Romancero gitano*): "They confuse my life and my character. I want nothing of that. The gypsies are a theme. And nothing more. I could just as easily be the poet of sewing needles and hydraulic landscapes" (III 902). In a similar vein is his statement in the Gerardo Diego poetry anthologies of 1931 and 1934: "If it is true that I am a poet by the grace of God—or the devil—it is also true that I am a poet by the grace of technique and effort, and of absolutely understanding what a poem is" (423). As these quotations suggest, there is a tension between spontaneity and control in Lorca, a self-consciousness of the unconscious and uncontrollable forces at work in his poetry and drama. Additionally, there is a significant intertextual ref-

erencing in a number of his dramas, which suggests a desire to acknowledge a certain temporal evolution and continuity within a context of production that also, and evidently, responds to "intentions" beyond his conscious control.

Chapter 1: Introduction

1. Lorca's overidentification with traditionalism and lyrical primitivism after the Spanish Civil War effectively erases his connection with continental Modernism as it authorizes the view that both his poetry and his theater glorify and embody "Spanishness." The attitude is epitomized in early influential essays by Dámaso Alonso—"Expresión" (1937) and "Generación" (1948)—propagating an idea about Spanish poetry of the 1920s and 1930s that persists unto this day, that it aimed to continue a literary tradition "profoundly rooted in the Spanish national spirit" and consciously rejecting any participation in "other aesthetic movements that cross the national borders in the years immediately preceding the jelling of our generation" ("Generación" 661).

2. Antonio Cao is among the first to study formal aspects of Lorca's theater in relation to avant-garde movements outside Spain, followed by Miriam Balboa Echevarría, who asserts Lorca's alignment with Surrealism.

3. This misdirected candor has had the unfortunate yet undeniable effect of limiting the scope of Lorca's dramatic vision and of authorizing critics to use the homosexual dimension as a convenient explanation for apparent inconsistencies in Lorca's scripts. See, among many other examples, Felicia Hardison Londré's unproductive interpretation of *Yerma* as a mask for "the anguish of a homosexual who knows he will never have children" (*Lorca* 40). In a somewhat more positive vein are studies by Binding and Sahuquillo.

4. Although the Jaussian response model has been criticized recently—Jean Alter has noted that "reception texts usually convey the horizon of expectations of professional critics who, for one reason or another, are likely to deviate from the actual reception by real audiences, and hence from real expectations" (218)—nevertheless, the most significant study to date of Lorca's theater to align itself with a tendency in performance studies, by Luis Fernández Cifuentes, does indeed adopt the Jaussian model with felicitous results.

5. See Hannah Arendt (92–93) for a cogent discussion of authority and its relation to the concepts of power and freedom.

6. Dru Dougherty and María Francisca Vilches offer a view of the state of professionalism of the Madrid theater scene as Lorca begins his career: "During this period the function of the stage director is barely defined, in relation to the way in which we presently understand it. The concept of 'regisseur' was known by a few critics . . . but in actual practice the figure of the stage director was blurred with that of the lead actor or the theatrical producer" (52–53).

7. See Manfred Pfister (19–22) for a description of the standard formal components of the 19th- and early 20th-century stage.

8. In part because of his experience as director of the La Barraca theater group, Lorca's evolving notion of theater dynamics brings him to an understanding of the need for a more global stage authority than simply a stage director. His *autor* thus resembles the legendary figures of the Spanish classical stage, often called *autores*, who participated in all aspects of the theater process, which included acting and directing as well as the writing of dialog.

9. Peirce considers that a *"symbol* is a sign which would lose the character which renders it a sign if there were no interpretant. Such is any utterance of speech which signifies what it does only by virtue of its being understood to have that signification" (170).

10. Peirce considers "a great distinguishing property of the icon is that by the direct observation of it other truths concerning its object can be discovered than those which suffice to determine its construction" (158).

11. Peirce further instructs: "Anything which focuses the attention is an index. Anything which startles us is an index, in so far as it marks the junction between two portions of experience" (161).

12. Peirce specifically characterizes the photograph as an index since it is produced under circumstances that force it "to correspond point by point to nature" (159). See also Krauss for a further explanation of why "drawings and paintings are icons, while photographs are indexes" (26).

13. For a general discussion of the tradition of visual-verbal interrelationships in a European and Modernist context, see W. J. T. Mitchell and Wendy Steiner.

14. Byrd also mentions Lorca's impressive use of lighting "with target focusing of the lights upon the central figures and the simple set pieces behind them" as well as the removal of the prompter's box in order to eliminate physical barriers between actors and audience (*Barraca* 73).

15. The Club Anfistora was originally called the Club Teatral de Cultura. Margarita Ucelay offers an excellent portrait of Lorca as director of "those works of his that the commercial theater rejected" ("Anfistora" 54), which he brought to the Anfistora group. That he had such outlets at all meant that for practical, if not commercial purposes, Lorca had considerable artistic freedom in Madrid. That Lorca remained in Madrid—to continue to "travel around my garden" (II 304) rather than to follow in the footsteps of Dalí and Buñuel who found freedom and fame in France—suggests, among other things, that by 1936 there were enough incentives and rewards for Lorca to consider that his intentions with regard to the reform of the Spanish stage were meeting with some success.

Chapter 2: The Early Theater

1. Lorca communicates his growing awareness of this necessary function rather negatively, however, in the form of characters who intrude upon a preexisting scene. Beginning in earnest with Cristobita's abrupt intrusion into Rosita's domestic life in *Tragicomedy of Don Cristobal and Miss Rosita*, the phenomenon intensifies with Pedrosa's disruption of Mariana's secluded life in *Mariana Pineda*.

2. It is tempting to cite Fernández Cifuentes's (29–44) and Lima's (55–64) eloquent reasons for considering this a misunderstood work of early genius. In fact, the prolog is self-consciously aware of the play's failure to explain itself on its own terms. Although elaborate and detailed, the scenario only serves to intensify the distancing of the audience from the story.

3. Anderson confirms as much when he further states that the prolog "is imagining an ideal audience for this play" (*"Prólogos"* 215). At this early point in his evolution, Lorca is more concerned with his private imaginative world than with the exigencies of performance. He has approached his task here as would a puppetmaster who, in addition to directing the movements of his characters (and speaking their dialog), is also the most prominent member of the audience.

4. Lorca alludes to Shakespeare throughout his career (see Andrew A. Anderson "Shakespearian"). In addition to the inspirational value and authority of Shakespeare, Lorca and other contemporaries, especially Cernuda, are attracted to what they perceive, correctly or incorrectly, to be Shakespeare's sympathy toward unorthodox sexual orientations. For Lorca, by now well aware of his homosexuality, Shakespeare's apparent endorsement of the involuntary and accidental nature of love and love's objects in *A Midsummer Night's Dream* (and the *Sonnets*) lends tremendous justifying authority to a theater struggling to define its own attitudes to this very issue.

5. For a discussion of Lorca's considerable juvenile production, see Martín (147–253).

6. Sahuquillo has noted a number of homosexual allusions in the play, not the least of which are the butterfly, which as a derogatory term (*mariposa*) is also frequently used to refer to homosexuals, and Alacranito, whose voracious appetite for body parts also parodies a homosexual orientation. While not specifically attributing the underlying tensions of the play to Lorca's anxiety over his homosexuality, Ruíz Ramón suggests that a personal anecdote, "a crisis of growth," an "eruption of a new force that disturbs the order of the senses and the spirit bringing forth a new anxiety" (*Historia* 178), lies at the heart of the pessimistic vision that governs the play.

7. This seems to be another holdover from Lorca's juvenile writing, concerned in works such as *Christ* (*Cristo*), *Shadow* (*Sombra*), and *Mystics* (*Místicas*) with reconciling the tenets of orthodox Christianity with personal expressions of religiosity and faith. See Martín (200–54) for a discussion.

8. Grasses are also part of the symbolic geography of Lorca's lyric poetry and on occasion serve as visual correlatives for activity in the unconscious in the poetry of Aleixandre, Alberti, and Cernuda.

9. The concept *burla* also carries consistent negative associations in Lorca's poetry, for example, in the "Double Poem of Lake Eden" of *Poet in New York* where he laments his early tendency to disguise the truth in allusions by means of "the deceptiveness (*burla*) and suggestiveness of the word" (I 490). As is deducible from the goals and purposes of Lola's version of theater, the same critique of superficiality and unworthiness, albeit more indirectly, also applies in the present context.

10. In correspondence, Lorca describes Mosquito in the following terms: "Mosquito is Shakespeare's Puck, half spirit (*duende*), half child, half insect" (Maurer II 166). Lorca also uses Mosquito as the spokesperson for the prolog, which was appended to the original text in 1932, when Lorca wrote the companion piece *Don Cristobal's Little Puppet Stage* (*El retablillo de don Cristóbal*). I shall discuss the appended prolog in chapter four.

11. This abrupt curtailment of the theatrical illusion effectively serves to shift the locus of the representation at this moment from the stage proper to the puppetmaster, since Mosquito and Cristobita, as embodiments of the theater functions, mutually expose each other's limitations. As the disruption of self-referentiality continues in Lorca's subsequent theater, the phenomenon of indexicality, signaling the presence of a more authoritative referent beyond the visible and audible stage, also intensifies.

12. The most comprehensive treatment of this play is offered by Robert Havard (*Pineda*), who places perhaps too much emphasis on the historical Mariana Pineda who bears only a mild resemblance to Lorca's character. Although an historical

approach to this play is not inappropriate, it ultimately serves to reinforce the mistaken impression of Lorca's creation of a straightforward realism.

13. Silence is an important theme throughout Lorca's theater (see Dougherty "Silencio"). In this play, the physical site of Mariana's silence, her throat, is prominently featured. Besides emphasizing the mortal consequences of remaining silent about the names of her fellow conspirators, the prominence of the image of the throat is also related to an emerging avant-garde agenda in which the production of language is often represented as originating in the throat rather than the intellect, at times involuntarily in the form of a cough. (Besides the earlier cited poem by Alberti, see also, among many others, Aleixandre's "On the Same Earth" ("Sobre la misma tierra") from Destruction or Love (La destrucción o el amor). This wider artistic context underscores the importance of silence, for it suggests that the throat is the locus of more than simply political secrets.

14. The name Pedrosa also brings with it a possible allusion to the contemporary stage criticism since simultaneous with the writing and staging of this play is the prominence of Manuel Pedroso, the most forceful Spanish advocate for a strong, even dictatorial, stage director. Dougherty and Vilches relate that Pedroso "questioned the supremacy of the dramatic text" (53) and that "the authority of the stage director was crucial for any reform of the theater since he brought a new mode of organizing the theatrical spectacle" (53–54). The image of Pedrosa as a destructive public eye, an unassailable authority who dictates the conditions under which Mariana will live or die on the executioner's stage, is offset only by Mariana's refusal to speak, which limits his leverage over her and which forces him to remain "the one / who awaits, like always, your news [noticias] (II 255), words which further allude to the vulnerability of all those involved in theater production, including stage directors, to "news"—that is, the reviews provided by theater critics.

15. Mariana's conjecture about her possible rescue by Don Pedro is ironic, in the larger context of Lorca's poetry, since her specific words, "Don Pedro will come on horseback / like a madman" (II 251), strongly recall Lorca's satiric ballad "Ridicule of Don Pedro on Horseback" ("Burla de don Pedro a caballo") which depicts the trivialization of a character who also fails to fulfill the expectations of his amorous role.

Chapter 3: The Farces

1. The dates of these dialogs are approximately between 1925 and 1927, which coincides with the completion of Mariana Pineda and the writing of The Shoemaker's Prodigious Wife and Perlimplín.

2. Lorca calls "Buster Keaton's Walk" ("El paseo de Buster Keaton") a "photographed dialog" (III 930) intended to be read rather than performed (Havard "Keaton" 14) while the "Mute Dialog of the Carthusians" ("Diálogo mudo de los cartujos") is expressed, in the absence of words, exclusively by punctuation marks.

3. Margarita Ucelay suggests that "by the early months of 1926 . . . we may consider Perlimplín a finished work" (Perlimplín 129). Owing perhaps as much to Lorca's intention to cast a retired military officer (Gibson Lorca I 590) in the principal role as to its content, censors canceled the production of Perlimplín during preparations for a February, 1929 premiere and confiscated the existing copies of the script, which were taken to police headquarters where they remained for three years (Gibson I 590–92). At Lorca's urging, along with the enticement to let the

Club Teatral de Cultura (later renamed the Club Anfistora) premiere the play, Pura Maórtua de Ucelay, assisted by the friendlier political climate of the Second Republic, retrieved a copy of the manuscript, not the original, from the censors (Ucelay "Aleluyas" 92), thereby allowing her group to stage an in camara production in April, 1933 (Gibson II 232).

4. By Buñuel's account, of questionable reliability, he is rather brutal in his assessment of the piece ("excrement" [*mierda*] [100–1]), with which Dalí strongly concurs.

5. In the absence of professional directors Spanish stage companies of the twenties and thirties were typically managed by a lead actor or actress. Theater productions were often dominated by impresarios motivated usually by profit, which favored scripts that pandered to audience gratification.

6. In this context, fear further refers to the consequences of the audience's incapacity to acknowledge innovation. The "other surroundings" may refer to private scenarios of the imagination to which the desire for a more original theater must retreat.

7. The proof for this assertion is *Perlimplín*, itself a farce like *The Shoemaker's Prodigious Wife*, but with a radically different box-office history. The conventional setting facilitates *The Shoemaker's Prodigious Wife's* commercial success and tremendously enhances Lorca's standing in the theater while *Perlimplín's* premiere is not only delayed for over four years but plays before a severely reduced audience.

8. Resistance within conformity becomes perhaps the most distinguishing feature of Lorca's female characters throughout his later theater. Geraldine Cleary Nichols (335) interprets the Wife's resistance in relation to crossing the threshold from childhood to adulthood, a view that reinforces her imaginative separateness. Farris Anderson stresses the Wife's resistance in metatheatrical terms as a "resistance to being dramatized" ("Metatheatre" 288), that is, to becoming part of a scenario.

9. Farris Anderson portrays the exchange between the Wife and the *autor* as a struggle to dominate the stage "embodied in an argument between two characters who possess differing measures of authority in the theatrical process" ("Metatheatre" 282).

10. The Wife's story does not rightly conclude but is abruptly interrupted with the threat of real brutality by an impatient onstage audience of townspeople, a prophetic presentiment of the fate of the "unstageable plays" (III 674), made so by "the spectators [who] would arise indignant and would prohibit the representation from continuing" (III 557).

11. This figure is resurrected in the Magician (Prestidigitador) of *The Public*. The *burla* motif reappears to reinforce the idea of a retreat from a more forceful intention. Reed Anderson's assertion that Lorca is attempting to instruct his audience how to respond and cultivating them for something unfamiliar is implausible ("*Prólogos*" 216–17). See also Morris ("Divertissement" 797) and Elvira Aguirre (57).

12. Nichols (336) reports that Lorca himself played the role of the *autor* on opening night.

13. Even after the Shoemaker abandons her, the Wife's reaction is continued resistance: "I will not resign myself. I will not resign myself" (II 334). Resistance becomes even more prominent in the later plays. Inés Marful has commented upon

the continuity between the earlier characters and the later plays with more overtly serious themes such as *Yerma*, calling the Wife, in fact, an "*alter ego* of Yerma at the level of farce" (54).

14. There is a greater overlap in the range of activities of characters who embody a principal theater function. In comparison to *Mariana Pineda*, the boundaries are somewhat blurred, as the imagination-centered Wife takes an active interest in the baser aspects of reality, such as money. This has prompted Balboa Echevarría to see her as a "director [of the affairs of the house] who transforms herself into a stage director" (51). A better explanation is that the "poetic creature" is contaminated by factors that diminish her principal role, to speak and to have others listen.

15. Beginning with *The Butterfly's Spell*, the probability or certainty of childless marriages is a constant feature of Lorca's couples.

16. The allusion to theater criticism is not accidental. Fernández Cifuentes notes that, especially during this period of his career, Lorca "paid close attention to the reviews of his productions" (102).

17. In so doing, she transforms the Shoemaker's imagined fears into reality. The theme of "the house that is no longer my house," enunciated in "Somnambular Ballad," becomes by this moment a consistent and increasingly intense theme. Confinement to the "four walls" is also a clear allusion to the four-walls setting of conventional theater, another strong indication of the domestication of this "poetic creature."

18. This theme appears prominently in the poetry in "The Unfaithful Married Woman" ("La casada infiel") of *Gypsy Ballads*, in which a gypsy becomes obsessed with telling the story of his deception at the hands of a married woman who told him she was a maiden.

19. There is at present no critical consensus about the ending to this play. Edwards, however, who sees it as "happy, optimistic" (45) represents a decidedly minority position. Indeed, the true site of any "ending," happy or otherwise, lies in the imagination of the theater audience.

20. Fernández Cifuentes observes that "the work returns then to the point of departure, without any resolution whatsoever, without having canceled or modified the conflict and/or the character" (107).

21. Allen (37–38) discounts any idea of adult eroticism and considers that, since the *aleluya* in its last manifestation is a children's genre, the play is actually dealing with regressive infantile sexuality. The fact that the *aleluya* evolves from both a religious and a satirical tradition only to conclude as a lesser version of itself suggests that its attractiveness for Lorca is precisely the emptiness of its literary authority in relation to its more substantial past.

22. Setting the Shoemaker's shop completely in white suggests as well the insipidness and colorlessness of his imagination.

23. For the sake of consistency, I have chosen to follow the version of the play as it appears in the *Obras*. I am aware of certain differences, which I do not consider significant, between this edition and Ucelay's more recent version.

24. In the context of Spanish classical theater in which the age of the marriage partners at times offers a tacit commentary about the appropriateness or inappropriateness of a given union (for example, Calderón's *The Painter of His Dishonor* [*El pintor de su deshonra*] and Moratín's *The Yes of the Girls* [*El sí de las niñas*]), in

comparison to the Shoemaker and the Wife, Perlimplín and Belisa are more accept-able as partners.

25. As opposed to *gente* ("people"). Lorca's use of *gentes* here and in subsequent plays alludes to a heterogeneous group more extensive than the stage society, that includes the actual theater audience.

26. This initiates a conscious attitude that is repeated throughout Lorca's sub-sequent theater, for example, in *The Public* where the First Student says: "The pub-lic must not traverse the silk screens and pasteboards that the poet devises in the privacy of his bedroom" (II 653). Even more explicit is the Autor of *Play Without A Title* who declares: "Paying for theater stalls does not imply the right to interrupt the one who is speaking, much less to judge the work" (II 1071).

27. This effectively reenacts the *autor*'s lament in *The Shoemaker's Prodigious Wife* as he surveys the state of theater only to find that "poetry retreats from the stage in search of other surroundings." Belisa also recalls the butterfly's detached attitude in *The Butterfly's Spell*.

28. Lyon, in an otherwise perceptive study that recognizes a strong relationship between *The Shoemaker's Prodigious Wife* and *Perlimplín* (235), nevertheless con-siders Belisa to be as devoid of imagination as are Perlimplín and the Shoemaker (237). It is fairer to say, however, that Belisa possesses an ungrounded fancy only minimally connected to the scene.

29. Freudian readings stress Marcolfa's motherly role (her name alludes to two prime maternal symbols, *mar* ("sea") and *golfa* ("gulf"). In whatever capacity, how-ever, the servant becomes a prominent fixture of Lorca's theater from this point forward.

Chapter 4: Experimental Theater

1. According to Andrew A. Anderson, work for both plays had begun by the spring of 1930 and had concluded by the summer of 1931 ("Strategy" 212). There is a continuing tendency, nevertheless, to isolate these plays from their chronologi-cal context (see Fernández Cifuentes, Vitale).

2. The first major study of *As Soon As Five Years Pass* was not until 1966 (Knight) while Rafael Martínez Nadal's critical study of *The Public* in 1970 actually predated the play's publication by some eight years. Unfortunately, the play has generated more speculation about Lorca's homosexuality (see Belamich "Polos" 79–85, "Claves" 108; Granell 110–14) than about avant-garde playmaking.

3. A long list of critical commentators—Knight, Sapojnikoff, Klein, Londré ("Metamorphosis"), Doménech, Zdenek, and others—consider the Youth to be the dream projection of himself.

4. A more pessimistic interpretation is offered by Farris Anderson, for whom the play depicts "the breakdown of personality . . . cast . . . in the languages and processes of theatre itself" ("Design" 250).

5. Fernández Cifuentes maintains that the Old Man's insistence upon tomor-row means that "tomorrow belongs to old age" (265). I consider, however, that "to-morrow" signifies a return to the conscious present, the literal "tomorrow" at the conclusion of the dream: not old age but the more distasteful prospect of mature adult life in today's world.

6. The Bride exists in multiple images, each corresponding to a different space (or plane) and moment within the dream.

7. This exchange also underscores the play's arbitrary quality since the multiple spaces and vast stretches of time in fact refer to activities contained within a compact medium "without distance beneath your face."

8. Indeed, his attraction to the Bride begins in earnest only after she spurns him.

9. This "open-air" setting is clearly another level within the dream just as the "theater in the open air" in *The Public* may simply refer to another plane or state of consciousness rather than to an actual public site.

10. Greater maturity brings the consciousness that living is synonymous with performing.

11. Fernández Cifuentes (274) considers the three assassins to symbolize three different times corresponding to childhood, adolescence, and old age. However, since they are very much like the Youth, they may simply embody the expectations from beyond his private domain that he has failed to meet.

12. This is the decisive feature of the experimental theater. The spectator must accept or reject these plays completely on their own terms.

13. The horses have been identified with sexuality. María Clementa Millán calls them the "expression of the impulses of amorous passion" (*Público* 59) while Martínez Nadal understands them in relation to "sexual energy" (205). Gullón, however, sees them as positive forces that "seek the renovation of the theatre that the Director refuses to accept" ("Radiografía" 85). My understanding is that they visually embody the relationship between the Director and his imagination. Once his imagination is drained of its vitality, symbolized in his lack of capital, the horses abandon him.

14. In addition to associations with Shakespeare's Globe Theater and the "open-air" theater in *As Soon As Five Years Pass*, the poles formed by the "theater in the open air" and the "theater beneath the sand" also invoke the sunken depths of Dante's *Inferno*, specifically Cantos XV and XVI, which feature a scenario of burning sand where the homosexual orientation of four public figures—Brunetto Latini and the three Florentines—is finally exposed. More than referring to a specific locale, these theaters exist primarily as states of mind-imagination, as the character Federico García Lorca reminds in the *Dialog with Luis Buñuel:* "from North to South on the weathervane on the roof there is the same distance as from one Pole to the other Pole" (II 304).

15. This is simply a more explicit exposition of the representational paradigm developed in *As Soon As Five Years Pass*.

16. This is also underscored in the "Solo by the Idiot Shepherd," which in the script precedes the sixth tableau (Rubia Barcia proposes it as a prolog or first tableau [*Público* 240–41]). The Idiot Shepherd, something of a wardrobe man in charge of the characters' masks, embodies the arbitrariness and irrationality by which identities are assigned.

17. Edwards also observes: "In *The Public* there is no separation between its action and its audience" (68).

18. *Blenamiboá* is also a hieroglyph, an icon of reversal, which succinctly describes how the characters function: not as autonomous subjects but as extensions of, visual shorthand for, the force that has authorized them.

19. There is no critical agreement about the role of the Emperor. Belamich sees him as a "titanic power . . . genie of masculine love" ("Polos" 83) whereas Millán associates him with the First Man and the Red Nude "in that each one represents

one of the distinct planes of the hidden force" ("Verdad" 22). Edwards offers a view closer to my own when he suggests that the "one" for which the Emperor calls is to be equated with "perfect homosexual love" (74). "Perfect" homosexual love for Lorca, however, means unconsummated love.

20. Often associated with shallow artistry (Londré Lorca 51), the Magician's contribution is nevertheless integral to the mature theater paradigm (see Rubia Barcia "Naked" 251), as will become apparent in the later theater.

21. While Lorca spectacularizes his play in a manner perhaps befiting the tastes of the Magician, the script remains relatively unchanged. The prolog, however, is substantially different from the earlier version.

22. It should be noted that, while it is possible that he could be cast as simply another puppet character, the Director here fulfills a human role, as puppetmaster, while the Poet is a puppet.

23. This is quite similar to the phenomenon in The Public of the Director's defense of the theater beneath the sand after the demise of the First Man.

Chapter 5: *Blood Wedding*

1. Among the many early advocates of this position are Barea (34–56) and Busette (29–45). Edwards (151–56) and others, however, continue to echo this "realistic" view.

2. Other noteworthy studies in this vein include Allen (161–212), Correa (Mítica 82–116), Feal Deibe (Eros 229–59; "Sacrificio" 270–87), and Palley (74–79), among many others.

3. For example, Cao (98) sees very little carry over from the experimental plays. Andrew A. Anderson takes the somewhat ambivalent position that Lorca was "simultaneously 'social' and 'avant-garde' " ("Strategy" 218) in the "rural dramas." Fernández Cifuentes, while he reads the plays "as something of an alternative to the most authoritative theater conventions of the time" (146), namely, the theater of Benavente, does not discuss the play in relation to the experimental theater. Londré (145–80), however, recognizes a much closer relationship between the more mature theater and the experimental plays, as has Balboa Echevarría who provides one of the strongest endorsements that in the mature theater Lorca is continuing rather than abandoning an avant-garde agenda: "The creation of As Soon As Five Years Pass and The Public will move Lorca to widen his vital aesthetic vision and will permit him to project these works in subsequent plays. The surrealistic theater of Lorca is not a theater left behind but rather a key to the final search, it is for Lorca an intense and desperate search to find a dramatic form that can contain his wider vision of the world" (26).

4. The fact that Lorca calls this play a "poem" testifies to his awareness of its difficulty within conventional contexts of mimetic space. As of this statement, The Public remains a two-dimensional written script, perhaps to be read to others but not ready to be performed.

5. Plans to stage As Soon As Five Years Pass are announced as early as 1933 (III 527) and an actual rehearsal had begun during the spring of 1936. In declarations to Martínez Nadal and others, Lorca made it clear that he believed that there would also come a time "within ten or twenty years" (Caballos 19) when The Public would be produced.

6. The reference to the window may also be an allusion to classical conven-

tions in painting, whereby scenes are rendered in a manner that recreates the act of looking out of a window.

7. Part of such an understanding includes the Magician, present in the earlier plays in the form of *burlas* and disguises. In *The Public*, this aspect of the theater process is personified as a pragmatic consciousness interested less in idealistic experimentation than in devising illusions that will have success in front of audiences. His suggestion to the Director that *A Midsummer Night's Dream* would have been a much better choice for adaptation than *Romeo and Juliet* is sound. The utilitarian caution of the Magician, vital to the success of Lorca's commercial theater, is perhaps acknowledged here in the choice of a rural, backwater scenario which, in contradistinction to the Director's desire to "express what happens every day in all the large cities" (II 664), offers a much simpler set of social relationships. This will become especially significant in the quasipastoral setting of *Yerma*.

8. In Lorca's poetic circle, the two-dimensional plane as a metaphor for consciousness is rather common. In Guillén, planeness or compactness is closely associated with an epiphanic experience, for example, the planeness of a tabletop in "Nature Alive" ("Naturaleza viva") becomes a correlative for the activity of consciousness. The two-dimensional compactness of the Youth's dream world, however, is but a prelude to its corruption and destruction.

9. Relating his reaction to Lorca's presentation of the play to friends at his home, Carlos Morla Lynch makes a fundamental observation about the title's effect on the spectator: "The title does not seduce me. I find it excessively melodramatic, 'Echegarayesque,' . . . inadequate for a work so beautiful, so full of light within the context of the cruelties that it contains. Besides, the word 'blood' reveals, even before the curtain is raised that the plot will culminate in an atmosphere of murder or suicide" (285–86). The title encourages the viewer to project a conclusion, to look for blood before there is blood. Likewise, the expressionistic use of color, the yellowness that dominates the visual scene of the Mother's house, not only reflects her bitterness but has the effect of discrediting the Bridegroom's desire to make a fresh start. The visual space of the drama is from the outset dominated by the blood discourse that precedes everything.

10. Although caves are part of the Andalusian geography, in the context of the experimental theater, situating the Bride's house in a cave also serves to allude to the tunnel from *The Public*, a truer configuration of Lorca's idea of the stage. Indeed, the Bride's cave opens a window to the "open air" as it also extends "beneath the sand."

11. There are two routes to the church. The ten-league route via the road is exactly double the more direct route on horseback "through the brook" (II 738) that Leonardo is prevented from taking by his wife, who insists that he drive their carriage. The outline of the routes forms an equilateral triangle, which again underscores Leonardo's role, and now his impotence, in the love triangle. Equally significant regarding the vast distances alluded to in the play is the apparent ease with which such distances can be circumvented (see note 15), which further enhances the idea of the imaginative variability of space.

12. In relation to other Modernist positions regarding the relation of dreams to empirical reality, Lorca's is a moderate one, as the Harlequin emphasizes in act III of *As Soon As Five Years Pass*, in which other possible configurations of this relationship are examined.

13. There is a strong similarity between this scene and sentiments expressed in

"Waltz in the Branches" ("Vals en las ramas") of *Poet in New York*, set in a wood that also features the accompaniment of waltz music from stringed instruments.

14. This is an ingenious vehicle for Lorca to allude, in a licit way, to the homosexuality and illicit violence prominent in the unstageable plays. A salient aspect of Dante's narration is the exposure of the homosexuality of his former teacher. Fear of public exposure has also been a prominent concern of a number of Lorca's characters, which makes the parallel with this episode in *Inferno* all the more compelling.

15. There is further evidence in the text that the association with Dante is carefully crafted, the likely intention of which is to disassociate this landscape further from a mimetically reproducible "Andalusian" time and space. For example, when the Mother greets the Bride's father in act I after remarking that the journey has taken four hours by carriage through desolate, treeless terrain, they engage in a brief exchange in which it is suggested that there are other possible routes. The father remarks that "you have come by the longer route" to which the Mother replies, "I am too old to walk across the mounds [*terreras*] of the river" (II 25), which suggests that the trip is actually much shorter, even walkable, if one is willing to cross the river at a fordable point by means of the *terreras*. Since *terrera* refers to a mound or an accumulation of earth, the Mother may be referring to a slide of earth or rocks that affords a much more direct crossing of the river on foot to the Bride's cave.

This reference is another detail that corresponds to the Dantesque geography of the seventh circle of Hell in that, as a consequence of a rockslide during Christ's harrowing of Hell, a natural bridge forms that affords Dante a much easier passage into this circle. The father's remark about the "longer route" strongly alludes to the pretext under which *Inferno* itself proceeds, the need to take another route, *altro vïaggio* (Canto I, v. 91), and not the shorter way, *il corto andar* (Canto II, v. 120). Finally, the fact that the lovers are intercepted by a group of horsemen at and in the river is also suggestive of the scene around the bloody Phlegethon patrolled by centaurs. The allusions to great distances and spaces in the play are directly contradicted by others, further enhancing the notion that space is a variable imaginative construct. As the spectator becomes conscious of his or her imagination as authoritative in regard to the representation, there is a simultaneous disruption of the comfortableness and predictability of the viewer-dominated scenario. Beginning with act III, the play reveals other dimensions that transform it into something unimagined.

16. Fernández Cifuentes concludes his discussion on a somewhat similar note: "the discourse of *Blood Wedding* constitutes a type of language object; verse and prose are better understood as conflictive physical presences than as conceptual vehicles" (159). Indeed, the theater signs are surpassing self-referentiality in order to become indexes of the more authoritative agency working through the visual-verbal entities on stage.

Chapter 6: *Yerma* and *Doña Rosita, the Spinster*

1. This recalls Lorca's reference to *The Public* as "a poem to hiss at."

2. For a discussion of tragedy and tragicomedy in the context of Spanish Golden Age theater, see Gail Bradbury. To date, there is no consensus as to whether *Yerma* is a tragedy or something else, perhaps a consequence of the failure to con-

sider that Lorca is actually offering a critique of classical tragedy. Gustavo Correa invokes the play's "Spanishness" to suggest that "[v]ery possibly *Yerma* would not even be a tragedy outside Spain," suggesting that it is a type of honor drama since "social honor . . . becomes the highest regulatory principle of society" ("Honor" 99–100). Sumner Greenfield ("Yerma" 18) and Ruíz Ramón (*Historia* 203) interpret Yerma's violence as an affirmation of her personal integrity and indomitability, which further situates the play within the *comedia* tragicomic tradition. Carlos Feal Deibe, however, associates the play with Euripidean tragedy since he considers that Yerma's incapacity for satisfaction transforms her into a type of death goddess who rejects all men ("Euripides" 512–16). Finally, Philip Silver does not consider *Yerma* a real tragedy since Yerma simply becomes unhinged as a consequence of subscribing to an "anti-natural" view of the world (184–88).

3. A. A. Parker, in fact, has advocated that a principle of poetic justice is at work in all Golden Age plays. Although Parker's ideas have less acceptance today, few scholars are willing to advance the thesis that the classical idea of tragedy is a significant dimension of Golden Age theater.

4. The invitation to analysis so prominent in *Yerma* has, unfortunately, also been accompanied by a tendency among critics to psychoanalyze Lorca. For example, Grace Alvarez-Altman considers that "Yerma is Lorca himself crying in the wilderness for his son" (96) while María Carmen Bobes interprets the obsessive behavior of a "character in disagreement with her existence, with her appetites, with her own desires" as the only acceptable expression "not only for society, but, especially, for the author" (85).

5. Victor describes Juan's ambitions in terms of capital: "He wants to bring together [*juntar*] money and he will do it" (II 815). *Juntar* recalls the Padre's lament in *Blood Wedding* about the separation of the properties of the Bridegroom and Bride. Juan effectively fulfills such an ideal over the course of the play by his purchases of land.

6. Many critics—to name but a few, Morris ("Anchor" 288, 291), Reed Anderson (*Yerma* 53), Baumgarten (296), and Greenfield ("Yerma" 19)—accept unquestioningly the peasant opinions regarding the relationship between attitudes toward sex and infertility, in regard to which Yerma seems lacking. I believe, however, that these attitudes are actually more expressive of city people—that is, attitudes toward sexuality more likely to be encountered in members of Lorca's actual theater audience—than of 19th-century peasants. This is also in keeping with a pastoral scenario—the shepherds in pastoral are refugees from the court in the guise of shepherds—as opposed to a starkly naturalistic peasant setting.

7. This strongly recalls the Mother's vision in *Blood Wedding* at the end of act II where she also suggests that events have actually been moving "backwards" in anticipation of the "hour of the blood."

8. The *comedia* abounds in examples in which civil authorities intervene merely to affirm the actions of parties who take the law into their own hands (e.g., *Fuenteovejuna, The Doctor of His Honor*). A similar possibility applies here as well, especially if Juan's proposition to Yerma may be considered "unnatural." Parr suggests that "Juan wants her to kiss him in a perverse way, and not in the mouth" (27). See also Baumgarten (297).

9. For Pfister, the basis for the modern stage is a scenario in which when "the audience looks into a room, one of whose walls is missing—apparently without the actors within that room being aware of this" (22).

10. Fernández Cifuentes' suggestion—"not things or deeds but words rule the course of the work; and further: words are the things and deeds in the work" (169)—is misleading because autoreferential verbal signs are themselves superseded by Yerma's more profound awareness of a hidden force residing beyond the visual, and audible, field of reference.

11. To affirm the totality of forces working through Yerma is, in relation to the theater functions, a tacit reaffirmation of the premises of the experimental plays, the idea of theater as a competition or struggle between antithetical forces. The physical site of that struggle is Yerma's imagination, limited by the constraints of her society and eventually overwhelmed by the power of a force whose mode of expression surpasses the visual orientation of imagination.

12. The consequences of Victor's earlier observation, "to whom will he leave it when he dies?" (II 815) now manifest themselves. Since his holdings are quite extensive, Juan's death will also diminish the community. More immediately, however, it diminishes the audience, whose powers of vision are also abruptly terminated.

13. Tragedy as expressed here is also associated with the insufficiency of the imagination as a strictly visual medium. The visual-material values of Yerma's society that have rendered her effectively invisible are superseded by an insubstantial medium which reveals to Yerma the true depth of the insufficiency she confronts.

14. Monleón notes a close relationship between *Doña Rosita, the Spinster* and earlier plays, calling it, in fact, "the tragedy of *Yerma* . . . corrected and expanded" (65).

15. Fernández Cifuentes also suggests that for the play's separate acts to become dramatically viable, the spectator's participation is required: "in this cooperation between the spectator and the work is where time is materialized. . . . In this way, the success of *Doña Rosita* is configured precisely as a concession or surrender by the audience to the author; its failure, on the other hand, is nothing more than a resistance by the spectator, a refuge in the old theatrical horizons" (219).

Chapter 7: *The House of Bernarda Alba* and *Play Without A Title*

1. Lorca's uncompleted works, collected by Laffranque (*Teatro inconcluso*) fully continue his innovative agenda. Lorca had completed the better part of the first act of *The Dreams of My Cousin Aurelia* and had written at least one act of *The Destruction of Sodom*, possibly a shorter version of the play to be expanded later (Byrd "Sodoma" 105–6; Andrew A. Anderson "Strategy" 218). Perhaps the most daring of his proposed plays is *The Black Ball*, intended to raise the issue of homosexuality (see Laffranque *Inconcluso* 77–78; the neologism "epentic" [*epéntico*] of the subtitle is a reference to creative individuals who do not marry or procreate).

2. The space of the town corresponds physically to backstage (see Magdalena Cueto 103; Ruíz Ramón "Espacios" 94–95; Taylor 19).

3. Lorca's critics have been as obsessed with qualifying the play's realism as with affirming it. It has been called a work of "magic realism" (Rubia Barcia), "classist realism" (Rubio 172), "poetic realism" (Cabrera 466; García Posada "Transfiguración" 167, among others), "erotic realism" (Alberich 9), as well as the more traditional "social realism" (especially Reed Anderson, Morris *Casa*). The story itself,

in fact, is not original but is taken from actual newspaper stories and photographs. The plot appropriates the real-life story of Francisca Alba Sierra, from the village of Valderrubio, who sealed off her house and her daughters for an extended mourning period (Morris *Casa* 16). Hers is a household with which Lorca was personally familiar since his family owned a nearby house in the same village. It is this house, and not Francisca Alba's, that provides the design for the house in the play (Morris *Casa* 9–10). Although this information may seem to suggest an enhanced realism, to my view it underscores precisely the opposite. The realist idea of an autonomous literary world is, in fact, contradicted and undermined by the presence of outside referents.

4. Ronald Cueto has documented the many instances of "queerness" in the play, aspects that simply do not fit within a realistic context. His assertion that "whatever *La casa de Bernarda Alba* with its accumulation of queerness upon queerness may be, it cannot, by any stretch of the imagination, be treated or produced purely and simply as a 'photographic documentary' " (24–25), however, is correct only if the scope of photography is restricted to mechanical reproduction, an understanding that a host of photographers during the 1920s and 1930s had categorically refuted.

5. Numerous critics have commented on the significant metatheatrical dimension in Lorca's theater, including the present play. See, for example, Farris Anderson ("Metatheatre" 291), Feal Deibe ("Póstumo" 56–57), Silver (170), Balboa Echevarria (26), and Vitale (130). Fernández Cifuentes, in fact, has characterized Bernarda's utterances themselves as essentially metatheatrical, as if they reproduced fragments from a preexisting text or script: "Bernarda's most basic and abundant sentences are quotations or fragments from a superior and unappealable text, a type of moral or ideological code whose representation in the house she has taken over exclusively" (200).

6. Ruíz Ramón has also noted that these are "spaces [that] do not exclude each other . . . since the destruction of one automatically determines the destruction of the other" ("Espacios" 94–95).

7. Havard ("Hidden") has speculated about the economic relationships in the house upon the death of Bernarda's husband, suggesting that his leaving of the bulk of his estate to his stepdaughter is evidence of a carnal relationship between the two as well as being a severe posthumous slap at Bernarda Alba (102, 105).

8. John Crispin has also emphasized Bernarda's vulnerability and weakness, that her will to dominate actually masks an acute sense of insecurity (178).

9. As Vicente Cabrera has suggested, there are numerous Christian references in the play, including the name La Poncia, a feminine derivation of Poncio, an allusion to Pontius Pilate. Indeed, La Poncia ultimately "washes her hands" of active involvement with the house, yielding to Bernarda's stronger will.

10. As Sandra M. Gilbert and Susan Gubar amply demonstrate in the literature by and about women during the nineteenth and early twentieth centuries, the insane woman kept from public view is emblematic of the repressed aspect of the public female self. Evidently, María Josefa's role underscores this tradition but more importantly suggests a deeper space within the house where Bernarda's restrictive understanding of sanity is invalidated. Such "insane" thinking—that is, any thinking in opposition to Bernarda's—is also manifested in the spectator who, like La Poncia, is able to "see through the walls" (II 1014). Adriana Berguero has characterized the discourse in the house as being dominated by the set phrase (303), which

in Bernarda's authoritarian dominion serves to reaffirm a "set" mode of thinking, which is actually no thinking at all: "I do not think. There are things that should not be nor cannot be thought. I command" (II 1030). Any form of independent thinking, therefore, is an "insane" threat to the autonomy of the house, which effectively collapses the distinction between sanity and insanity in a manner that fully parallels the relationship between inside and outside space.

11. Only away from the house and the village does sexual desire seem to empower the parties involved. As La Poncia is quick to point out regarding the case of Paca la Roseta, her tryst is with outsiders because "the men around here are not capable of that" (II 989). In the sense that Pepe's effects are ultimately self-destructive, her statement is also true with regard to Pepe, who is not capable of using his sexual authority to benefit himself.

12. The allusion is to the instantaneous, automatic production of sound, the visual parallel of which is the instantaneous production of the photographic image. The croaking of frogs is also prominent in Lorca's "Ridicule of Don Pedro on Horseback" of *Gypsy Ballads* and the more fully surrealistic "Girl Drowned in a Well" of *Poet in New York*.

13. *Broma* and similar terms connote for Lorca situations producing effects far more severe than expectations warrant. *Broma*, a bad joke that has gotten out of hand, in fact, offers perhaps a better characterization of developments in the play than does "tragedy."

14. The most interesting indexical allusion occurs in Adela's reference to St. Barbara after hearing thunder while confessing her ignorance as to what it means. Bernarda has no explanation either, replying that "the ancients knew many things that we have forgotten" (II 1049). St. Barbara was martyred for her Christian beliefs by her own father who had kept her prisoner and who was himself subsequently killed by a lightning bolt (Bull 118). The logical inference from the biblical story is that something equivalent to a lightning bolt, yet another index powerful enough to "break down the walls" (II 1042) will destroy those who are persecuting Adela. As it turns out, literally everyone involved with the house becomes a recipient of this dubious "wisdom of the ancients," a legacy with effects indeed as severe as being hit by lightning.

15. A real-life index, the shotgun blast, becomes the equivalent to the lightning bolt in the story of St. Barbara.

16. Bernarda's final scream of "Silence!" underscores that the word she had valued most no longer has meaning. In the sense that the house will no longer be above critical commentary, there will never be silence again. Her house has now become the occasion for a public performance, in the imaginations of the townspeople, of perhaps interminable duration.

17. A majority of critics interpret the play's conclusion to signal a defeat for Bernarda, to a greater or lesser degree. A consensus, however, has yet to emerge fully. Londré conjectures that nothing may change for Bernarda (*Lorca* 179) while Edwards sees her "victorious" (255) but controlled by the very things she sought to dominate. Morris, on the other hand, understands Adela's death "to consolidate Bernarda more firmly in power" (*Casa* 116). Although this last reading seems implausible, a stronger form of authority does emerge at the conclusion, but at the expense of Bernarda and all those associated with her house.

18. The issue in *The House of Bernarda Alba*, of course, was not who had the

right to interrupt the representation but rather which offstage domain possessed sufficient authority to sustain such an interruption.

19. The possession of the necessary *finanza* for mounting a theatrical spectacle, which throughout Lorca's career has been as well a moral issue inseparable from the person in need of such support—for example, the early heroines, the Director, and Bernarda Alba—is no longer presented in such conflated terms. The possession or nonpossession of capital is not relevant here as a measure of the worth of the artist or his or her theater project. This marks a qualitative step forward and a further subtle indication of the growing authority of Lorca's theater, which, although still dependent on "the economy of the theater," is nevertheless in a better position to define itself on its own terms.

20. These words strongly recall Bernarda's characterization of the stallion whose powerful hooves against the walls of her house sound as if they will knock them down. The Autor's desire here is exactly opposite that of Bernarda Alba, for he wants his theater to include the outside space that Bernarda so zealously attempts to banish from her private domain.

21. During the writing of *Play Without A Title* Lorca was involved in rehearsals for *As Soon As Five Years Pass*. The much more severe test, of course, was a premiere of *The Public*, which Lorca himself knew would have to wait, at least for the foreseeable future.

WORKS CITED

Abel, Lionel. *Metatheatre.* New York: Hill and Wang, 1963.

Aguirre, Elvira. "Una farsa violenta: *La zapatera prodigiosa* de Federico García Lorca." *Explicación de textos literarios* 13 (1984–85): 53–57.

Aguirre, J. M. "El llanto y la risa de la zapatera prodigiosa." *Bulletin of Hispanic Studies* 58 (1981): 241–50.

Alberich, J. "El erotismo femenino en el teatro de García Lorca." *Papeles de Son Armadans* 39 (1965): 9–36.

Alberti, Leon Battista. *On Painting.* Tr. John R. Spencer. New Haven: Yale UP, 1966.

Alberti, Rafael. *Poesía (1924–1967).* Ed. Aitana Alberti. Madrid: Aguilar, 1972.

Alighieri, Dante. *Inferno.* Ed. John D. Sinclair. New York: Oxford UP, 1975.

Allen, Rupert. *Psyche and Symbol in the Theatre of Federico García Lorca.* Austin: U of Texas P, 1974.

Alonso, Dámaso. "Federico García Lorca y la expresión de lo español." In *Obras completas.* Vol. 4. Madrid: Gredos, 1975. 758–66.

———. "Una generación poética (1920–36)." In *Obras completas.* Vol. 4. Madrid: Gredos, 1975. 653–76.

Alter, Jean. *A Sociosemiotic Theory of Theatre.* Philadelphia: U of Pennsylvania P, 1990.

Alvarez-Altman, Grace. "Poly-Anthroponymical Onomastic Technique in *Yerma* by Federico García Lorca." *Names* 30 (1982): 93–103.

Anderson, Andrew A. "Some Shakespearian Reminiscences in García Lorca's Drama." *Comparative Literature Studies* 22 (1985): 187–210.

———. "The Strategy of García Lorca's Dramatic Composition, 1930–36." *Romance Quarterly* 33 (1986): 211–30.

Anderson, Farris. "The Theatrical Design of Lorca's *Así que pasen cinco años.*" *Journal of Spanish Studies: 20th Century* 7 (1979): 249–78.

———. "*La zapatera prodigiosa:* An Early Example of García Lorca's Metatheatre." *Kentucky Romance Quarterly* 28 (1981): 279–94.

Anderson, Reed. *Federico García Lorca.* New York: Grove Press, 1984.

———. "The Idea of Tragedy in García Lorca's *Yerma.*" *Hispanófila* 25 (1982): 41–60.

———. "The Idea of Tragedy in Lorca's *Bodas de sangre.*" *Revista hispánica moderna* 38 (1974–75): 174–88.

———. "*Prólogos* and *Advertencias:* Lorca's Beginnings." In *"Cuando yo me muera . . . ": Essays in Memory of Federico García Lorca.* Ed. C. B. Morris. New York: U Presses of America, 1988. 209–32.

Arendt, Hannah. "What is Authority?" In *Between Past and Future.* New York: Viking Press, 1968. 91–141.

Artaud, Antonin. *The Theater and Its Double.* In *Collected Works.* Vol. 4. Tr. Victor Corti. London: Calder and Boyars, 1974.

Balboa Echevarría, Miriam. *Lorca: El espacio de la representación. Reflexiones sobre surrealismo y teatro.* Barcelona: Ediciones del Mall, 1986.

Barea, Arturo. *Lorca: The Poet and His People.* Tr. Ilsa Barea. London: Faber and Faber, 1944.

Baumgarten, Murray. "Body's Image: *Yerma, The Player Queen,* and the Upright Posture." *Comparative Drama* 8 (1974): 290–99.

Belamich, André. "Claves para 'El público.' " In *Federico García Lorca. Saggi Critici nel Cinquentenario della Morte.* Ed. Gabriele Morelli. Fasano: Schena, 1988. 107–15.

———. "*El público* y *La casa de Bernarda Alba,* polos opuestos en la dramaturgia de Lorca." In *La casa de Bernarda Alba y el teatro de Federico García Lorca.* Ed. Ricardo Doménech. Madrid: Cátedra, 1985. 77–92.

Ben Chaim, Daphna. *Distance in the Theatre: The Aesthetics of Audience Response.* Ann Arbor, Mich.: UMI Research Press, 1984.

Berguero, Adriana. "Federico García Lorca: Frases hechas y prejuicios para la delimitación del asfixiante espacio de la tragedia." In *"Cuando yo me muera . . . ": Essays in Memory of Federico García Lorca.* Ed. C. B. Morris. New York: U Presses of America, 1988. 295–322.

Binding, Paul. *Lorca: The Gay Imagination.* London: GMP, 1985.

Bobes, María Carmen. "Lectura semiológica de *Yerma.*" In *Lecturas del texto dramático. Variaciones sobre la obra de Lorca.* Ed. Gómez Ubaldo. Oviedo: U de Oviedo, 1990. 67–86.

Bradbury, Gail. "Tragedy and Tragicomedy in the Theatre of Lope de Vega." *Bulletin of Hispanic Studies* 58 (1981): 103–11.

Brecht, Bertold. *Brecht on Theatre.* Tr. John Willett. New York: Hill and Wang, 1964.

Bull, Judith M. " 'Santa Bárbara' and *La casa de Bernarda Alba.*" *Bulletin of Hispanic Studies* 47 (1970): 117–23.

Buñuel, Luis. *Mi último suspiro.* Barcelona: Plaza y Janés, 1982.

Bürger, Peter. *Theory of the Avant-Garde.* Tr. Michael Shaw. Minneapolis: U of Minnesota P, 1984.

Busette, Cedric. *Obra dramática de García Lorca.* Long Island City, N.Y.: Las Américas, 1971. 29–45.

Byrd, Suzanne. *La Barraca and the Spanish National Theatre.* New York: Ediciones Abra, 1975.

———. "*La destrucción de Sodoma:* A Reconstruction of Federico García Lorca's Lost Drama." *García Lorca Review* 4 (1976): 105–8.

Cabrera, Vicente. "Poetic Structure in Lorca's *La casa de Bernarda Alba*." *Hispania* 61 (1978): 466–70.

Cao, Antonio. *Federico García Lorca y las vanguardias: Hacia el teatro*. London: Tamesis, 1984.

Cernuda, Luis. "Historial de un libro." In *Prosa completa*. Ed. Derek Harris and Luis Maristany. Barcelona: Barral, 1975.

———. *La realidad y el deseo*. 4th ed. Mexico City: Fondo de Cultura Económica, 1983.

Correa, Gustavo. "Honor, Blood, and Poetry in *Yerma*." *Drama Review* 7 (1962): 96–110.

———. *La poesía mítica de Federico García Lorca*. Madrid: Gredos, 1970.

Crispin, John. "*La casa de Bernarda Alba* dentro de la visión mítica lorquiana." In *La casa de Bernarda Alba y el teatro de García Lorca*. Madrid: Cátedra, 1985. 171–85.

Cueto, Magdalena. "Transgresión y límites en el teatro de García Lorca: *La casa de Bernarda Alba*." In *Lecturas del texto dramático. Variaciones sobre la obra de Lorca*. Ed. Gómez Ubaldo. Oviedo: U de Oviedo, 1990. 97–116.

Cueto, Ronald. "On the Queerness Rampant in the House of Bernarda Alba." In *Leeds Papers on Lorca and on Civil War Verse*. Ed. Margaret A. Rees. Leeds: Trinity and All Saints' College, 1988. 9–39.

De Marinis, Marco. *The Semiotics of Performance*. Bloomington, Ind.: U of Indiana P, 1993.

Diego, Gerardo, ed. *Poesía española. Antología*. Madrid: Signo, 1934.

Doménech, Ricardo. "Aproximación a *Así que pasen cinco años*." In *Estudios en honor a Ricardo Gullón*. Ed. Luis González-del-Valle and Darío Villanueva. Lincoln, Nebr.: Society of Spanish and Spanish American Studies, 1984. 101–14.

Dougherty, Dru. "El lenguaje del silencio en el teatro de García Lorca." *Anales de la literatura española contemporánea* 11 (1986): 91–110.

Dougherty, Dru and María Francisca Vilches. *La escena madrileña entre 1918 y 1926: Análisis y documentación*. Madrid: Fundamentos, 1980.

Eco, Umberto. *A Theory of Semiotics*. Bloomington: U of Indiana P, 1979.

Edwards, Gwynne. *Lorca: The Theatre Beneath the Sand*. London: Marion Boyars, 1980.

Eich, Christoph. *Federico García Lorca: Poeta de la intensidad*. Madrid: Gredos, 1970.

Elam, Keir. *The Semiotics of Theatre and Drama*. New York: Methuen, 1980.

Eliot, T. S. "Tradition and the Individual Talent." In *Selected Prose of T. S. Eliot*. Ed. Frank Kermode. New York: Harcourt, Brace, Jovanovich, 1975. 37–44.

Feal Deibe, Carlos. *Eros y Lorca*. Barcelona: Edhasa, 1973.

———. "Euripides y Lorca: Observaciones sobre el cuadro final de *Yerma.*" In *Actas del Octavo Congreso de la Asociación Internacional de Hispanistas.* Vol. 1. Madrid: Istmo, 1986. 511–18.

———. "El Lorca póstumo: *El público y Comedia sin título.*" *Anales de la literatura española contemporánea* 6 (1981): 43–62.

———. *Lorca: tragedia y mito.* Ottawa: Dovehouse, 1991.

———. "El sacrificio de la hombría en *Bodas de sangre.*" *MLN* 99 (1984): 270–87.

Felman, Sharon G. "*Perlimplín:* Lorca's Drama About Theatre." *Estreno* 17 (1991): 34–38.

Fernández Cifuentes, Luis. *García Lorca en el teatro: la norma y la diferencia.* Zaragoza: Prensas Universitarias de Zaragoza, 1986.

Fox, Dian. *Refiguring the Hero.* University Park: Pennsylvania State UP, 1991.

García Lorca, Federico. *Obras completas.* 3 vols. Ed. Arturo del Hoyo. Madrid: Aguilar, 1986.

———. *Sonetos del amor oscuro.* Intro. Miguel García-Posada. Epilog Amancio Prada. Madrid: Centro Dramático Nacional, 1986.

García Lorca, Francisco. *Federico y su mundo.* Ed. Mario Hernández. Madrid: Alianza, 1981.

García Posada, Manuel. "Realidad y transfiguración artística en *La casa de Bernarda Alba.*" In *La casa de Bernarda Alba y el teatro de García Lorca.* Ed. Ricardo Doménech. Madrid: Cátedra, 1985. 149–70.

Gibson, Ian. "En torno al primer estreno de Lorca (*El maleficio de la mariposa*)." In *La casa de Bernarda Alba y el teatro de García Lorca.* Ed. Ricardo Doménech. Madrid: Cátedra, 1985. 57–75.

———. *Federico García Lorca.* 2 vols. Barcelona: Grijalbo, 1985 and 1987.

Gil, Ildefonso-Manuel, ed. *Yerma,* 5th ed. Madrid: Cátedra, 1980. 13–35.

Gilbert, Sandra M. and Susan Gubar. *The Madwoman in the Attic.* New Haven: Yale UP, 1984.

González-del-Valle, Luis. *La tragedia en el teatro de Unamuno, Valle-Inclán y García Lorca.* New York: Eliseo Torres, 1975.

Granell, E. F. "Giroscopio de presagios." In *Lecciones sobre Federico García Lorca.* Ed. Andrés Soria Olmedo. Granada: Comisión Nacional del Cincuecentenario, 1986. 101–14.

Grant, Helen F. "The World Upside-Down." In *Studies in Spanish Literature of the Golden Age Presented to Edward M. Wilson.* Ed. R. O. Jones. London: Tamesis, 1973.

Greenfield, Sumner M. "The Problem of *Mariana Pineda.*" *Massachusetts Review* 1 (1959): 751–63.

———. "Yerma, the Woman and the Work: Some Reconsiderations." *Estreno* 7 (1981): 18–21.

Guillén, Jorge. *Cántico.* 2d ed. Madrid: Cruz y Raya, 1936.

————. "Una generación." In *El argumento de la obra*. Barcelona: Sinera, 1969. 7–42.

Gullón, Ricardo. "Perspectiva y punto de vista en el teatro de García Lorca." In *La casa de Bernarda Alba y el teatro de García Lorca*. Ed. Ricardo Doménech. Madrid: Cátedra, 1985. 13–30.

————. "Radiografía de 'El público.' " *Homenaje a Federico García Lorca*. Ed. Manuel Alvar. Málaga: Ayuntamiento de Málaga, 1988. 79–93.

Havard, Robert G. "The Hidden Parts of Bernarda Alba." *Romance Notes* 26 (1985): 102–8.

————. "Lorca's Buster Keaton." *Bulletin of Hispanic Studies* 54 (1977): 13–20.

————, ed. *Mariana Pineda*. Warminster, England: Aris and Philips, 1987.

Hernández, Mario. *Libro de los dibjos de Federico García Lorca*. Madrid: Fundación Federico García Lorca, 1990.

Hornby, Richard. *Script into Performance*. Austin: U of Texas P, 1977.

Hutman, Louise. "Inside the Circle: On Rereading *Blood Wedding*." *Modern Drama* 16 (1973): 329–36.

Issacharoff, Michael. "Postscript or Pinch of Salt: Performance as Mediation or Deconstruction." In *Performing Texts*. Ed. Michael Issacharoff and Robin F. Jones. Philadelphia: U of Pennsylvania P, 1988. 138–43.

————. "Stage Codes." In *Performing Texts*. Ed. Michael Issacharoff and Robin F. Jones. Philadelphia: U of Pennsylvania P, 1988. 59–74.

Jameson, Fredric. *Fables of Aggression: Wyndham Lewis, the Modernist as Fascist*. Berkeley: U of California P, 1979.

Jauss, Hans Robert. *Toward an Aesthetic of Reception*. Minneapolis: U of Minnesota P, 1982.

Klein, Dennis A. " 'Así que pasen cinco años': A Search for Identity." *Journal of Spanish Studies, 20th Century* 3 (1975): 115–23.

Knight, R. G. "Federico García Lorca's *Así que pasen cinco años*." *Bulletin of Hispanic Studies* 43 (1966): 32–46.

Krauss, Rosalind. "The Photographic Conditions of Surrealism." *October* 19 (1981): 3–34.

Laffranque, Marie. *Federico García Lorca: Teatro inconcluso. Fragmentos y proyectos inacabados*. Granada: U de Granada, 1987.

————. "Poeta y público." *Cuadernos ("El público")* 20 (1987): 29–35.

Lewis, Wyndham. *Wyndham Lewis On Art: Collected Writings, 1913–1956*. Ed. Walter Michel and C. J. Fox. New York: Funk and Wagnalls, 1969.

Lima, Robert. *The Theatre of García Lorca*. New York: Las Américas, 1963.

Londré, Felicia Hardison. *Federico García Lorca*. New York: Frederick Unger, 1984.

———. "Lorca in Metamorphosis: His Posthumous Plays." *Theatre Journal* 35 (1983): 102–8.

Lyon, John. "Love, Imagination, and Society in *Amor de don Perlimplín* and *La zapatera prodigiosa.*" *Bulletin of Hispanic Studies* 63 (1986): 235–46.

Marful, Inés. "Apuntes para una psicocrítica del teatro loquiano: de la obra juvenil a las farsas." In *Lecturas del texto dramático. Variación sobre la obra de Lorca.* Ed. Gómez Ubaldo. Oviedo: U of Oviedo, 1990. 43–66.

Martín, Eutimio. *Federico García Lorca, heterodoxo y mártir.* Madrid: Siglo XXI, 1986.

Martínez Nadal, Rafael. *El público: amor, teatro y caballos en la obra de Federico García Lorca.* Oxford: Dolphin Book Co., 1970.

Martínez Nadal, Rafael and Marie Laffranque, ed. *El público/Comedia sin título.* Barcelona: Seix Barral, 1978.

Maurer, Christopher. *Epistolario/Federico García Lorca.* 2 vols. Madrid: Alianza, 1983.

Millán, María Clementa, ed. *El público.* Madrid: Cátedra, 1988.

———. "La verdad del amor y del teatro." *Cuadernos ("El público")* 20 (1987): 19–27.

Mitchell, W. J. T. *Iconology.* Chicago: U of Chicago P, 1986.

Monleón, José, ed. *Doña Rosita la soltera o el lenguaje de las flores.* Madrid: Centro Dramático Nacional, 1981.

Morla Lynch, Carlos. *En España con Federico García Lorca.* Madrid: Aguilar, 1958.

Morris, C. B. "The 'Austere Abode': Lorca's *La casa de Bernarda Alba.*" *Anales de la literatura española contemporánea* 11 (1986): 129–41.

———. "Divertissement as Distraction in Lorca's *La zapatera prodigiosa.*" *Hispania* 69 (1986): 797–803.

———. *García Lorca: La casa de Bernarda Alba.* London: Grant and Cutler-Tamesis, 1990.

———. "Lorca's Yerma: Wife Without an Anchor." *Neophilologus* 56 (1972): 285–97.

Mukarovsky, Jan. "Dialectical Contradictions in Modern Art." In *Structure, Sign, and Function.* Tr. John Burbank and Peter Steiner. New Haven: Yale UP, 1978. 129–49.

Nichols, Geraldine Cleary. "Maturity as Accommodation: Lorca's *La zapatera prodigiosa.*" *MLN* 95 (1980): 335–56.

Oliver, Roger W. *Dreams of Passion. The Theatre of Luigi Pirandello.* New York: New York UP, 1979.

Palley, Julian. "Archetypal Symbols in *Bodas de sangre.*" *Hispania* 50 (1967): 74–79.

Parker, A. A. "The Spanish Drama of the Golden Age: A Method of Analysis and Interpretation." In The Great Playwrights. Vol. 1. Ed. Eric Bentley. New York: Doubleday, 1970. 697–707.

Parr, James A. "La escena final de *Yerma.*" *Duquesne Hispanic Review* 10 (1971): 23–29.

Pavis, Patrice. *Languages of the Stage: Essays in the Semiology of the Theatre.* New York: Performing Arts Journal Publications, 1982.

Peirce, Charles Sanders. "The Icon, Index, and Symbol." In *Collected Works.* Ed. Charles Hartshorne and Paul Weiss. 8 vols. Cambridge: Havard UP, 1931–58. 2: 156–73.

Pfister, Manfred. *The Theory and Analysis of Drama.* Cambridge: Cambridge UP, 1991.

Pound, Ezra. *Ezra Pound and the Visual Arts.* New York: New Directions, 1980.

Pound, Ezra and Ernest Fenollosa. *The Chinese Written Character as a Medium for Poetry.* San Francisco: City Lights, 1936.

Ramond, Michèle. *Psychotextes: La question de l'Autre dans Federico García Lorca.* Toulouse: Eché, 1986.

Rojas, Carlos. *El ingenioso hidalgo y poeta Federico García Lorca asciende a los infiernos.* Madrid: Destino, 1980.

Rubia Barcia, José. "*El público,* Naked and Unmasked." In *"Cuando yo me muera . . . ": Essays in Memory of Federico García Lorca.* Ed. C. B. Morris. New York: U Presses of America, 1988. 233–57.

———. "El realismo mágico de *La casa de Bernarda Alba.*" *Revista hispánica moderna* 31 (1965): 385–98.

Rubio, Isaac. "Notas sobre el realismo de *La casa de Bernarda Alba.*" *Revista canadiense de estudios hispánicos* 4 (1980): 169–82.

Ruíz Ramón, Francisco. "Espacios dramáticos en *La casa de Bernarda Alba.*" *Gestos* 1 (1986): 87–100.

———. *Historia del teatro español. Siglo XX.* 5th ed. Madrid: Cátedra, 1981.

Sahuquillo, Andrés. *Federico García Lorca y la cultura de la homosexualidad masculina.* Alicante: Instituo de Cultura "Juan Gil-Albert," 1991.

Sapojnikoff, Victor. "La estructura temática de *Así que pasen cinco años.*" *Romance Notes* 12 (1970): 11–20.

Schlueter, June. *Metafictional Characters in Modern Drama.* New York: Columbia UP, 1979.

Schmelling, Manfred. *Métatexte et intertexte: aspects du théâtre dans le théâtre.* Paris: Minard, 1982.

Scott, Nina M. "Sight and Insight in *La casa de Bernarda Alba.*" *Revista de estudios hispánicos* 10 (1976): 297–308.

Sherry, Vincent. *Ezra Pound, Wyndham Lewis, and Radical Modernism.* Oxford: Oxford UP, 1993.

Silver, Philip. "El metateatro de Federico García Lorca." In *La casa de Anteo*. Madrid: Taurus, 1985. 157–90.

Smith, Paul Julian. *The Body Hispanic*. Oxford: Oxford UP, 1989.

Soufas, C. Christopher. *Conflict of Light and Wind: The 'Generation of 1927' and the Ideology of Poetic Form*. Middletown, Conn.: Wesleyan UP, 1989.

Steiner, Wendy. *The Colors of Rhetoric*. Chicago: U of Chicago P, 1982.

Taylor, Diane. "Interiority and Exteriority in García Lorca's *La casa de Bernarda Alba*." *Estreno* 15 (1989): 19–22.

Ubersfeld, Anne. *Semiótica teatral*. Madrid: Cátedra, 1989.

Ucelay, Margarita, ed. *Amor de don Perlimplín con Belisa en su jardín*. Madrid: Cátedra, 1990.

———. "De las aleluyas de Don Perlimplín a la obra de Federico García Lorca." In *Federico García Lorca. Saggi Critici nel Cinquentenario della morte*. Fasano: Schena, 1988. 89–106.

———. "Federico García Lorca y el Club Teatral Anfistora: el dramaturgo como director de escena." In *Lecciones sobre Federico García Lorca*. Ed. Andrés Soria Olmedo. Granada: Comisión Nacional del Cincuecentenario, 1986. 51–64.

Uspensky, Boris. "The Structural Isomorphism of Verbal and Visual Art." In *A Poetics of Composition*. Tr. Valentina Zavarin and Susan Wittig. Berkeley: U of California P, 1973. 130–72.

Vitale, Rosanna. *El metateatro en la obra de Federico García Lorca*. Madrid: Pliegos, 1991.

Whiteside, Anna. "Self-Referring Artifacts." In *Performing Texts*. Ed. Michael Isaacharoff and Robin F. Jones. Philadelphia: U of Pennsylvania P, 1988. 27–38.

Wood, Michael. "Austere Fireworks." *New York Review of Books* 39 (July 16, 1992): 36–40.

Zdenek, Joseph W. "Alter Ego and Personality Projection in García Lorca's *Así que pasen cinco años*." *Revista de estudios hispánicos* 16 (1982): 303–13.

OTHER WORKS CONSULTED

Alvarez Harvey, María Luisa. "Lorca's Yerma: Frigid . . . or Mismatched." *College Language Association Journal* 23 (1980): 460–69.

Anderson, Andrew A. " 'Un dificilísimo juego poético': Theme and Symbol in Lorca's *El público.*" *Romance Quarterly* 39 (1992): 331–46.

Bejel, Emilio. "Las funciones dramáticas de *Bodas de sangre.*" *Hispanófila* 80 (1984): 87–94.

———. "Las secuencias estructurales de *Bodas de sangre.*" *Dispositio* 3 (1978): 381–92.

Busette, Cedric. "Mariana Pineda as Religious Martyr." *Revista de estudios hispánicos* 18 (1984): 115–22.

Cabrera, Vicente. "Cristo y el infierno en *La casa de Bernarda Alba.*" *Revista de estudios hispánicos* 13 (1979): 135–42.

Colecchia, Francesca. "The 'Prólogo' in the Theatre of Federico García Lorca: Towards the Articulation of a Philosophy of Theatre." *Hispania* 69 (1986): 791–96.

Dolan, Kathleen. "Time, Irony, and Negation in Lorca's Last Three Plays." *Hispania* 63 (1980): 514–22.

Doménech, Ricardo. "Nueva Indagación en *Doña Rosita, la soltera.*" *Anales de la literatura española contemporánea* 11 (1986): 79–90.

———. "Símbolo, mito y rito en *La casa de Bernarda Alba.*" In *La casa de Bernarda Alba y el teatro de García Lorca.* Ed. Ricardo Doménech. Madrid: Cátedra, 1985. 188–209.

Edwards, Gwynne. "Lorca and Buñuel: *Así que pasen cinco años* and *Un chien andalou.*" *García Lorca Review* 9 (1981): 128–43.

Esslin, Martin. *Antonin Artaud.* New York: Penguin, 1966.

Esteban, Alfonso and Jean-Pierre Etienne, eds. *Valoración actual de la obra de García Lorca.* Madrid: Casa de Velázquez–Universidad Complutense, 1988.

Feal Deibe, Carlos. "Lorca's Two Farces: *Don Perlimplín* and *Don Cristóbal.*" *American Imago* 27 (1970): 358–78.

———. "La idea del honor en las tragedias de Lorca." In *"Cuando yo me muera . . . ": Essays in Memory of Federico García Lorca.* Ed. C. B. Morris. New York: U Presses of America, 1988. 277–93.

Figure, Paul. "The Mystification of Love and Lorca's Female Image in *El público.*" *Cincinnati Romance Review* 2 (1983): 26–32.

González-del-Valle, Luis. "Justicia poética en *Bodas de sangre.*" *Romance Notes* 14 (1972): 236–41.

Greene, Naomi. *Antonin Artaud: Poet Without Words.* New York: Simon and Schuster, 1970.

Greenfield, Sumner. "Lorca's Tragedies: Practice Without Theory." *Siglo XX/20th Century* 4 (1986–87): 1–5.

Hart, Stephen M. "The Bear and the Dawn: Versions of *La casa de Bernarda Alba.*" *Neophilologus* 73 (1989): 62–68.

Jerez-Farrán, Carlos. "La estética expresionista in *El público* de García Lorca." *Anales de la literatura española contemporánea* 11 (1986): 111–27.

Josephs, Allen and Juan Caballero, ed. *La casa de Bernarda Alba.* Madrid: Cátedra, 1983.

Kowsan, Tadeusz. *Littérature et Spectacle.* Paris: Mouton, 1975.

Martínez Lacalle, Guadalupe. "*Yerma:* 'Una tragedia pura y simplemente.' " *Neophilologus* 72 (1988): 227–37.

Menarini, Piero, ed. *Lorca, 1986.* Bologna: ATESA, 1987.

Morris, C. B. "Voices in a Void: Speech in *La casa de Bernarda Alba.*" *Hispania* 72 (1989): 498–510.

Newberry, Wilma. "Patterns of Negation in *La casa de Bernarda Alba.*" *Hispania* 59 (1976): 802–9.

Nickel, Catherine. "The Function of Language in García Lorca's *Doña Rosita, la soltera.*" *Hispania* 66 (1983): 522–31.

Ortega, José. "Surrealismo y Exotismo: *Así que pasen cinco años* de García Lorca." *García Lorca Review* 10 (1982): 75–93.

Richards, Katherine C. "Hypocrisy in *La casa de Bernarda Alba.*" *Romance Notes* 22 (1981): 10–13.

Rude, Roberta N. and Harriet S. Turner. "The Circles and Mirrors of Women's Lives in *The House of Bernarda Alba.*" *Literature in Performance* 3 (1982): 75–82.

Sáenz de la Calzada, Luis. *"La Barraca." Teatro universitario.* Madrid: Revista de Occidente, 1976.

Schechner, Richard. *Between Theatre and Anthropology.* Philadelphia: U of Pennsylvania P, 1985.

———. *Performance Theory.* New York: Routeledge, 1988.

Schechner, Richard, and Willa Appel, eds. *By Means of Performance.* Cambridge: Cambridge UP, 1990.

Smoot, Jeanne J. "*Yerma:* Artistic Triumph or Narcissistic Defeat?" In *Selected Proceedings of the 32nd Mountain Interstate Foreign Language Conference.* Ed. Gregorio C. Martín. Winston-Salem, N.C.: Wake Forest University, 1984. 321–28.

Sullivan, Patricia L. "The Mythic Tragedy of *Yerma.*" *Bulletin of Hispanic Studies* 49 (1972): 265–78.

Timm, John T. H. "Some Critical Observations on García Lorca's *Bodas de sangre.*" *Revista de estudios hispánicos* 7 (1973): 255–88.

Ucelay, Margarita. "La problemática teatral." *Boletín de la Fundación Federico García Lorca* 6 (1989): 27–58.

Velázquez Cueto, Gerardo. "Actualidad y entendimiento de *Doña Rosita, la soltera* o *El lenguage de las flores* de Federico García Lorca." *Insula* 410 (1981): 1, 12–13.

Vilches de Frutos, Maria Francesca, and Dru Dougherty. *Los estrenos teatrales de Federico García Lorca (1920-1945).* Madrid: Tabapress, 1992.

Villegas, Juan. "Federico García Lorca: ¿Teatro de evasión?" *García Lorca Review* 4 (1976): 61–66.

Walsh, John K. "The Women in Lorca's Theatre." *Gestos* 2 (1987): 53–65.

Wells, C. Michael. "The Natural Norm in the Plays of F. García Lorca." *Hispanic Review* 38 (1970): 299–313.

Yndurián, Francisco. "*La casa de Bernarda Alba:* ensayo de interpretación." In *La casa de Bernarda Alba y el teatro de García Lorca.* Ed. Ricardo Doménech. Madrid: Cátedra, 1985. 123–47.

Zdenek, Joseph W., ed. *The World of Nature in the Works of Federico García Lorca.* Rock Hill, S.C.: Winthrop College, 1980.

INDEX